THE
INNER CHILD
WORKBOOK

This *Inner Work Book* is
part of a series that explores
psyche and spirit through writing,
visualization, ritual, and
imagination.

Other books in this series include:

The Artist's Way
BY JULIA CAMERON

The Adult Children of Divorce Workbook
BY MARY HIRSCHFELD, J.D., PH.D.

At a Journal Workshop
BY IRA PROGOFF, PH.D.

The Family Patterns Workbook
BY CAROLYN FOSTER

Following Your Path
BY ALEXANDRA COLLINS DICKERMAN

A Journey Through Your Childhood
BY CHRISTOPHER BIFFLE

The Path of the Everyday Hero
BY LORNA CATFORD, PH.D., AND MICHAEL RAY, PH.D.

Personal Mythology
BY DAVID FEINSTEIN, PH.D., AND MICHAEL RAY, PH.D.

The Possible Human
BY JEAN HOUSTON

The Search for the Beloved
BY JEAN HOUSTON

Smart Love
BY JODY HAYES

True Partners
BY TINA TESSINA, PH.D., AND RILEY K. SMITH, M.A.

Your Mythic Journey
BY SAM KEEN AND ANNE VALLEY-FOX

THE INNER CHILD WORKBOOK

What To Do With Your Past When It Just Won't Go Away

CATHRYN L. TAYLOR

M.A., M.F.C.C.

Jeremy P. Tarcher/Putnam
a member of
Penguin Putnam Inc.
New York

This book is
dedicated to
my mom, Gladys Taylor,
who had the courage
to love and let go;

and to my sister,
Suzy,
and my brothers,
Tom and John,
who know me
as no one else ever will.

Jeremy P. Tarcher/Putnam
a member of
Penguin Putnam Inc.
375 Hudson Street
New York, NY 10014
www.penguinputnam.com

ISBN 0-87477-635-X

Most Tarcher/Putnam books are available at special quantity discounts for bulk purchases for sales promotions, premiums, fund-raising, and educational needs. Special books, or book excerpts, can also be created to fit specific needs.

For details, write Special Markets, Putnam Publishing Group.

Design by Lee Fukui

Manufactured in the United States of America
40 39 38

CONTENTS

ACKNOWLEDGMENTS   vii

FOREWORD   ix

PREFACE   xi

INTRODUCTION   1

1   DISCOVERING AND HEALING   13
YOUR CHILDREN WITHIN

2   THE INFANT SELF   37
Welcome to the World
Birth to Eighteen Months

3   THE TODDLER SELF   70
From Dependency to Autonomy
Eighteen Months to Three Years

4   THE YOUNG INNER CHILD   90
Confronting the Good, the Bad, and the Ugly
Three to Six Years

5   THE GRADE-SCHOOL CHILD WITHIN   112
Judgment by One's Peers
Six to Twelve Years

6 THE YOUNG TEEN WITHIN   133
   Getting Comfortable with Discomfort
   Twelve to Fifteen Years

7 THE ADOLESCENT WITHIN   154
   Carving Out a Self
   Fifteen to Seventeen Years

8 THE YOUNG INNER ADULT   175
   The Bridge to Adulthood
   Seventeen to Twenty-one Years

9 DEVELOPING ONGOING RELATIONSHIPS   205
   WITH YOUR CHILDREN WITHIN

10 INTIMATE ADULT RELATIONSHIPS AND YOUR   216
   CHILDREN WITHIN

11 ADDICTIONS, RECOVERY, AND YOUR CHILDREN   229
   WITHIN

   EPILOGUE   240
   Life after the Pain
   APPENDIX 1: Glossary   243
   APPENDIX 2: The Twelve Steps of Alcoholics   244
   Anonymous
   APPENDIX 3: Herbs for Work with Your Inner   245
   Children
   BIBLIOGRAPHY   247

ACKNOWLEDGMENTS

To LAUREL KING for your professional consultation and personal inspiration, for providing a shoulder I could cry on and for giving birth to my godchild, Lillian. My life is much richer because of you.

To ESTHER VOGEL who struggled through draft after draft of this manuscript, and was a typist, a friend, and the lamaze coach to this birth. (We can finally cut the cord!)

To MARIE KANARR, HELEN HAYES and LINDA WESLEY for your contributions to the typing of this manuscript.

To MARGEE BARTLE, my oldest and dearest friend, BERYLENE ANDREA, LEAH CRANE, JOANNA DENKIN, SHEILA FAIRCHILD, and JEANNIE VOGEL for reading parts of this manuscript and encouraging me to continue.

To KATIE HEALY for reading chapter after chapter searching for inconsistencies, lack of clarity, and redundancy.

To SUE DEVEREAUX for your herbal advice and support.

To my editors CONNIE ZWEIG, and JENNIFER BOYNTON for your support, advice, and belief in this project.

To JEREMY TARCHER, for seeing value in this work.

To ALYSSA HALL and PAUL NORDSTRAND for your guidance and care, and to KAREN SAEGER and ROBERT GREEN for your professional and personal direction.

To SALLY REGAN for suggesting I write a book and to CATHIE ANDERSON for suggesting that it be on the children within.

To MARSHA NORRIS for your celebratory contributions and for teaching me so much about sisterly love.

To JOY SUTHERLAND for the morning phone calls, and for calming the little girl inside me any time she felt frightened or overwhelmed by this project.

To JANE MCCULLOUGH for your perserverance, to DON SUMMERS for the coffee breaks, to MARY BACKUS for your undying support, and to CANDACE KUNZ for your humor and excitement that I did it. (Oh yo! Oh yo!)

To DARLENE TURNER for being my spiritual advisor and friend.

To WALTER SHINE for inspiring much of the material on intimate adult relationships and for having the capacity to follow your dreams and honor that which was in your heart.

To the friends already mentioned, but also to TAMA ADELMAN, KIM KIRK BAILY, CHRIS BERGER, ANTHONY CARPENTIERI, KENNY DAHLE, BRYAN GOULD, LESLIE GOULD, PATTY-LYNN GREEN, SUSAN KING, JULIA PERSONS, JUDY SHEARD, LINDA SHORMANN, DAVID SKIBBINS, JONATHAN TENNEY, and JOHN WEIDERSPAN for supporting me in my growth.

To my brother TOM for your phone calls, to my brother JOHN for your jokes, and to my sister SUZY and her husband ALLAN for giving me free access to your home when I was in need of shelter or simply a retreat.

To GEORGE, ANDREW, SHIELA, and DAD for your unwavering yet invisible support and to the antelope medicine that embodied this work with its Higher Purpose.

To MAX, my faithful companion, who never lets me down.

I also want to pay tribute to those who inspired each chapter on the children within.

To LILLIAN BERGER, my godchild, for being the little beam of Light I could look forward to seeing at the end of my week and for being someone I could hold while I let go.

To SEAN TABOR, my nephew and kindred spirit, who at age two asked me to chase the "monsters" away from his bedside.

To MICHELLE TABOR, my niece, who at age three trusted me enough to at one moment say "I hate you," and the next say, "Won't you stay!" You will always be an angel on my shoulder.

To CHRISTOPHER BERGER, my adopted nephew, for igniting your own interests with the passion of a true ten-year-old.

To CATHY TAYLOR, my niece and namesake, for carrying on with the fourth generation, and for your depth of feeling and gentle pursuit of tranquility.

To WALTER SHINE, JR, for searching relentlessly for who you want to be.

To the many teens with whom I worked as you attempted to learn the skills needed to be on your own, and most especially to MARK, ANTHONY, DAVID, the TWO ERICS, DANIELLE, COVAN, and SCOTT, who all made a special impression on my heart. And to LEO, DORIS, CAROLYN, and MUKTI.

A special thanks to my Tuesday night group. You gave me a container for my grief and a place in which to explore new approaches.

And last, but not least, to all of the clients, students, and lecture participants who have shared your stories, your pain, and your hopes.

To all of you, I am forever indebted.

FOREWORD

Surprised and delighted! That was my experience in reading Cathryn Taylor's *Inner Child Workbook*. Let me explain why.

As with any word or phrase in popular usage, its constant application can begin to dominate our thinking in such a way that we don't see its full possibilities. The concept of the "inner child" as a symbol of the wounded self is now part of the vernacular of the recovery movement. While this definition is partly true it overlooks a very important point—that as Cathryn Taylor clarifies, we don't have merely *one* child within, we have many!

As this book makes clear, we all should progress through a series of developmental steps from infancy to childhood to adolescence to adulthood. For a wide range of reasons, most of us in dysfunctional families don't do some of these essential steps and, as a result, a part of us stops growing. The wounded or handicapped part then becomes an inner child figure that is trapped in that stage of growth. In a very complete and readable way, Cathryn addresses the unmet needs and ongoing issues of each of these children within at each stage of development.

From my own clinical experience, it has become clear that in order to heal an abusive past, we need to work with each inner child individually. We need to work with the inner infant, the one who screamed for attention and touch; the two-year-old, the one who was not allowed to get angry; the six-year-old, the one who had no friends; the eleven-year-old, who was a victim of incest; the fifteen-year-old, the one who felt fat and ugly. To become more fully present in our own lives, we must invite all of these children back into their interior home to be nurtured and healed.

By taking the reader step-by-step through the experiences of the past, Cathryn shows us how to re-parent each inner child. As we master the developmental tasks that were missed in earlier times, we can then choose not to reenact destructive adult behaviors. We learn that we no longer need to believe—as we did as children—that dysfunctional behavior will get our needs met.

grief. And there was absolute terror. All my life I had assumed I would grow up, get a job, get married, and have kids. Ending the relationship was not difficult, but letting go of the myth that I could find fulfillment through a husband was terrifying.

This period was one of many transitions. After getting divorced, I changed jobs, finished graduate school, and decided to quit smoking. Still, I was managing well until my apartment building sold and the new manager asked me to move out. With that, every aspect of my life that had represented security had dissolved or changed. The loss was unbearable. I had never been more depressed.

Although I felt suicidal, I was, even then, too metaphysically minded to attempt it. I strongly believed in a power greater than self, and this belief enabled me to feel there was something to be learned from the pain I was experiencing. But that belief did not lessen the pain. I prayed a lot, cried a lot, and trembled with raw emotion. I felt as if every feeling I had ever repressed was emerging, demanding expression.

I was so emotionally overloaded that I went to a psychiatric unit begging for relief. I do not remember the name of the psychiatrist I saw, but I am forever indebted to her. After hearing my story, she said she would not honor my request for antidepressants. She felt I was mourning everything I had ever been dependent on—my Dad, Mom, husband, work, my home, even cigarettes—and that medication would simply give me something else to depend on. She recommended I try to get through this crisis without drugs, but promised that if, in four days, I still wanted them, she would prescribe them for me.

I left her office terrified. But, oddly enough, I also felt stronger. Someone who did not even know me saw someone inside me who could pull through. And because she saw that part of me, I started to see it also.

I spent the next eight months in hibernation. My only sanity check was that I could still function at my job at a residential treatment center for adolescents. I would be in tears until I took the turnoff leading to the center. Somehow, magically, the tears would subside and I would do my work. Later, when I returned to the safety of my car, my eyes were once again full.

I was vulnerable, raw and open. I didn't feel strong enough to live alone, so I moved in with my sister and her family. Their home provided the safe harbor I needed while I began to heal. I was intolerably sensitive. Someone would look at me crossly, and I would feel shame;

someone would gently brush against me while in line at the store, and I would take offense. I was absolutely aware of everything going on around me, as if I were constantly on alert. It was the closest I ever came to being psychotic—totally open with no sense of self—but my role at work kept me sane. It was the one place in my life I still knew who I was. Without it, I would have found myself back at the psychiatric unit once again begging for relief.

Shortly after my visit to the psychiatric unit, a friend and I were discussing how our relationships with our fathers had affected our lives. After he finished talking about his own experiences, I replied, "You think *you* had it bad . . . when Dad had *my* nervous breakdown, I really felt scared!!" He stopped me. "Do you know what you just said?" he asked. Only then did I realize how much responsibility I had taken on for Dad's nervous breakdown. It wasn't even *his* anymore!

The day I went to that psychiatric unit was the day I finally had my own nervous breakdown. No one called it that, but that's what it was. At a different time, and a different place, with a different doctor, I could have ended up on medication or been given shock treatments to dull my pain; I could have ended up with the same limited options and made the same choices as my Dad. I was so bonded with him and had taken on his nervous breakdown to such a degree that, before I could get on with my life, I had to know I could survive his. I had recreated my Dad's depression to see how I would react.

One of the ways I reacted was to compulsively talk about what I felt. In reaction to Dad's not talking about his feelings, all I did was talk about mine. Acknowledging this compulsion gave me the courage to experiment with not talking, an experiment that proved to be quite interesting. Although I didn't know much about my inner child during that time, I certainly could not escape her pain. I felt I was crying every tear I had ever held back. The feelings were overwhelming and undifferentiated.

With time, and with the help of friends, my therapist, and the safe harbor of my sister's home, my life did stabilize. I spent the next several years reclaiming and redefining the real me. I began to meditate. I slowly worked through what my Dad had been unable to resolve. He did not have the support or the understanding—perhaps not even the motivation—that I had to confront what he feared. I had adopted this fear and it had become one of my life's themes. I had to struggle to resolve it or live with the pain of repeating it.

Most of us adopt the fears of those we love, and recreate what haunts us. I have seen the daughter of a woman who committed suicide struggle with the same choice. I have seen a friend whose father was murdered battle her fear of death, and the son of a psychotic mother fight with his own fear of being "crazy."

Studies of dysfunctional families continually suggest there is a generational connection among physical and sexual abuse, insanity, alcoholism and infidelity. For instance, if you grew up in a home where anger was abusively expressed, you can either repeat the behavior, or you can refuse to express anger. Both extremes are dysfunctional, but I don't believe we recreate these patterns because we are self-destructive. Rather, I believe it is because we have a will to master what our caretakers were unable to master. Some of us succeed; some don't. Others simply numb themselves to the task through their addictions. With the help of friends and by the grace of God, I was able to work these issues through.

At first my recovery demanded that I spend a great deal of time alone. But eventually I realized I was ready to begin to search for an intimate relationship. The search didn't take long.

I was in Washington, D.C. attending a conference and visiting an old friend. We were having fun and I was certainly not consciously looking for an intimate relationship.

But one morning I was jogging at the mall, enthralled. I had never seen the Capitol or the Washington Monument before. I was running along and suddenly I looked up and there he was . . . sitting peacefully on a bench. We exchanged hellos—and I kept running. But I felt a strange pull to go back. I wrestled with myself for another half mile, trying to decide what to say and what to do and finally turned around. I knew I was going back, and I knew it didn't matter what I said.

I had never before felt this kind of connection. It was as if fate were in control and I was merely following its direction. Once more I nonchalantly ran by him. Again we exchanged hellos. I finished my run and then walked back to where he sat. All the opening lines I had rehearsed evaporated. I simply asked if I could sit down. We started talking—and even though many things were new, many were familiar. It was as though we were acting out a play that had been written long, long ago. We spent the rest of the day talking, and somewhere inside, each of us knew our lives would never again be the same. There were many complications, but he ended up making a move to California.

The first three months were great. Everything I had learned about myself was holding true when I related to him. I succeeded in staying connected to myself and open to him at the same time. It was easy; staying open to him was being connected to me. It was when the garbage within us started to rise to the surface that it became difficult. I didn't know the term *codependent* then, but my codependency definitely emerged. As long as we were infatuated with each other, we were fine. However, the real work began when the newness wore off, and it became time to deepen our emotional connection and negotiate our differences.

We battled with our egos and struggled with our hearts as we tried to determine how we fit together. It was taxing, but it was working. We were confronting and resolving every reason we had for not loving each other, peeling away the layers of doubt and fear and need. We plunged on until we hit a layer that stopped us cold: his ambivalence about having moved away from his children to be with me surfaced and I knew there was no way to compete. I had never loved anyone as deeply as I had allowed myself to love this man. When he told me of his plans to return, I understood, but I was devastated. The thought of his leaving was almost more than I could bear.

I began to search for answers, for reasons, for anything that would ease the pain. In desperation, I went to a woman to have a "spiritual reading." She told me to go home, sit in front of the mirror, and talk to the little girl inside who felt so afraid. I thought back to that cold December day when my feelings about Dad had thawed, and I remembered the feelings of that inner child. But this inner child felt younger. At first I felt awkward, but gradually the pain started to emerge. I sat in a rocker, and rocked back and forth. I began to sob as I heard the little girl speak fearfully of having trusted someone and, again, having them leave. I then heard an older voice assure the child that she would survive and that she would not be alone. I spent hours releasing and healing this inner fear of abandonment.

I bought a giant-sized teddy bear that was soft and cuddly. Anytime I felt this pain I would take my teddy bear and sit in my rocker. I would imagine my inner child sitting in my lap as I cradled and comforted her through her distress and the feelings of fear and loss would subside. Working with my pain in this way let me to stay open to the love that I felt for this man. I didn't have to hate him or berate him or refuse to see him as he prepared to go. The older voice within me could accept and support him in his decision, and the younger, frightened voice could be heard and consoled.

I began using this tool anytime I felt discomfort and found that I could be much more intimate in my relationships because I was much less afraid of being hurt. Over time I developed a very nurturing relationship with this inner voice or child within. I also began to become aware that there was more than one inner child. I had a three-year-old, who was spunky and alert. I had a ten-year-old, who was angry and sullen. I had a teenager, who was rebellious and afraid. I started to listen and respond to each voice, and slowly began to heal my family within.

I started using these same techniques with my clients, and was amazed at their effectiveness. Abused women began to heal their wounded and violated little girls within. A man reclaimed and healed his inner teenager by compassionately setting limits on his adolescent behavior. A middle-aged woman shed tears as she held her imaginary inner child in her arms, saying she felt a part of her had come home.

From these experiences, coupled with my views on addictions and recovery, I began to form my model of recovery. I developed a flow chart mapping out the progression of addiction and recovery that included healing the inner child. I started teaching classes and conducting workshops. But I truly understood the significance of the inner children when my Dad got sick again.

Dad had been battling depression for several years and, even though he was again psychiatrically hospitalized, he simply continued to get more depressed. However, this time as he got more depressed, he also got more volatile and suicidal. To our shock, he was diagnosed as having Alzheimer's disease. He was released from the hospital, but was too difficult for my mother to handle. My family met and decided he needed out-of-home care.

The day we had to take him to the county hospital was perhaps my longest day. The rest of the family was busy elsewhere. My Dad and I spent the day alone, waiting for the family doctor to give the orders for admission. As we waited, we talked and I reminded him that he had been violent the previous night. "It's not safe for you to be home," I said. Like a child he looked at me and said he would do better. He had meant no harm. I continued to explain that I understood, in fact, we all understood. And because we understood we also could admit that it was important he live somewhere where he felt safe.

The day went on. Sometimes I just held him. Other times we sat in silence or talked. Periodically he would ask me to walk him through the house. "Just one last time," he would say. We both knew it would be the last day he would live in his own home. At one point, he fell asleep. I sat on the couch looking at the body of this frightened old man whom I so admired. I closed my eyes for a moment and—quite unexpectedly—had one of the most incredible experiences of my life. I felt myself go into an altered state of consciousness. It felt as if every child within me surfaced simultaneously and had their last say. Some were angry. Some were sad or full of shame. But each said what she needed to. The experience was over in about two or three minutes and was followed by an incredible sense of calm. I had a sense of turning my Dad over to his Higher Power, releasing him so that he could die. Dad suddenly jerked in his sleep and I opened my eyes. The experience faded from my immediate awareness. I got Dad ready and drove him to the hospital. I got him settled, and said what I felt was our last good-bye. On the plane ride home, I recalled the experience of my inner children's goodbyes, and suddenly the feeling of finality made sense. I flew back to my life in California, a life without the daily reminder of my Dad's pain. When I felt guilty about being so far away, I would convince myself that I had done all that I could do.

Then, one night, while teaching class, I suddenly went blank. For thirty seconds I was completely disoriented, then in a split second it all came back, and I continued the class. I put the incident aside, but when I was driving home, I flashed back. I felt a moment of panic as the thought Alzheimer's rushed through my mind, but I quickly dismissed it, telling myself I was not going to spend the next thirty years worrying about that.

The next day as I began to meditate, I recalled the incident. Casually, I heard myself ask my Higher Power what the incident was about. In my mind's eye I saw a small figure appear out of nowhere. She looked like me when I was about eight years old and she was furious. She defiantly snapped, "If you won't go back and help him through this, I'll show you what it's like to be him." I was dumbfounded. In all the work I'd done, I had never come across a child so angry or one who sought so much control. I sat and listened while she challenged me to return. "After all he's done for you, how can you abandon him now?" Then the image finally faded. Taking a few deep breaths, I heard myself say, "What the *hell* was that?"

For the next several weeks I battled with the feelings and the voice of this inner child. I thought that if I just accepted this guilt-ridden little girl, the feelings would finally subside. They didn't. They became more intense.

I finally realized I could use my residential experience with acting-out teens to help with this demanding internal voice.

The next time I meditated, she again appeared in my mind's eye.

As she began to chastise me, I pictured my adult self walking over and putting her arms around the little girl. Calmly, but firmly, I said, "Enough. I am *not* going back to take care of him. I cannot afford to do that, and I do not want to do that. I know how hard it is for you to see him now, and I know how hard it is for you to let go. I will not desert you. I will help you as you grieve, but I am not going back."

She collapsed in my arms and began to sob. From then on, I was able to help her grieve. In my daily meditations, this inner child would talk to me about her Dad. I said nothing out loud, but had a continuous dialog going on in my head. She told me how much she adored him and what good pals they were. She told me about the time he had promised to buy her roller skates, but had forgotten. When he saw her disappointment—even though it was Saturday evening and the store was closed—he phoned them and asked if they would open. They would. He took her down and bought the skates.

She talked of the trips she made to the country with him and about the time he got her a cowgirl suit. She laughed as she recalled funny stories about him. She told me about the time she had asked him about where people went when they died. He had said he did not know. They had made a pact promising that whoever died first would come back and tell the other what it was like. He had smiled at her, she said, and then willingly shook her hand to seal their pact.

Sometimes she'd get sad to think of him as he was now. When she did, I would assure her that I would now be providing for her and keeping her safe. I told her that, as much as we loved him, we had to let him go.

She had a lot of difficulty with her feelings of abandonment. So she would not feel so alone, I began including her in my activities. If I had to write, I would imagine she was coloring; if I had to make phone calls, I would picture her playing with the typewriter; if I had to do a mailing, I would pretend she was licking stamps.

For several months, I worked with my grief by picturing it as the pain of my eight-year-old child. I was able to separate from it and guide "her" through it. Had I collapsed into the pain, I would either have become immobilized by the guilt of not returning home, or I would have left everything and gone back. Working with her in this way enabled me to stay open to the pain without having to act on it and, slowly, I began to feel a shift. Her alliance with and dependence on Dad began to move to the adult part of me. As she began to accept and trust my adult self, she began to accept the loss. Then one day she said she desperately wanted to see him.

With my eyes closed, I told her to sit on my lap and together we could imagine contacting Dad. Suddenly, in my mind's eye I saw my Dad appear. As soon as he did, my inner child went running over to him. She threw her arms around him and told him she loved him and forgave him. She understood, she said, that he needed to do what he was doing. Then, my Dad looked up at me—the adult me—and said, "You've done a wonderful job with her." The adult part of me watched in total astonishment. I burst into tears and felt a peace about his wanting to die that I had not before known. I am still in awe of this encounter.

Whether my Dad experienced anything or not, I'll never know. More aware of his own loss of his abilities, he simply stopped eating. Consciously or unconsciously, he was starving himself to death. He would only live if he were fed intravenously. Two months earlier his weight had gotten so low and his health so bad that the doctor had ordered an IV. Yet, my Dad had fought the IV so fiercely that it had taken four people to hold him down long enough to put it in his arm. Now, the same decision had to be made once again.

My mother telephoned us. We agreed that we should not force him to have an IV, but I also felt that he should be asked what he wanted. Mom said she could not bring herself to talk to him about it— it was too painful. I volunteered. The therapist in me thought that, if anyone in the family had the experience of such life and death questions, it was me.

There was another part of me, however, that did not have a clue how to ask her father if he was really ready to die.

But I made the call. Dad answered, his voice weak. I told him about the IV, and asked him how he felt about it. He said he did not want it. My voice cracked with emotion as I asked if he knew what that meant. He said he did.

"You know it means you will die?" I asked.

Softly, he said, "That's what I want. I want it to be over."

Taking a deep breath, I told him that we respected his choice. We loved him, but we were willing to let him go if his pain was too great.

I asked if he was scared. He said yes. I asked if he wanted me to tell him what I had read about death. He said yes. I began to talk.

I shared everything I had read with him. I talked about the Light, the tunnel, the relatives and friends who supposedly are escorts to the other side.

I asked him if it all sounded crazy or weird. I almost felt he smiled as he said no. I told him everything I valued about him, and asked if he remembered our promise to communicate after death. He did. I asked him to honor it. He agreed. It was the sanest exchange we had had in months.

I kept talking, feeling more inspired by the moment. There were long silences on his end, but he would answer when I addressed him directly—until one question received no response.

"Dad, are you there?"

My heart stopped. Had the man died right there on the phone? Again I said, "Dad? Dad?" No answer, just silence. Then I heard a big snore. He had fallen asleep!!

I laughed—then called the hospital from my other phone and asked the nurse to go wake him. We said our goodbyes and the call was over.

He was not put on an IV. I waited for the call that would say the end was near. Two weeks later it came. I flew home to spend the last five days of my father's life with him. I have never felt more loving and more at peace than I did then. I was able to tell him how much I loved him and all that I had learned from him. And I reminded him of our pact. At the moment of his passing, with tears streaming down my cheeks, I whispered "Go into the Light." I continued whispering this as he gently took his last breath. Those last moments of his life were perhaps the richest moments of mine. I believe I was able to be so present in the process of his death because I had worked so intensely with my inner children.

My work with my inner children continued after he was gone, but the grieving was gentle and our connection'was strong. On Memorial Day of 1988, my Dad kept his promise to my little girl. He did return—during my morning meditation. The encounter was clumsy and joyful and brief, but there is no doubt in my mind that it was him.

Two weeks later, I was thinking of my Dad, missing him and feeling sad that he would never see the me I was meant to be. Then I suddenly realized that he had. In those last days of his life I *had been* the best I am to be.

As that realization sank in, I imagined a mirror shattering in front of me. All the reflections I had about my relationship with Dad were suddenly freed and entered into the very center of my heart. The experience of my Dad was no longer outside me—it was now a part of me.

After the experiences with my Dad, my professional and personal work with the children within changed, becoming more than just a therapeutic technique. It evolved into a truly tangible process that enriches one's ability to live and love and let go without fear.

Every tool I have learned and used both professionally and personally is contained in the pages of this book. Some of them will work for you, others may not. The suggestions that follow are offered as a gentle guide. They are useful regardless of your childhood experience. For some, that experience was more wounding than for others. Because of this, each person's healing process will vary in its depth and in its intensity. Use your imagination. Create and develop other tools that are specific to your needs. Making this process truly your own is the best way for you to heal the pain of your past so you can experience the joy of your present.

INTRODUCTION

Do you worry that you will do to your children what your parents did to you? Do you shy away from commitment, or cower at the thought of saying "no"? Do you eat too much, drink or smoke too much, love, shop, work or worry too much? Do you blame others for your pain? Do you wish your past would just go away?

Many people suffer in this way, and most of you are haunted by your childhood. It was then that you learned how to relate to others and how to get their love and approval. It was then that you absorbed your parent's patterns of behavior and formed your values. These lessons became the foundation of your adult lives. If your foundation was faulty, the present structure of your life will be weak. You will be prone to recreating the patterns from your past and reliving the wounds you experienced as a child.

WHAT YOU CAN EXPECT FROM THIS BOOK

This book helps you rebuild your faulty foundation. It offers you a step-by-step formula for returning to your childhood and repairing the wounds that left you weak and vulnerable. It helps you fill in the gaps in your feelings and your abilities that exist because you were unable to progress successfully through the developmental stages of a healthy childhood. It leads you through a process of healing those wounded feelings by helping you personify and get to know these feelings as the children within.

Who are the children within? They are the voices inside you that carry the feelings you were unable to express as a child. They carry your fear, anger, shame and despair. They also carry your excitement, joy, happiness, and love, but many of us have had to deny those feelings as well. Whether you were ignored, belittled, or abused, you learned very early that it was not safe to *feel*. You learned that to feel meant to be vulnerable and to be vulnerable meant that you might not survive. Because you wanted to survive, you learned not to feel.

Many of you learned that it was not safe to feel because you were raised in a time when feelings were unimportant. If you were raised by parents who experienced the Great Depression or suffered through World War II, then you were raised by parents who had little opportunity to feel. They were more concerned with being able to keep food on the table, a roof over their heads, and money in the bank for the future. Their sense of security depended on fitting in and being part of a community that offered stability.

World War II marked the end of that permanence in our society. In the '50s, as the economy and technology improved, we became more mobile. Relatives, communities, and stability were left behind. As we moved into the '60s, we left our idealism behind. Assassinations, the struggle for civil rights, and a senseless war left us wounded and apathetic. The '70s brought Watergate, the nuclear arms race, and disillusionment. By the time we moved into the '80s we found ourselves in limbo—disconnected from others, yet not reconnected to our feelings or ourselves.

Now, as we begin the '90s, this connection is imperative. Those of us who are part of the baby-boomer generation are discovering that we were raised to become part of a society which no longer exists. A connection to our intuition or real self and an ability to identify and process feelings are basic to our emotional well-being.

As a result, many of us feel displaced and unprepared for today's challenges. We need ways to deal with these feelings. We need to learn how to identify, express, release, and transform what we feel. Learning to do this demands that you reexperience what you felt in childhood because that was when you first learned about feelings. This book is designed to help you with this healing task.

WHAT THE WORKBOOK WILL AND WILL NOT DO

This Workbook will

- show you appropriate ways to deal with your feelings toward your parents and children;
- give you the tools you need to confront and grieve your past so you can change how you relate to your past;
- cope more effectively so you can live without addictions and with deeper feeling;
- teach you to have feelings without acting them out;

- enable you to release others from being responsible for your feelings;
- give you the skills you need to act from choice instead of obsession;
- introduce you to the use of ceremony to help ritualize the steps of your growth; and
- help you discover and reclaim your creative potential.

The Workbook will not

- answer all your questions about your pain; it will teach you to find the answers yourself by asking the right questions;
- cure or fix you; you will do that yourself by the honesty of your own efforts;
- eliminate your need for other people; it will simply help you be more dependent on yourself than you are on them.
- demand that you confront your parents unless you choose to do so
- teach you how to feel good; it will teach how to feel.

HOW THE WORKBOOK IS ORGANIZED

Chapter 1, "Discovering and Healing Your Children Within," explains how this material should be used and what will be needed from you in order to use it. It introduces you to the concept of the inner child and gives you a brief background on the development of this concept. It also expands this concept from the idea of one inner child to that of many different children within. Next, a six-step formula is introduced to help you deal with the pain carried by your inner children: identifying your pain, researching your pain, regressing to your pain, objectifying and interacting with your pain, and grieving and healing your pain.

The last section of this chapter provides you with the information you will need to complete the exercises. You will meet your adult self and create a form for a concept we will later define called your Higher Power. It is essential to know both of these characters before you work with your inner children because your adult will oversee the work, and your Higher Power will be an image from which you will draw support.

Chapter 2, "The Infant Self," applies the six-step formula to your infant within. The exercises help you identify, confront, and resolve the problems you may have trusting yourself and others, feeling safe, and knowing how to nurture and be nurtured.

Chapter 3, "The Toddler Self," will help you identify your difficulties with being autonomous, setting limits, and saying and being told no. The six-step formula is then applied to help you confront and resolve these issues.

Chapter 4, "The Young Inner Child," helps you identify the difficulties you may have with accepting your positive and negative qualities. This is perhaps the most difficult developmental stage because so many traits and values are learned at this age. How you learn to relate to yourself and others, how you relate to your body and your sexuality, and how comfortable you feel with being curious all originate in this stage.

In chapter 5, "The Grade-School Child Within," the formula helps you explore and heal problems you may have fitting in with your peers. You also identify and work on difficulties you may experience with beginning and completing projects, public speaking, and attaining professional success.

Chapter 6, "The Young Teen Within," helps you understand how you deal with awkwardness. Your young teen self carries these feelings of awkwardness and your ability to tolerate discomfort. The formula teaches your adult self to help your teen self learn how to manage this discomfort.

Chapter 7, "The Adolescent Within," enables you to confront your feelings about your identity, the issues against which you rebel— tasks that are associated with your adolescent self. Exercises that escort you through the six steps to help you deal with this conflict and pain.

Chapter 8, "The Young Inner Adult," completes the process of working with your developmental stages. You learn or revise the skills needed to move into the adult world. Many of us fail to make this move successfully. Chemical dependency, emotional dysfunction, or family loyalty prevent us from growing up. The exercises help you assess your readiness for the adult world and help you learn the skills needed to become a mature adult. A "Rite of Passage" ritual helps you ceremonially move into adulthood and concludes your work with the different ages within.

Chapter 9, "Developing Ongoing Relationships with Your Children Within," consists of exercises that help you deal with issues unrelated to age. They help you cultivate relationships with your inner children and offer techniques for dealing with inner children's issues that could get triggered in daily life.

Chapter 10, "Intimate Adult Relationships and Your Children Within," shows how your inner children can influence your most intimate adult relationships; how they can sabotage your efforts to be close or keep you in relationships that are no longer satisfying. There is also an exercise that shows you how to deal with your feelings if and when a relationship dissolves.

Chapter 11, "Addictions, Recovery, and Your Children Within," is for those who are in early recovery from chemical or behaviorial addiction.

ABOUT THE EXERCISES

You will find that most chapters contain exercises that elicit both cognitive and creative responses. The cognitive exercises will help you identify problematic personal issues and research the circumstances that caused them. They will help you think about your pain and identify the wounds of your children within.

The creative exercises use writing and art to help you explore your feelings and uncover your childhood memories. They will give you an opportunity to reexperience how you felt as a child and to experience, perhaps for the first time, new ways of being, after you have healed some of your pain.

Journal Writing. I recommend that you record your responses in a journal. Use it for stream-of-consciousness writing, recording without censure whatever thoughts and feelings come to mind. By the time you have finished your inner work, you will have a rich collection of the feelings you identified, experienced, resolved, and healed. It will be similar to having a photo album that documents your inner journey. Just as your childhood emotional development should have followed a predictable progression, so does the material in this book. For this reason, I recommend that you complete the exercises in order. This is especially true when you are working with the developmental stages. If you do not feel that a specific age carries much pain for you, I still advise you to read the information in Step one of that age. You will then have a clear notion of those tasks, and that knowledge will help you work with the stages that do need attention. Also, a trauma that occurred when you were older can affect issues related to younger tasks. For instance, if at age thirteen you had been molested, then your young inner teen would need to be healed, but your infant self also would have issues regarding trust and safety that would need to be addressed. In addition, your toddler self would have to relearn how to set limits after the experience of violation. So it is best if you work with each age in sequence.

Feel free, however, to choose the exercises that fit for you. General instructions for all exercises are provided in both chapter 1 and in the chapter on the infant self. The purpose of each exercise is explained, and there are suggestions about how to cope with your own resistance. There are guidelines on how to keep the pace of your internal work manageable, and instructions on how to prepare for that particular exercise. If, when working with the exercises in later chapters, you need to review the general instructions, the page number is listed to expedite that review. When necessary, instructions that are age-specific are presented at the beginning of the exercises.

Do not force yourself to complete an exercise that feels uncomfortable for you. Push your comfort zone, but do not abuse yourself by doing an exercise that may be too provocative for you at this stage. Write about the feelings you have in response to the exercise. Then, if you choose, make a note to return to it and complete it later.

The Tools You Need For Healing

The tools for these exercises are guided imagery, verbal and written dialogue, mirror work, drawing or finding pictures that represent your pain and the characters within, and ceremony and ritual. The purpose is to elicit your early memories, to unblock your buried feelings, and provide you with ways to heal.

Guided Imagery. Sometimes these are meditations that need to be pre-recorded or can be read aloud by a friend. In these you listen to the entire meditation and then record your responses. At other times, guided imagery appears as a series of statements that you read, react to in your imagination, then record your responses. People respond to guided imagery differently. Some visually experience what they hear or read; others simply feel sensations associated with the images presented. There is no right or wrong way to respond. Accepting and recording your responses honestly is all that is important.

Verbal and Written Dialogues. Dialoguing is a tool that involves talking to the different parts within you; orchestrating an interaction so that a healing can occur. It can be done verbally, when you are actually stating the feelings of the different parts involved in the exercise, or it can be done by writing the responses of each character.

When you are dialoguing between the adult self and a younger inner child, I suggest you use your least dominant hand to write your inner child's responses. It was difficult, as a child, to master the skill of writing. Sentences were shorter, words more direct. By using your least dominant hand, you will find that this experience is recreated. The more mature response of the adult self is experienced by using the hand you are most accustomed to using.

Mirror Work. Mirror work involves sitting in front of a mirror and having a dialog with your selves in order to observe the body and facial movements that accompany these parts within. It allows you to see for yourself how your shoulders slump when you speak from your child self, or how you wince when you express your inner child's fear. It also helps you see more clearly your physical demeanor from your adult point of view.

Looking at yourself in a mirror is also one of the most effective ways of finding that higher, more evolved part of yourself. By facing yourself eye to eye, you can look beyond your physical deficiences and see the wise self within you.

Drawing. Drawing your pain frees your creativity and lets you give form to the feelings and to the different internal characters without using words. Describing the voice of the critical self with words can be limiting; drawing often gives you a richer symbolic means of expression.

Using Pictures from Magazines. You are asked to find pictures that represent your inner children or your inner adult, or pictures that capture the traits you are attempting to acquire. Cutting these pictures from a magazine, for example, and pasting them in your journal gives you another, sometimes more concrete way to document the progress of your work.

Activities. Activities are suggested, whose purpose is to assist you in re-experiencing the sensations from your earlier years. For instance, when working with your toddler self, I suggest you throw a tantrum.

Rituals. A ritual is a ceremony that is planned and implemented for a specific purpose. Sometimes rituals are used in these exercises to assist you in completing a phase of your work. At other times they are used to pay tribute to the growth you have attained. Again, if any of these are uncomfortable for you, I encourage you to ignore them. The intent is to use ritual to enhance your work, not to hinder or complicate it.

Creating a Safe Place

It is important to do the exercises in a place that feels safe and comfortable and where you will not be interrupted. If you live alone, it will be easier for you to create such a place; but if you live with others, you may have to use your imagination. Your special place should be designed according to your specific needs and tastes.

After you have selected your special place, take a moment, sit there quietly, and see how you feel. Is it a place where you can feel calm and not worry about other people intruding? Can you hear the phone, the traffic, or bothersome noises from outside? Look around you. Are there objects, photographs, or anything that could be potentially upsetting to you? For instance, is there a picture of you and your father that might distract you if you were doing an exercise that involves your relationship with him? Are there mementos that trigger certain memories? Are the memories comforting? Would they induce a sense of inappropriate loyalty?

Choose very carefully those things you want around as you do your internal work. Use them as a source of support. You might want to use a special pen or a special journal given to you by a friend, a teddy bear, a scenic picture, or any other item that could enhance your work. The point is to make the area yours and to have the area confined to a certain place in your home. It is important, once you have completed your work for a session, to be able to leave that special place. If you do your work at the kitchen table and then just put the work away and prepare the family meal, there may still be feelings that hang in the air. Just as it is important to be able to feel safe and relaxed so you can concentrate on your internal work, it is also important to be able to get away from it—to have a boundary separating the time you spend reexperiencing your past and the time you spend living your current life.

Alloting the Time You Need

I recommend the amount of time each exercise will take, but obviously this can vary greatly for each person. Feelings are not always predictable. I often will suggest that you take a break after forty-five minutes to an hour. Walk around, get a drink of water, have a snack, and let your body take a rest. It is also good to take a ten- or twenty-minute walk after you have finished working on the day's material. It helps you bring your focus back from the emotional realms to the physical. When focusing intently on our emotions, we tend to lose awareness of our bodies. So treat your body well during the exercises.

As you are completing the exercises for each stage, keep a record of the stages that carry the most pain. Then go back later and do more in-depth work with these ages. I recommend that you work through the entire book at least once. It is not unreasonable to assume this could take between twelve and eighteen months, though the length of time depends on your intensity and consistency. You may even want the support of a professional if you feel your wounds are very deep.

The exercises are designed to be done repeatedly and the book to be used as a lifetime resource. Personal change takes place in layers. You may have worked with a certain age and felt its problems resolved only to have a life event trigger another level of pain related to those age-specific issues. You can always return to this book and the appropriate exercises. Your experience will be different each time because you will be coming to the exercises after having integrated your previous work.

Use Props to Enhance Your Work

Throughout these exercises I suggest that you burn sage, candles, or incense. These scents produce a calming effect. Burning sage is traditionally used in ceremonies to cleanse and purify a working area. A sage stick contains sacred plants tied in a bundle, which is lit and waved through the air; the smoke is said to absorb the air's negative energy. The Native Americans used sage sticks to carry their prayers to the spirit world.

You can purchase many forms of incense at herb shops, health food stores, or New Age establishments. Or you can buy the herbs and prepare them yourself, by grinding them with a mortar and pestle or in a coffee grinder. They can then be burned over a charcoal stick.

If you want to use the herbs in the bathing ritual, tie them up in a square of cheesecloth, place it in the tub, and squeeze it to release the essential oils and properties of the herbs.

You can also use bath salts or oils. Salt crystals are especially useful in baths because the fragrance assists healing and the rock salt has properties that absorb tension from the muscles and relax the body. Put them into the tub as you are running the water, so that the crystals are fully dissolved.

Another prop that can enhance your work is music. I recommend soft, soothing, wordless music. Sound can slow you down and can complement the contemplative mood you will be creating when you begin your work.

Working Alone, in a Group, or with a Professional

Most of these exercises can be done privately, but that is not necessarily the best way. They will often be most effective if you are in a group and everybody is working on the same material. This structure can offer a safe place to obtain the support you need as feelings emerge, and give you a chance to share with others and listen to their reactions. Another advantage is that it can both help you keep focused and provide a kind of safety net. If an exercise provokes too many feelings, you will have the other members of the group to help you accept what you feel. You may decide that you want to have a paid professional or therapist facilitate your group. The therapist can help keep the group on track, anticipate difficulties, and help you accept feelings that might otherwise be too traumatic to confront.

Working privately with a therapist is also an option. The exercises provide the structure and your individual sessions with the therapist provide a safe place and professional guidance to pursue your inner work. This inner journey can often be a difficult one. Its whole purpose is to release feelings and relive experiences that part of us would rather keep hidden. Some of these can be quite frightening and may be too overwhelming to experience alone. For some, working with a trained professional may be the answer.

This is not to discourage you however, from making the journey on your own. For many people, the sense of self-discovery and the increasing feelings of self-worth and independence that come from doing it on their own is the most valuable part of the process. Don't do it *all* on your own, however. Choose a friend with whom you can share your feelings and discoveries. You may have first experienced these feelings in isolation, but it is not necessary to be alone now.

Hints for Therapists

The exercises in this book work very well in group therapy. I have modified this material to meet the needs of a ten-week group, and I have presented its bare bones in a two-day workshop. Obviously, neither presentation is as comprehensive as the material found in this book. In the ten-week group, some of the exercises were completed at home and some were conducted in the group setting. The weekly group served as a support where the members could discuss their reactions to the assignments.

The material also can be used to provide a structure for private sessions. Individual therapy is an ideal format for guided imagery. The writing exercises can be completed outside of the therapy, but understood more effectively with your professional support.

When Not to Use the Workbook

Do not use this book if you are not interested in being able to feel your feelings. The children within are your feelings—they are the feelings from your past. You cannot make your past go away unless you are willing to experience the feelings of your past in a safe and nurturing way.

Do not use this book if you are on prescription mood-altering drugs unless your work is supervised by a professional. These exercises will affect your mood; reexperiencing the pain from your past always does. For your own safety, have a professional monitor your progress so you do not provoke feelings too fast and upset the balance the medication is supposed to maintain.

Do not use this book if you are in early recovery from chemical dependency. Working an intense program such as this helps you uncover underlying feelings from childhood. This material can provoke stress and could threaten your abstinence because it would trigger feelings you are unable to deal with non-addictively.

After you have twelve to twenty-four months of abstinence, and have a viable recovery program that includes meetings and a sponsor, this material can be very beneficial in helping you resolve your childhood issues. This is done most effectively if you have learned how to cope non-addictively with stress from your day-to-day life.

Do not use this book in isolation. Part of the pain resulting from childhood is that you had no one there to help you deal with the trauma or to meet the needs that were not getting met. While you are reworking the pain from your past it is important to share your discoveries with others. It helps you integrate your new knowledge into your daily life and creates the supportive atmosphere you may not have had as a child.

A Note on Vocabulary

Definitions vary. All technical or unusual terms are defined in the text, when they first appear. A glossary can also be found in the appendix.

There was a time
when you were not
a slave,
    remember that.
You walked alone,
    full of laughter,
you bathed bare-
    bellied.
You may have lost
all recollection of it,
    remember . . .
you say there are not
    words to describe it,
you say it does not
    exist.
But remember.
Make an effort
    to remember,
Or, failing that,
    invent.
        Monique Wittig
        Les Guerilleres

1

DISCOVERING AND HEALING YOUR CHILDREN WITHIN

As Monique Wittig states ... her poem *Les Guerilleres,* I too believe there was a time for each of us when we were not a slave to our past, a time when we were connected to our true selves and felt innocent, trusting, and free. It is our childhood pain that prevents us from remembering that time and precludes our living as adults with a sense of freedom and inner peace. This book will help you heal your childhood pain, and enable you to once again remember that time, or failing that, inspire you to invent the childhood you never had. To accomplish this, you will need to change the experience of your past and reclaim and heal the child within you.

THE INNER CHILD EXPLAINED

Change often begins with the child because a child embodies the process of change. In his anthology *Reclaiming the Inner Child,* editor Jeremiah Abrams says that the "inner child is the carrier of our personal stories, the vehicle for our memories of both the actual child and an idealized child from the past. It is the *truly alive* quality of being within us. It is the soul, our experiencer throughout the cycles of life. It is the sufferer. And it is the bearer of renewal through rebirth, appearing in our lives whenever we detach and open to change."

It is no wonder that we return to the child to find the solution to the reduction of emotional pain. The first move by professionals toward the prevention of mental anguish was inspired by the discovery that problems of children who became delinquent actually resulted from frustrations originating in their families. A connection was made to the behavior of the adult criminal. The movement to rehabilitate criminals was born as psychology shifted from seeing them as aberrations of society who carried a mental disease, to tormented souls who could be helped. The transition began with the observations of the troubled child. Again, the child embodied the process of change.

Now, as you seek change in yourselves, you once again return to the child. But this time you return to the child *within.*

Although the inner child concept seems to be a recent development in psychological healing, it has actually been known for some time. According to Charles Whitfield, author of *Healing the Child Within,* "the concept has been around for over two thousand years. Carl Jung called it the divine child, Emmett Fox called it the wonder child. Psychotherapists Alice Miller and Donald Winnicott refer to it as the true self."

American psychiatrist W. Hugh Missildine, author of *Your Inner Child of the Past,* was one of the first to address the issue of working with one's inner child. Dorothy Corkille-Briggs, in her book *Celebrate Yourself,* and Eric Berne, founder of Transactional Analysis, were among the first to discuss the "wounded" or "not okay" child. They began addressing the issues related to that part of us that is damaged in childhood and feels ashamed and afraid. Nathaniel Branden has more recently linked low self-esteem to the traumas experienced in childhood. In his books *How to Raise Your Self-Esteem* and *Experience High Self-Esteem,* he offers concrete ways of raising our self-esteem through exercises which reclaim, heal and integrate the unresolved feelings from childhood.

Therapists Claudia Black and Sharon Wegsheider-Cruse were among the first to introduce the concept of the dysfunctional family to the field of chemical dependency. In *It Will Never Happen to Me,* Claudia Black identified particular characteristics that were common in children raised in alcoholic homes. She coined the phrase "adult children of alcoholics" because, in her own recovery and in her work with others, she began to notice that many adults from alcoholic homes carried certain childhood patterns into their adult lives. Sharon Wegsheider-Cruse, in *Another Chance,* added even more insight into the family dynamics found in alcoholic homes. Finally, John Bradshaw connected the concepts of the inner child, the dysfunctional family, and addiction. With his public television series and his books, *Bradshaw: On the Family: Healing the Shame That Binds You* and *Home-*

coming: *Reclaiming and Championing Your Inner Child,* the world of self-help experienced an explosion and the pieces of the puzzle began to form one big picture.

THE INNER CHILD AND RECOVERY

For many, healing the inner child became synonymous with recovery. Abstaining from destructive behavior became dependent on dealing with one's past. The main concept of the inner child theory is a person-ification of this past. It gives individuals a way to relate to their past in a tangible, rather than abstract, manner. As illustrated in my own story, I was better able to deal with the painful feelings associated with my Dad's death or the loss I felt as my relationship dissolved when I objectified those feelings and related to them as the feelings of my in-ner child. This allowed me to experience the part of me who felt the pain as well as the part of me who could respond to the pain.

The inner child embodies the characteristics of the innocent part of the self. But as you continue your internal work, you soon discover that there is more than one voice crying out for help. These voices rep-resent different sets of needs that require unique and age-appropriate responses. Some emerge at a particular age, others appear carrying cer-tain feelings. But distinct differences between them do become appar-ent. That is why I use the plural—inner children.

I have found it useful, when working with the inner children, to draw on the discoveries that Erik Erikson and Jean Piaget made in their studies of the real child. They observed there was a natural progression to the stages of development from childhood into adulthood. Each stage has specific tasks that need to be mastered if you are to move suc-cessfully to the next stage. What you do not master in childhood reap-pears in your adult lives as inappropriate responses to people, places, or things. It is these inappropriate responses that cause you discomfort. They are outgrowths of the pain and fear experienced in childhood when basic needs were not filled.

Learning what you need to learn in each childhood stage is con-tingent upon your needs being met. You need to feel safe with your caretakers and receive the support necessary to accomplish the other tasks that accompany each stage of development. If your needs at each stage are not met, you do not have the foundation needed to master these tasks. Of course, life does not stop because you are unable to learn and master these tasks. It continues, and you survive by developing faulty ways of responding to others and to the events that take place in your lives.

In childhood these faulty behaviors are functional because they help you survive. But in adulthood, they become inappropriate. They no longer bring you what you want and need. You continue to repeat these faulty behaviors as adults, however, because you know no other way to respond. These behaviors express your fear of love, your inability to say no, your criticalness, your shame. And they result in patterns that interfere with your professions, your self-esteem, and your capacity to claim your place in the world as an adult.

Faulty behaviors and inappropriate responses can be attributed to the different inner children who live inside us because we learned and developed these ways of behaving as children. They are associated with certain emotional events that occurred at specific times in our lives. This is the reason the inner children often appear as various ages. For some people, each age or feeling is portrayed by a different child. For others, the same child appears at different ages carrying different feelings.

Your inner children may appear in daily life in several ways. Sometimes this is positive, such as the childlike joy you feel when you fly a kite or the excitement you experience at a ball game. They also can be responsible for the times you feel angry, alone, or confused. These painful feelings get triggered whenever you confront a situation that involves a developmental task that you did not successfully master. For example, a skill that was to be learned by you as your grade-school self was "task completion." Between the ages of six and twelve you are given the task of completing homework assignments and school projects. If, instead, you had to focus your attention on a painful situation at home, if you were worried about getting beaten or trying to second-guess whether your father would be drunk, the emotional and intellectual energy you needed to learn the skills to begin projects and to follow them through might not have been available. You then might have been labeled as lazy or stupid because you were unable to complete assignments. In response, you may have been embarrassed, and thought of yourself as incompetent. As an adult, when faced with a similar situation, such as writing a college term paper or completing a report for your boss, you may now experience the same feelings of embarrassment and the same fears of humiliation. To heal that pain, you would need to return to that age and help your grade-school self within learn the skills necessary to succeed. Knowing now that task completion is learned in this developmental stage would help you focus your inner child and help him or her develop these skills.

Introduction to the Six Steps

As I worked with the children within, it became evident that the steps of healing were predictable—certain events were necessary if healing was to take place. That progression evolved both into a formula that I now use when working with an inner child's pain. I have organized the work with each developmental stage of the child around this formula. It consists of six steps.

- Step one introduces you to the tasks that needed to be mastered at each developmental stage and helps you identify the pain that resulted if you were unable to complete these tasks.
- Step two helps you research childhood events and attitudes that influenced your development at each stage.
- Step three helps you reexperience the feelings and sensations of that time.
- Step four helps you objectify those feelings and see them as separate from your adult self.
- Step five helps your inner child grieve.
- Step six completes the healing process with a ceremony to emotionally, physically, and spiritually heal each of your children within.

The steps of the formula were inspired by many therapeutic models. Step one was inspired by traditional psychoanalytical principles, which help you identify childhood pain and help make the subconscious material conscious. Step two was inspired by Family Systems therapists Virginia Satir and Jay Haley, who emphasize the need to understand the context of destructive patterns in our family backgrounds. Step three embraces the principles first introduced by Gestalt therapist Fritz Perls, who professed that if we wished to heal our pain, we must first be willing to *experience* that pain. Step four was influenced by Eric Berne, who introduced the concept of multiple selves in his Transactional Analysis approach to healing. He suggested the benefits of interacting with the different ego states existing within each individual. Techniques devised by David Quigley in his Alchemical

Hypnotherapy approach to working with the children within were also illuminating. Step five was inspired by Elizabeth Kubler-Ross and Alice Miller, who emphasized the need to grieve for that which is lost. Alice Miller has stated, "There was something you once needed in childhood that you did not get. You will never get it and the proper response is grief." To heal, one must acknowledge what was not there and then release the self from wanting it any longer. Step six, the final ceremony of healing, is inspired by the recognition, as pointed out by mythologist Joseph Campbell, that we need to ritualize change to make it tangible. Our process of inner healing is incomplete unless we are willing to give it symbolic form and to celebrate it.

STEP ONE: IDENTIFYING YOUR PAIN

Your first task for each age will be to identify the pain you carry from that stage of development. To begin, it is necessary to understand what tasks were to be mastered at that stage, and each stage's introduction contains this information. You will also find a discussion of the childhood needs that were fulfilled if you had successfully mastered the tasks, as well as an explanation of how mastering these tasks prepares you for the next developmental stage. Examples are included that illustrate the application of the six-step formula. I hope these stories will bring life to the formula before you begin work with your inner child's pain. Then you will be ready to identify your own pain.

The first exercise, "How You Respond Today," asks you to respond to a series of statements that will help determine how past pain influences your current life. Your responses to the statements will help you identify areas you need to explore further. There are instructions on how to interpret your responses, and how to determine the direction you may need to pursue.

In the second exercise, "How You Carry These Issues in Your Life Today," you are asked to write in your journal about specific situations in which you may have felt discomfort. For instance, when working with your adolescent self, I ask you to write about a recent time you felt you wanted to rebel. In the introduction to that chapter, you would have already learned that this rebelliousness is a carry-over from your teen years. By recognizing it as belonging to your inner teen, you begin to identify the source of the rebelliousness and more accurately assess the current situation that triggered that same need.

Drawing on your own responses to questions in these exercises, you then make a list of the weaknesses and strengths you have carried from each developmental stage. Exploring the circumstances that created these will be the focus of your research in Step two.

STEP TWO: RESEARCH YOUR PAIN

Now you gather information on the events that occurred to your caretakers before your birth in your childhood, the attitudes that existed during each developmental stage, and the external factors that may have interfered with your development.

As young children you are self-centered. Everything in your world revolves around you. You do not have the capacity to understand that some event, totally unrelated to you, influenced the care you received. Your mother's lack of attention therefore might have been experienced by you as a sign that you were not worthy of her love. You could carry this feeling of unworthiness into adulthood and feel shame for being unlovable.

In researching this pain, the adult part of you, who is not self-centered, can comprehend the effect of external factors. You understand the shortcomings of those who raised you. Understanding these factors arms your adult self with the information needed to help the inner child dissolve the shame, grieve, and finally resolve the pain.

This is essential to working with your children within because it frees you both from carrying your caretakers' pain, and from blaming yourself for it. This kind of pain is carried from generation to generation through a process called "mimicking." As a child, you mimicked everything your caretaker did, and their pain was passed on to you in all your interactions. For instance, if your mother's father died right before you were born, your experience of birth and the following months of your life would have been influenced by your mother's grief. *Her* grief would have become *your* grief because of your symbiotic tie with her. You would have sensed her pain in every touch, heard it in every word. You would have inherited an aspect of her grief because you would have mimicked and responded to her grief-stricken behavior. Mimicking is evident in many second-generation Holocaust survivors, who inherit their parents' grief. They also inherit the guilt their parents felt for having survived. While they may not have experienced this atrocity directly, it was woven so deeply into the fabric of

two parts within you who can relate to each other. You can talk then with your inner child, comfort your inner child, and heal your inner child.

The first exercise, "Meeting Your Children Within," involves guided imagery that introduces you to the inner child of that stage. Guided imagery is a tool each person responds to differently because it asks you to draw on your imagination to see pictures in your mind. It is similar to daydreaming, except that it is intentional; it is similar to night dreaming except that you are conscious.

Once you have met that inner child, I suggest that you try to find a photo of yourself at that age. If you can't, try to find a picture from a magazine that reminds you of who you were then, physically or symbolically. Don't be concerned if you choose a picture that doesn't look like you. Trust that there is something in that picture that represents your pain.

The first inner child I ever worked with was my five-year-old—the part of me who carried my shame. When I imagined her, she looked like a child from one of those old Keane pictures that were so popular in the '50s and early '60s. She had dark straight hair and piercing brown eyes. Physically, she looked nothing like me but her sad face and haunting look symbolized how I felt when I experienced shame.

The second exercise, "Creating a Dialogue with Your Children Within," offers questions that will help you get to know the many facets of that inner child. Exercise three, "Talking In the Mirror to Your Children Within," furthers the experience of the separation by giving you the opportunity to observe the changes that may occur when talking from the different parts of yourself. Louise Hay, author of *You Can Heal Your Life,* often recommends mirror work because it so effectively brings you face-to-face with that which you fear most.

The Protector and the Critical Voice

Objectifying and interacting with your pain is not just giving your inner child form, it is also giving form to a protector and to a critical voice. These characters will be used repeatedly in your work with your children within. They may be the same at each stage, or you may experience a variety.

In the fourth exercise, "Creating Your Protector," you and your inner child create a form for the protector. As you continue your work with each inner child, this protector may take on different forms. Your inner children will direct you. If asked, they will know who they want to protect them.

In the fifth exercise, "Detecting the Critical Voice," you give form to the critical voice that abuses that inner child and perpetuates the negative self-talk. The critical voice carries the internalized censuring messages you heard from your parents and society in general. For instance, if you were told as a child that you were stupid, you may refer to yourself as stupid today. If you were told as a child that you were ugly, you may still feel ugly now. Your critical voice carries these feelings.

Your critical voice is evident whenever you hear yourself make statements that begin with "you should," "you should not," or "you can't." These phrases echo messages you heard as a child, and each stage carries its own critical voice. Some of these messages were meant to protect and guide you, others served to shame and restrict you. In each stage it is important to uncover these messages and to understand their intent. Only then can you transform them from statements that wound to statements that nurture. Writing exercises that elicit a dialogue between this voice and the inner adult's voice will assist you in doing this.

The exercises for each stage are designed around these tools. Objectifying the feelings and interacting with the younger selves are often the hardest steps for people to feel comfortable doing and to remember to do. It feels awkward and crazy. We are not used to talking to our many selves. We're told that this is a sign of being crazy, so we resist. Also, the pain of our inner children gets triggered so quickly that we sometimes fear acknowledging it.

When I first started working with my inner children, I would often forget to stop and relate to them. Panic, anger, or rejection would surface, and I would become so engrossed in those feelings that I would not stop to ask who inside was feeling pain. When I did remember to check in, I usually felt instant relief because I had accessed my adult self and objectified my pain. I can still sometimes forget to become quiet enough to ask. It's amazing that almost every time I do ask, however, I get a response and can deal with the feelings within minutes.

In talking to your inner children, it is important to refer to each directly, as "you." Using "you" is already creating a separation, a dyad. For those who are just beginning to explore feelings, this may be confusing.

Separation from a feeling you have not felt or embraced is not possible. Separating, or what I refer to as "objectifying" your feelings, becomes important when you are ready to begin the healing process. Emotional health is "living-with-feeling." It is experiencing what you feel and then letting go. Objectifying your feelings is necessary when you are unable to let go. When you experience a negative feeling that lingers on, and you keep mulling it over and over and over, it is time to objectify that feeling. Immersing yourself in this negative self-talk is debilitating and can be harmful to you and to others. Dealing with your critical voice is a way to confront the negative self-talk, while viewing the uncomfortable feelings as the feelings of your inner child is a way to objectify the pain. This is an approach you can use to establish some distance from the pain, thus allowing an interaction with the pain. And with that interaction the healing process begins.

Exercise six, "Changing Your Inner Child's Experience of Childhood," is designed to help you retrieve the wounding scenes from your past, and then change your experience and perception of those scenes as an adult. The scenes you retrieve may be real or imagined. Wounds may have resulted from your parents' unintentional errors, or they may have been the result of negligence or intentional abuse.

For some, the life events may have been physical or emotional abuse. For others, the trauma may have resulted from a dysfunction in the family: alcoholism, terminal illness, unemployment, or divorce. It also may simply have been the trauma experienced from being raised at a time when being a parent was not geared to building the children's self-esteem. What is important is that as a child, you were unable to defend yourself against these wounding life events.

To transform this experience you must begin to focus on the times you felt discomfort. This is done by closing your eyes and assessing where your body felt this discomfort. Feelings of rage or fear, abandonment or shame may surface. You then begin to see, sense, or feel the younger child within you. At that point you ask, "When have I felt this way before?" Usually, by conducting this kind of internal dialogue, a memory or childhood scene will surface.

You will then review this scene—it may be a real or a symbolic recreation—to see which characters are there. Then have the characters interact.

At this point, you will be able to determine who in the scene needs help and decide exactly what they need. Sometimes the intervention process means responding to each character in the scene. At other times it simply means rescuing the inner child by removing him or her from the scene. Whatever the situation is, the adult self is the one who enters the scene, intervenes, stops the destructive behavior, or meets the unmet needs of that particular age.

If the adult self confronts a scene that he or she feels ill-equipped to handle, bring into the mind's eye other figures who can help, for instance, an adult whom you admire. What is useful about guided imagery and the use of imagination is that you can create whatever intervention is necessary. Research has shown that the body does not know the difference between what the mind imagines and what actually occurs. If you can imagine it, you can experience it. If you can imagine healthy and responsible interactions taking place, you can negotiate and meet the needs of characters in the scene. As a dialogue takes place, the tension and discomfort are addressed. As they are addressed, they dissipate.

Sometimes the interaction is simple. The inner child or wounded self may merely need to be told and reassured that he or she is safe and valued. At times, the inner child may need to be rescued from an abusive scene or may need to get the parents' help so he or she can get on with being a child. Most importantly, their needs are heard, responded to, and met. Creating an internal dialogue is a way to reassure your inner child that he or she is no longer alone. The adult assumes responsibility for the things the inner child was unable to comprehend and can do things the child was unable to do. You will have all of your personal research to draw from to help you comfort and assure the child that it was not his or her fault that the needs were not met.

As you rework each scene, you rewrite your personal history. Painful memories are replaced with nurturing ones. An experience is created that transforms that stage. Needs are met that were not met, tasks are mastered that were not mastered. Through this repetition you reclaim and heal each of your children within.

STEP FIVE: GRIEVING YOUR INNER CHILD'S PAIN

Once you have learned how to objectify your pain and interacted with the inner child who carries that pain, you are ready to help your inner child grieve. Each inner child's unique issues will need to be grieved, and to be of assistance, you, as the inner adult, will need to know how to grieve.

The Stages of Grief

The grieving process is one that most of us know little about. We are not taught to grieve; we are taught to survive. This is unfortunate, because I believe that we are always in some state of grief, which we go through when we experience a loss. And loss occurs every moment we are alive. Loss ranges from the traumatic to the banal. It is experienced when you lose a loved one through death or divorce, or when you lose a job or your career suffers a set–back. You suffer loss when a fire or flood destroys your property, or if you are injured or ill. Trust severed by betrayal is a devastating form of loss. Self-esteem may be wounded through shame. You can even feel loss when you miss a phone call, or say something that makes you feel foolish.

Whenever you feel a sense of panic or fear, you are probably experiencing a loss because panic is the first stage of grief. It is through panic that you break your denial and free yourselves to feel the fear. When you feel fear, you try to control, and you begin the second stage of grief, called bargaining. You try to make deals with what you fear you have lost. For instance, if you are hospitalized after a near-fatal car accident, you may make a bargain with God, promising never to drive fast again if he will only let you live.

As a child we were bargaining when we promised our parents that we would be good, be quiet, be *anything,* as long as they wouldn't hurt us anymore. We were bargaining when we promised God we'd be good if only he'd make our parents stop drinking. Sometimes our bargaining is irrational, sometimes it is not. But when it doesn't work— when our parents don't stop drinking even though we've been a model child—we get angry. We have to face our loss.

Anger is the third stage of grief. Most of us, once we break our denial, vacillate between these first three stages of grief. We feel panic and anger and then try to bargain or control. With time, we exhaust ourselves and collapse into despair, the fourth stage of grief. It is out of the tunnel of our despair that acceptance and resolution emerge. Accepting our loss is the fifth and final stage of grief. We may always have feelings about what we have lost, but our lives can continue even though we have suffered this loss.

It is this grieving process that your inner children go through when you begin to help them heal. They feel grief in response to the original loss of caretaking. They will experience grief as they release their parents or caretakers of the responsibility to meet their needs, thus forming an alliance with you as their main support. They will experience grief as you surpass your parents' limits and capabilities and they will experience grief when you release the multi-generational pain that you have inherited. Exercise one, "The First Four Stages of Grief," in Step five of the formula lets you address all of these forms of grief in each age.

Here is an example of how your inner children's grief occurs. If as a child you were unable to manage this panic, you tried to bargain and make deals. You tried to be a good little kid so your daddy wouldn't drink. You tried to keep the house spotless or get good grades so your mommy would not be sad. These attempts to bargain with your situation led to feeling shameful because nothing that you tried ever worked. You didn't know it then, but the situation was out of your hands. So repeatedly you tried to make things better. These attempts to bargain with your pain gave you a false sense of comfort and seemed to keep the panic at bay.

This pattern is virtually always found at the root of codependent behavior. The obsession with making bargains with others and trying to control their behavior keeps the focus off the fear that they would abandon us. As a child, this pattern of behavior enabled us to survive, because to have faced the reality of our situation would have been overwhelming. Attempting to control our caretakers was the only way we could stay safe.

Using Anger to Heal

Anger is the only emotion that can empower us to move *through* the panic so we can combat and interrupt our bargaining behavior. Few are willing to embrace anger. We would rather do anything than feel the anger. We ingest, protest, reject, addict, deny—anything to keep us from the power of rage, because the ultimate fear is that expressing our anger will permanently damage whatever structure we're hoping to create. Without hope, our inner children believe they will cease to exist.

In childhood this belief may have been true because that hope did keep you alive. As an adult, however, you can experience anger and escort your inner child through this stage of grief. Remember, embracing anger empowers the inner child, and makes the child able to accept that the dysfunction was in the family. This enables your inner child to begin the process of letting go. Anger lets the child realize that the caretakers will never change—a necessary realization if the child is to establish an alliance with you. As long as your inner child holds on to the hope that the situation will change, he or she is unable to accept the reality of the past. If he or she embraces this hopeless situation, your inner child collapses into despair. It is important to note that your inner child can only experience this despair with your adult self in close contact. Isolation, loneliness, and defeat are much too profound to be endured alone.

The suggestions in this step of the formula aid your inner child in the experience of that grief. Remember, grief is an ongoing process and the exercises may be used repeatedly. After expressing the emotions at one layer, you may experience a reprieve only to uncover yet another layer of loss that needs to be grieved. Although this may seem alarming when it happens, it is a natural process, a progression we all go through.

Generalized Grief

There may be times when your grief extends beyond your personal experience. The cycles of abuse and neglect are beginning to be confronted. And as you confront this pain, you often touch the pain of others who have experienced something similar. Therefore, whatever cloak of identity your pain and grief wears will be the pain you feel most intensely.

If you have been a victim of sexual abuse, you may relate to the pain of all sexual-abuse survivors. If you have been victimized because of your race, religion, sexual preference, or gender, you may relate to the pain of others who have suffered these same insults. If you are a Vietnam vet, you carry not only your pain, but the pain of every soldier and person who had to participate in the terror of war. You may find you need to release this "generalized grief" as well. Until recently, there have not been many resources for learning how to deal with these feelings. But now we have the time, the tools, and the desire to help ourselves.

STEP SIX: HEAL YOUR PAIN, RECLAIM YOUR JOY

The final stage of grief is acceptance and resolution. In Step five you helped your inner child express pain; the ritual in the exercise "Healing Your Inner Child," will help him or her ceremonially release that pain. In this stage you make peace with the loss and help each inner child to let go.

Celebrate Your Health

Ceremony is a way to acknowledge an important event, to ritualize its passing or completion. Some common ceremonies in our culture include weddings, bar mitzvahs, and birthdays. For some of you, though, the idea of creating your own ritual may frighten you. You may associate the word with evil and the occult. This is certainly not the context in which I use this word. Ritual is a tool to make your resolution of grief tangible. The rituals offered in Step six will guide you as you release the feelings you identified, experienced, and expressed in the previous steps of the formula. It also will enable you to release your childhood pain at three levels: emotionally, physically, and spiritually.

In each age, you are first led through a ceremony in which you burn all the writings and drawings that represent your grief and then bury the ashes in the earth. Symbolically, you release the emotional tension and energy that each inner child has carried and that has been given physical form by you in these writings and drawings with respect to the past.

Once you have released emotionally, you can release physically. By paying tribute to your body and by releasing the feelings of your inner child from your body, you can begin to alter the physical postures and stances you have adopted to accommodate your childhood pain. The bathing ritual is a way to augment your healing process physically. I also recommend ongoing bodywork because it will help you learn ways of posturing yourself nondefensively.

After you complete the bathing ritual, you are ready to experience spiritual healing. Guided imagery leads you through this experience for each age. In this final phase of your healing, you introduce your inner child to your Higher Power, who then takes the inner child into a healing Light. After the inner child has been healed, the Higher Power returns your inner child to you and the true essence of this child is freed. You then reclaim the joy and gifts of that inner child by reintegrating him or her into yourself.

This will complete the formula for that particular age. You will then be able to take all that you have experienced, released, and healed and use it as the foundation for the next developmental stage. In working and reworking this formula you are, indeed, going back through childhood and changing your experience. You are developing the tools you need to continue your ongoing growth. You will have a model that you can continually use to deal with any residual pain left over from your childhood. Methods for coping with the pain of your everyday life will emerge. The formula teaches you how to deal with these feelings. If you can deal with feelings, you can *live-with-feeling,* and this is the basis of emotional health.

YOUR ADULT SELF

Before you work with your inner children there are several preliminary exercises that you must complete. Later in the book, you will work the exercises from your adult self, so it is essential that you first have a clear idea of who that part of you is. If your experience of being an adult is unclear, you must establish an adult figure who can act as your guide. The exercise "Finding Your Adult Self" will help you determine this and assist you in creating the adult figure you need.

The second exercise, "Creating a Form for Your Higher Power," will help you create a form for your personal image of God so that you have a clear image to draw on when this is recommended. The third exercise, "Exploring the Garden of Your Past," leads you through guided imagery that helps you envision your past as a garden. This imagery is used throughout the work with your children within as a metaphor for your growth and for the process of healing yourself.

EXERCISE ONE: FINDING YOUR ADULT SELF

In her book, *Celebrate Yourself,* Dorothy Corkville Briggs says that the responsible inner adult is "that part capable of thinking, in touch with reality, that postpones a present pleasure for a long-term gain. It estimates the probability of consequences of certain acts. It is the part of you that is responsible to yourself and to others."

It is important to find your adult self because it will oversee your work and negotiate between your critical characters within and your children within. The adult self is the part of you who makes sure that the needs of your inner children are met and works hand in hand with your Higher Power to determine the most effective way to meet those needs. Use the following suggestions to help you find your inner adult.

Purpose and Directions

The exercises below help you draw on the experiences you have had with people in your life who are responsible. They also will help you build on your own personal experiences of being responsible. Combining these two resources gives you a healthy model for your inner adult.

Guidelines and Pacesetters

Your inner adult will orchestrate the healing process. Take your time with this exercise. You are building the foundation for the most important character in this work. Keep in mind that we all have some experience with being responsible. You would not have purchased this book if there were not a part of you who is healthy enough to want to change.

If at any time your inner adult seems incapable, use a technique called "acting as if." This involves selecting an adult whom you admire and whom you feel would be able to deal with the task, and imagining that person completing the work. Or you can simply pretend that you *are* that adult by imagining how the person would respond. It helps to imagine how this person would move and speak, and to use words you think he or she would use. Play-acting is a great way to develop the strengths you need to do your internal work; it gives a model that you can draw on any time you feel doubtful of your own abilities.

At the end of these exercises, you should have a better idea of how strong your inner adult already is or what you need to do to develop your adult further.

Preparation

You will need your journal, pen, scissors, magazines, and tape. Find a time when you will be uninterrupted and allow approximately thirty to forty-five minutes. If you decide to work longer, take a stretch and walk around the room a bit, then resume your work.

Exercise

1. List in your journal five men and five women you know and would describe as responsible. Next to their names, describe the qualities you see in them that made you put them on your list.

2. List three fictitious men and women whom you have seen in the movies, on television, or read about. Describe the qualities they seem to have that make you feel they are examples of responsible adults.

3. Cut out magazine pictures representing people whom you would describe as having these qualities. Use these pictures to make a collage in your scrapbook.

4. Make a list of times in your life you were responsible. How did you handle that responsibility? Did you feel competent or insecure?

5. In your journal, write a description of your ideal responsible adult. List ten ideal qualities that a responsible adult would possess.

6. Rate yourself according to those ten qualities. Take an inventory of the qualities you have and the qualities you would need to develop in order to have an effective inner adult. Do not use this information to judge yourself; use it to assess what work needs to be done.

7. Close your eyes and imagine this ideal adult standing in front of you. Merge with this adult and imagine you become that adult. See how you feel, how you walk, talk, carry your body. Describe that experience in your journal.

Closing

You should now have a better idea of how strong your inner adult is and what you need to do to develop him or her. In your work with the inner children, you will be using the adult self a great deal. Always try to bring into your exercises the part of you who has been responsible. "Act as if" when you have to. Use role models when necessary. They can do what you are unable to do until your adult self is more solid and capable. You will be working in your imagination, so you can do whatever you want and need to do.

EXERCISE TWO: CREATING A FORM FOR YOUR HIGHER POWER

I have found that it is necessary to have faith in a power greater than yourself if you are going to heal your inner child's pain. Sometimes the pain is so excruciating that it cannot be contained by the adult self. If you have experienced painful feelings deeply, you often feel there is no place else to go with your pain. With a spiritual or religious belief that there is someone or something that you can ask to remove your pain, you can more easily let that pain go.

Purpose and Directions

You will be examining your beliefs concerning a Higher Power and then creating a form to represent that belief. For some it may be the image of a wise old being. For others it may be a sphere of Light, a guardian angel, or a spirit guide. For still others it will be experienced as part of you; or it will be a part outside of yourself. The image may be based on religious beliefs, and may appear in a human form, such as Jesus, Buddha, Mohammed, or a guru, or as an abstract symbol, such as a cross or a mandala. And some may picture an aspect of nature or envision a group to which you belong. Accept whatever form presents itself. If you feel uncomfortable with that form, then look for an image to which you can comfortably relate.

Guidelines and Pacesetters

If you are uncomfortable with the idea of a Higher Power by any definition, then feel free not to do this exercise. When you come across a reference to this character in the exercises, simply ignore it and proceed.

Preparation

Go to your private place where you will be doing your work. Place your journal and your pen by your side. You may want to play some soft, relaxing music so that you are more able to achieve a meditative state of mind. Either pre-record the imagery or ask a friend to read it to you.

Exercise

Close your eyes and take a deep breath. Take several more deep breaths and then bring your focus to the center of your being. When you feel that center within you, imagine that you see a ball of beautiful glowing Light taking shape in that area of your body. Imagine now that this ball of Light begins to illuminate and expand until soon it can completely encase your total physical form. When you feel surrounded by this Light, imagine you begin to walk forward.

Soon the Light fades and you see and feel a beautiful meadow all around you. You walk over to a path that leads you deeper into this meadow. A presence is accompanying you. This presence is your Higher Power. What form does your Higher Power have? How do you feel about this form? Is it a form that will enhance your work? If so, stay with this form and ask it if it will help you on your journey. When you have your answer, imagine that you and the form for your Higher Power walk out of the meadow, down the path and back into the center of the Light. Conclude this exercise by taking a deep breath and imagining that you bring the essence of your Higher Power back with you to your present time. Open your eyes when you feel comfortable to do so.

Closing

Record your feelings or reactions to this exercise in your journal. Describe the form you created for your Higher Power. Think of a symbol that you can use to represent the presence of your Higher Power. For instance, you might want to have a special crystal or a special stone that carries this essence. You may have a picture or a poem, or an item from someone close to you that carries a specialness about it. This token will help you make the presence of your Higher Power more tangible. You can carry it with you throughout your day and always have it present when you work with your children within.

EXERCISE THREE: EXPLORING THE GARDEN OF YOUR PAST

Purpose and Directions

You will envision a garden that symbolizes your past and revise the images at each stage as you work with your children within. As issues are identified, resolved, and healed, you and your children within will clear your garden of the weeds and overgrowth that result from each stage. The condition of your garden may shock you. You may feel as though you will never be able to make it beautiful and ready for new growth. However, just as your internal growth will take time so, too, will the cleaning of your symbolic garden. Each weed pulled and each shovel of dirt turned over will contribute to the transformation of your past. Use your garden as a tangible indicator of the progress of your growth.

Preparation

Go to your private place, relax, and get into a meditative state. Either pre-record this exercise or have a friend read it to you. Have your pen, journal, and drawing materials handy.

Exercise

Close your eyes and go to that place within you that is at the very center of your being. Picture the Light in this center expanding and creating a cylinder of Light all around you. Imagine that this Light fades and you find yourself back on the path in a beautiful meadow. Start walking down this path. Notice that there are garden plots all along the way. These plots represent the gardens of others. Continue until you come to the plot that is yours. You will intuitively know which one this is.

Stand before your plot. Notice the condition of your personal garden. Look at what grows on this plot that represents your past. You might see beautiful flowers that are being strangled with weeds. How do you feel as you gaze into this symbol of your past? As you work with each child within, you will be tilling the soil, pulling the weeds, preparing your soil for growth, and planting the contributions of each inner child. With this in mind, follow the path out of the meadow and come back into the center of your Light. Open your eyes when you feel comfortable to do so.

Closing

Draw a picture or describe your garden in your journal. This is an image that you will continuously work with throughout the healing process of your children within.

TIME TO BEGIN

You have been introduced to all the concepts and tools you need, and you are now ready to begin your work with your ages within. Take time to breathe and to feel what you were unable to feel when you were young.

2

THE INFANT SELF

Welcome to the World

The degree of nurturing, safety, and trust you feel toward others is a clue to the degree of nurturing, safety, and trust you felt when you were an infant. From birth to approximately eighteen months of age, the developmental tasks you needed to master were bonding with your caretaker and learning about nurturing and trust. Bonding is sometimes defined as feeling physically safe with our main caretaker, but actually it means much more. It is, most importantly, an emotional connection with another human being. Through this physical and emotional connection, you developed trust. When, as an infant, you were held and comforted, fed, bathed and kept clean, your world felt nurturing and safe. You felt welcome, and you learned to trust because your physical and emotional needs were met.

In our society it is typically our mother or mother figure who nurtures us and teaches us safety and trust. Gabriel Roth and John Loudon discuss this concept beautifully in their book *Maps to Ecstasy: Teachings of an Urban Shaman.*

> The birth cycle begins with conception and lasts for approximately five years. Mother is the sacred teacher of this cycle. She passes on her lessons through her body by example, guidance, attitude, energy, vibration. Men with maternal instincts know how to nurture themselves and how to take care of their children. But it is the mothers who pass the nurturing instinct on to their children. Body to body. It's that simple.

And what you learned from your mother, or your mother figure, you applied to yourselves and to others. From this relationship you built the foundation for the next stage of development, which was separating from your caretaker and establishing your independence. You could not separate from someone to whom you had never attached. You could not become independent from someone on whom you had never been able to depend.

Your relationship to your mother or mother figure also provided you with the model you later use for closeness in your adult intimate relationships. If this relationship was weak, if your needs for safety, trust, and nurturing went unmet, you may grow up to fear closeness or remain forever dependent on others to meet your needs. For instance, if you were left for long periods of time to cry, if your diapers went unchanged, if your cues for hunger were misread or ignored, or if the arms that held you were rejecting and rigid, you probably would not have felt safe. If you did not feel safe, you would not have been able to bond enough with your caretaker to develop trust. The inability to trust would directly influence your experience of nurturing. Having experienced your world as unsafe, you would most likely grow up either compulsively seeking closeness or habitually avoiding it.

When closeness is sought compulsively, it is most often an attempt to fill basic nurturing needs that were never met. Dependence can be disguised as closeness. The needs you want filled by others can far surpass the healthy expectations of an intimate relationship. The relationships that do last most likely mirror the parent/child dynamic because you enter them with your infant's unmet needs. If this is the case, you may find that many of your relationships terminate because of your "neediness."

On the other hand, you may avoid closeness for fear of getting hurt. You may fear it would result in rejection, abandonment, or abuse. You may fear that those in your current life will discover what you already assume—that you are not worthy of love. We suspect something must have been wrong with us, or our caretakers would have made us feel safe and loved. Feelings of unworthiness and shame cover up the fear that we will be abandoned, rejected, or abused.

Case History: Janie

Such was the case for Janie. She had recently ended a relationship and was in much pain. She came to see me, and as we talked she kept repeating how repulsive and shameful she felt. She kept saying she could not imagine anyone ever wanting to touch her or hold her again.

I talked with Janie about the concept of the inner child. I had her close her eyes and picture the first time she felt repulsive. As she did this, she saw herself as an infant. She was alone in her crib. Her skin was raw from eczema. Janie had been told by relatives that her mother had been repulsed and, in fact, had not wanted to touch her. She had also been told that she had been in so much pain that her body was too tender even to be touched.

Having identified the source of Janie's feelings, I led Janie through guided imagery in which she objectified her sense of repulsion by seeing those feelings as the shame of her infant within. Doing this enabled her to respond to the feelings, instead of collapsing into this pain of repulsion.

In her mind's eye, Janie became her nurturing parent. I asked her to go over to the infant and imagine that she put a magic salve on the baby's skin that began to heal the rawness of the wounds. For several sessions we worked with Janie's feelings of repulsion. In each session she would separate from the pain, see the pain as the infant's wounds, tend to the wounds and comfort the infant within her. When the child was healed enough to be held, I asked Janie to imagine herself rocking and cuddling the infant, nurturing her back to health. I had her assure the infant that she was not to blame for the wounds and that she would never be abandoned or alone again. As she reclaimed responsibility for this part of herself, dissolved the shame and responded to the fear of abandonment, Janie was freed to deal with the grief she felt over the loss of her present-day relationship. Her infant's shame and fear had covered up her grief and had kept her from progressing through it so she could heal and get on with her life.

STEP ONE: IDENTIFYING YOUR PAIN

In the following exercise you explore your issues with safety, trust, and nurturing. By examining how you react in your current life, you will begin to identify the feelings of both strength and vulnerability that have been carried over from this developmental stage.

EXERCISE ONE: HOW YOU RESPOND TODAY

Purpose

The statements in this exercise reveal whether your needs at the infant stage were met. They help you identify how often you feel the effects of the gaps you may have had in this developmental stage and help you see how these issues still emerge in your current life. Your responses will also show you the strengths you may have developed because of the attention you *did* receive.

Guidelines and Pacesetters

If you begin to feel overwhelmed, take a break. If the statements trigger strong memories or feelings, you could do some free-form writing in your journal, which is simply writing down the feelings you are experiencing. It provides a way to express and release what has been triggered. Write until you have expressed the feelings that have come up and you feel calm enough to continue, or skip to the next statement. You can always come back to the provocative statement when you feel more prepared to deal with the feelings.

Preparation

Go to your private place. Have your journal and pen handy. Play soothing music, light a candle, and prepare your space so that you are comfortable. If you so choose, call in the support of your Higher Power. Allow approximately thirty minutes for this exercise. The time will vary according to how much you write. If you need more time, get up and stretch before you proceed.

Exercise

Read each statement slowly. Take a deep breath and then check the option that best expresses how often you feel this way.

Safety	Always	Often	Sometimes	Rarely	Never
I do not feel I have a right to ask others to meet my needs.	_____	_____	_____	_____	_____
Feeling close to others frightens me.	_____	_____	_____	_____	_____
I feel a general sense of panic or restlessness.	_____	_____	_____	_____	_____
The world feels like an unsafe and fearful place.	_____	_____	_____	_____	_____

Nurturance					
I fear being touched or touching others.*	_____	_____	_____	_____	_____

	Always	Often	Sometimes	Rarely	Never
I have a difficult time acknowledging and responding to my own needs, desires, and accomplishments.*	_____	_____	_____	_____	_____
I have a difficult time giving attention to others.	_____	_____	_____	_____	_____

Trust

It is hard for me to determine what my needs are.*	_____	_____	_____	_____	_____
I have difficulty trusting that others will meet my needs so I try to take care of them myself.	_____	_____	_____	_____	_____
I lack trust in myself to take care of my needs.	_____	_____	_____	_____	_____
I am ashamed to show others how "needy" I really feel. I am afraid they will laugh or ignore me.	_____	_____	_____	_____	_____

Closing

Review your answers. Look at the group of statements under Trust. Does it seem from your answers that you have a problem with trust? What about safety and nurturing? For instance, if you checked mostly "never" or "rarely" in safety and nurturing, but checked mostly "often" or "always" for the category of trust, then your caretaker probably met your basic needs and was physically affectionate, but did not respond to your emotional needs. You may have felt cared for and safe, but not responded to enough to feel and develop trust. On the other hand, if your answers indicate that you feel safe and trusting but are uncomfortable with nurturing, then your caretaker may not have been very affectionate. Responding with either extreme ("always" or "never") could indicate a lack of flexibility or a need to always be in control. Use your own judgment to interpret the significance for you. For instance, in statement five under nurturance, if you responded by saying that you

were unable to trust your caretakers to meet your needs, you may have learned very early how to take care of yourself. Although there are wounds associated with this trait, there is also the strength of being able to meet your own needs. Record any ideas you have on how your experience at this stage may have contributed positively to your development.

℃ℑ

STEP TWO: RESEARCHING YOUR INFANT SELF'S PAIN

If you had more strengths than issues, you may have little to research in Step two. However, you should still explore the origins of those you did uncover. If, on the other hand, you discover there are many wounds from this stage, then you will want to research that time of your life more fully. This will help you identify the history of your pain. As mentioned in chapter 1, a great deal of your pain is not actually yours. It was inherited. You inherited the feelings or suffered from the impact of any tragedy or distraction that was occurring in the life of your mother or caretaker when you were a child. The kind of love and care you received were also deeply affected by your parents' own strengths and weaknesses. Failing to understand these circumstances, you may assume the problem was with you.

For instance, you may feel you were not good enough to receive the nurturing you so badly needed as an infant. You may feel you were not wanted, and therefore were not worthy of the love and attention you so desperately required. These feelings can result in your carrying a sense of shame that you had any needs at all. You can even feel shame for being born.

You may carry the belief that the inadequate parenting you received was your fault. The truth is that it was not your fault that your needs went unmet. It was your right to have your basic needs met in infancy. It was your right to receive the care and attention you needed at each stage. If this did not happen, there was a reason. Perhaps there were many reasons, but one of them was not you!

Identifying the history of your pain will enable you to construct the bigger picture of the reasons your needs were not met. Your inner adult will then be armed with the information needed to help your children within confront the pain related to this stage, which is rooted in the needs to feel safe, to experience trust and to feel nurtured.

EXERCISE ONE: INTERVIEWING YOURSELF

Purpose and Directions

The purpose of interviewing yourself first is that it will enable you to obtain an accurate record of what you remember. Every family member experiences family life differently. Your memory may be entirely different from everyone else. If you interview them first, you might doubt your own memories if they vary from those of family members. The same is true for family friends and other significant people as well. Specific accounts of your past may match, but it will be quite revealing if they do not.

Guidelines and Pacesetters

Your early memories will be based primarily on what you have been told or on what you intuit about that time. You may also stir up memories from your past when you reflect on old photographs or remember objects, such as trophies or ribbons that are associated with a particular time in your life. Even different tastes, scents or odors can trigger memories, such as the taste of cinnamon toast or the smell of a certain tobacco. These cues elicit pleasant or unpleasant memories depending upon their association. This period of your life may even be represented by symbolic scenes that depict how you felt at that time. For example, a scene I had when working with my three-year-old involved being encased in a large terracotta vase. Different members of my family walked by the vase, lifted the lid, and said something to me, but no one rescued me or lifted me out. Obviously this never really happened, but symbolically it represented a feeling I had that related to that time of my life. So give yourself permission to record any impressions you have of this time in your life. Metaphors for your experience may spontaneously emerge. Record them as well.

If you recall nothing, especially from the younger years, do not be alarmed. At this stage, you did not have the cognitive ability to remember consciously, and you may have been told very little about this time in your life. In the later years, however, the loss of memory may be due to a traumatic event or because you were using drugs or alcohol. If this is the case, rely on the information you obtain from others—but only others whom you trust.

Preparation

Go to your private place and prepare the room in any way that feels comfortable. Allow at least forty-five minutes to ponder and respond to these questions. If you need more time, take a stretch break.

Exercise

1. Record what facts you may know: the place and time you were born. What was the weather like? What events were going on that day? Where did you

live? Did you go to daycare? Were significant caretakers other than your parents involved in your life? Did you have siblings? Did your grandparents live in the home?

2. Record any images, impressions, or sensations you can uncover about the first eighteen months of your life.

3. Is there a symbolic image that expresses how you felt?

Closing

Write down what your impressions are of this time. In other words, what you have pieced together about your caretaking from this stage. Once you have recalled and recorded all that you can remember, prepare to proceed.

EXERCISE TWO: INTERVIEWING YOUR BODY

Purpose and Directions

As I've noted, if a feeling or emotion is not expressed, it is stored in the body. This exercise will determine where in your body the needs and feelings of your inner children are stored, and then explore what those needs and feelings are. Let the guided imagery below lead you step by step through this process. Someone else could read it for you, you could prerecord it, or you could simply read it yourself as you go along.

Guidelines and Pacesetters

Some people can't dialogue with their body, seeing it as a separate part of themselves. It feels too strange. If this is the case, don't worry about it. When it is time to work with your body, you will know it and at that time, the questions will be applicable. Review the guided imagery and if it feels too uncomfortable, disregard this exercise and move on.

Preparation

Find a time when you will be alone in your private place. Do anything you need to do to insure you will not be interrupted. You may want to do this exercise while looking into a mirror. Prepare the room with any special items, such as candles, music, incense, or fresh flowers, and pay tribute to your body before you ask it to speak. (I know it sounds strange, but it works.) Have your pen and journal by your side.

Exercise

1. Close your eyes. Imagine yourself surrounded with healing white Light, while you begin to breathe deeply. Take each breath more and more deeply,

until you seem to be breathing into the very center of your body. When you feel relaxed, continue.

2. Let your focus travel freely through your body. Now, either look into a mirror or pretend you are. Look at your body. See it without judging it. Acknowledge your body as though you were saying hello to an old friend.

3. Where do you feel tense? Ask this tension if it has something to say about your inner infant's pain. Be quiet and listen. Record any response you receive.

4. Now think of a time you felt abandoned. Where in your body do you hold that experience? Write about that experience. How is that experience related to your childhood? Record the response.

5. Think of a time that you felt a betrayal of trust, and then a time you felt a need to be held and were not. Where does your body hold these experiences? Write down what you feel.

6. Think of a time you felt needy and find where that experience is stored in your body. What does that experience tell you about your inner infant's pain? Record your findings.

Closing

When you have completed each question, use deep breathing to help you return your focus to the center of your being. Surround yourself with Light. Open your eyes when it feels comfortable to do so. You may be surprised at the information your body gave you, or perhaps you may have received no information at all. Do not be alarmed. Just reflect on the experience you did have.

EXERCISE THREE: HOW YOU TREAT YOUR BODY

Purpose and Directions

This exercise helps you assess the degree to which you have recreated your experience of childhood in the way you treat your own body. Use these questions as a jumping-off point. Allow yourself to ponder the thought that if your body were a child, what kind of care would that child be receiving from you. The way you treat your body is probably most linked to the way you were treated as an infant because your body is similarly dependent upon you to meet its needs.

Guidelines and Pacesetters

This exercise can evoke shame and guilt because it shows you the parental messages you internalized and how you may use them against yourself. Try not to be frightened or ashamed of your discoveries. Admitting that you may treat yourself as badly as you were treated is difficult, but our bodies naturally take the brunt of our abuse. You begin to nurture your body when you discover the ways you neglect, abuse, or molest it. Your honesty can help you rectify the situation and begin to give your body the care it deserves.

Preparation

Go to the place where you do your internal work. I suggest you surround yourself with Light, ask your Higher Power for support, and make sure you will not be interrupted. Allow approximately forty-five minutes for this exercise. Take a stretch break if you need more time.

Exercise

Answer the following questions in your journal.

1. Do you trust your body to tell you what it needs?
2. Do you respond to those needs when you know what they are?
3. How do you know when you are hungry? Do you eat when you are hungry? Do you eat when you are not hungry?
4. Do you eat when you are upset?
5. Do you try to push your body beyond its limits with stimulants, such as coffee or sugar?
6. Do you "go for the burn" when you exercise? Why? Ask your body how it feels about that.
7. Do you get enough rest?
8. What activities do you do that are nurturing to your body?
9. Do you like your body? Do you affirm and praise your body?

Closing

Write down other thoughts or feelings you have about the way you treat your body. Consider again, if your body were an infant who depended upon you for its care, what quality of care would it be receiving? How does that make you feel? Record your responses in your journal. When you have finished writing, I suggest you sit quietly with your eyes closed and imagine yourself surrounded by the healing Light. Thank your Higher Power, and be silent for a moment. Then say whatever you need to say to your body before you finish.

EXERCISE FOUR: INTERVIEWING FAMILY MEMBERS, RELATIVES, AND FRIENDS

Purpose and Directions

This last exercise helps you research the circumstances of this developmental stage by giving you questions for family members, relatives, friends, babysitters, nannies, and coaches. The answers you get will help you construct the history of your inner children's pain. I offer some guidelines that will help you determine the form of interview you want to use for each person. Consider the questions a starting point, but let the interview develop in its own way.

Guidelines and Pacesetters

It may be difficult to get information from others. Ideally, your questions will help determine what really happened. But they may not. You may discover nothing new. Family members may not remember, or choose not to remember, or become hostile because you even asked. Don't push. If they don't want to talk, let it go. If there is no one to ask, if family members and friends are dead or nowhere to be found, then let it go. The information will surface in other ways. Part of your inner child's pain, however, may have to do with the lack of recorded history. If this is the case, then you may want to write about this in your journal. If family members begin to humiliate or verbally abuse you, then back off. Do not put yourself at risk to do this exercise.

Carefully select the method of interviewing you wish to use. Face-to-face interviews will give you the most information, but they also will be the most risky. Decide if you are prepared to take that risk. You may feel more comfortable calling on the phone, or writing the questions in a letter and asking the person to respond. But no matter which method you use, if it becomes too uncomfortable, back off. What is too uncomfortable? If you cannot sleep at night because you are afraid to ask these questions, do not ask. If you are having a hard time eating, cannot concentrate, or feel anxious at the thought of asking these questions, then don't ask. These reactions indicate that it is too early in your healing to ask. Trust them. The time will come.

However, if the task seems manageable, even if you feel just a little frightened as you pick up the phone, sit down to write the letter, or meet the person with whom you will talk, be gentle with yourself, but continue. You can back off if and when it becomes unmanageable. If you find that the information you receive is overwhelming, find a friend, a religious or spiritual counselor, or a professional to help you sort through it.

There is no right or wrong way to do this. Gather what you can, include questions that seem appropriate, then move on. Remember, your intention is to gather information that will help you understand the circumstances of your childhood, so you can uncover the source of your pain. If your interviews don't seem to supply the right information, write in your journal about how that feels or discuss it with a friend or a professional. Then let it go.

Finally, remember that researching your pain is perhaps the most arduous step in this formula because it involves the most footwork. Give yourself time to integrate the information and protect yourself from becoming overwhelmed. If it does get too much for you, then take a break. Try to find at least one other person with whom you can share this information. (In fact, this work is done very effectively in a support group of others who are working the same program.) Your first experience of these feelings was in isolation; it is not necessary for you to recreate that experience.

Preparation

You will probably want to spread this exercise out over a period of time. A week or two for each stage is reasonable, but take longer if you choose. Research each age separately. Your questions about other stages of development may be based on the discoveries you make in earlier ones. It will also help you stay focused on the specific issues related to each inner child. If you just do one general interview it will be much more difficult to sort out the specific circumstances that affected the task at each stage. Go slowly and be as comprehensive as you can. Use your journal to record your own thoughts, reactions, and feelings and those of others.

Exercise

Use the following format for each interview.

1. Make a list of the people you want to interview. Decide how you want to do the interview: person to person, by phone, or by letter. Review the following list of questions and write down the ones you wish to use. Create an interview sheet for each interview.

2. First ask parents, friends, or relatives to tell you general impressions about this time in your life.

3. Now be more specific. (Questions that pertain to developmental stages are listed in later chapters.) Following are examples for the infant. What were you like as an infant? Was your birth planned or was it an accident? How did your parents feel about your birth? Find out as many reactions to your coming into this world as you can. What was happening the day of your birth? What was your birth like? Were there any complications? If you were adopted, ask about the circumstances that led to that adoption. Was your mother your main caretaker? If not, who was and why? How did your mother feel about being a mom? Did she nurse you? For how long? How were you weaned? Was your mother or caretaker affectionate? Were there any medical complications that first year and, if so, what were they? When did you crawl, talk, etc.?

4. Next, ask about family events during this period of your life. Did your family move? Did someone change jobs or lose a job? Did anyone die, get married, or give birth? Were there any medical or financial crises, tragedies or traumatic events that would have influenced the quality of your care? Was there any alcoholism or drug abuse? Record your findings in your journal.

5. What was going on in the world at this time? Were there any political scandals, religious upsets, or any events that may have had an influence on the care you received. Were any of your family members affected by these events. If so, how? Record the information you gather in your journal. Record your thoughts as well as their answers.

6. Are there any specific questions you want to ask each person you are interviewing?

Before you begin your interviews, determine the order in which you want to interview. Review the plans you have for your interview with a friend and talk about any resistance or anxieties you may have about doing the interview. Before you leave for each interview, take a few moments to pray or meditate, and to write your feelings in your journal.

Closing

When you have completed each interview, take a few more moments to comment on how you felt interviewing each person. How do you feel about the information you received? Based on what you learned, what assumptions can you make about your care? Use the information from the exercises in Steps one and two to construct the profile of your infant's pain. In one column, list issues you compiled in Step one. In another column, indicate the circumstances that may have caused these issues. In a third column, indicate how this issue is evident in the way you treat your body. See below for an example.

Issue	Circumstances	Evidenced in the way I treat my body
I do not trust that others will respond to my needs.	My father was in a bad car accident three months after I was born. For about four months, I was often left with a babysitter while my mother was at the hospital. When she was at home, her attention was focused on the survival needs of the family, not on the basic needs I had as an infant.	I focus on my work and on my relationship with others and often ignore the basic needs of my body.

Developing this structure will enable you to construct the profile of your infant self's pain. It will also arm you with the information you need to help your infant heal. Once you have obtained this information, move to Step three.

❧

of trust experienced by your infant within. This frees the adult self to respond to the needs of this younger self. It allows you to establish the part of you who feels the fear and the shame (the infant self) as distinct from the part of you who can respond to this discomfort (the adult self).

EXERCISE ONE: MEETING YOUR INNER CHILD

Purpose and Directions

This exercise uses guided imagery to get you in touch with all that each inner child carries. Once those feelings are identified, you will separate from them by personifying them as the child self. Once the separation is made, have your adult and children within interact.

Guidelines and Pacesetters

Keep in mind that each person responds differently to guided imagery. Some will see a clear image of the inner child, others will sense a vague presence, and others will relate to their children within entirely emotionally. There is no right or wrong way, so give yourself permission to accept whatever method works.

If, when meeting your inner children, you find that one frightens or offends you, it is probably because it carries traits you have not been able to accept in yourself. It may take time for you to feel comfortable with this part of yourself. In this case, continue doing the exercises, but ask your Higher Power for assistance. Have your Higher Power interact with your inner child until it feels safe for you to interact yourself. When you create the protector for this inner child, it will also be able to assist you in this inner child's care. Continue your work, however, because this inner child represents a part of you that you have disowned. When you reclaim him or her you will make peace with yourself as well.

Preparation

There are several ways to use this imagery. You can read each sentence, close your eyes and imagine, and then respond to what you have read. You can prerecord the imagery and play it back. You can have a friend read the imagery to you. Select the way that feels most comfortable to you. When you are ready to begin, go to your safe place and make sure that you will not be interrupted for at least thirty minutes. This will give you time to meet your child within and to relate to it before you interact.

Exercise

Close your eyes and surround yourself with the protective Light. Take a few deep breaths. Imagine you are walking in a beautiful garden, noting its smells and colors.

Feel the sense of peace and safety. As you walk through this garden you come across a beautiful wooden cradle. You look into this cradle and you see a baby. As you look closer at this baby you realize that it is the infant within you.

How do you feel when you first see your infant within? Notice how vulnerable the infant is. What is your infant self doing? Is it sleeping, crying, cooing or lying there quietly waiting for someone to appear? Reach down and touch the child. How does the infant respond? See if you can determine what this child self needs. Without using words, express to the infant that you are its future. You are proof that he or she survived. Tell the infant within that you will help it heal. You have come back to rescue it, to heal the loneliness and fear.

All your fears about closeness, all your shame of being vulnerable, and all your worries of being abandoned are carried by the child who rests in this cradle. Spend a few minutes with your infant within. When you feel you have had enough time with your infant for now, assure it that your work with the pain is beginning. The hurt is over. He or she will not be left alone again. Conclude by bringing your focus back to your breathing and to the Light that surrounds you. Take several deep breaths and, when it feels comfortable, open your eyes.

Closing

This first meeting can be emotional. Sometimes it is like meeting a stranger, sometimes it's like meeting an old friend. Record your responds in your journal. End this experience by asking your infant self to help you find a photo or a picture from a magazine that looks like him or her. Paste that picture in your journal so you can look at it as you begin to ask more in-depth questions, and then write about how the picture makes you feel.

EXERCISE TWO: CREATING A DIALOG WITH YOUR INNER CHILD

Purpose and Directions

This exercise will help you separate further from your children within by helping you determine their likes and dislikes. It also gives your child self a chance to ask you questions. You will imagine having a conversation with your child within, and record its answers in your journal. Sometimes, it is helpful when asking these questions to look at a photo or picture you selected to represent this part of you, but you can also simply imagine this inner child.

Guidelines and Pacesetters

Infants can communicate, but they can not use words. If you do not get verbal answers from your infant within, try to interpret body language or sensations that you intuit. Some people feel they communicate best with this self using a form of telepathy. If that works for you, use it. As you work with the older children within, their ability to communicate will mature.

Preparation

Go to a safe place and have your pen and journal ready. Begin your dialogue. Allow at least thirty uninterrupted minutes for this exercise. Write the question in your journal using your dominant hand. Use your least dominant hand to record your inner children's response.

Exercise

1. What is your infant's favorite color?
2. Does your infant have a favorite story? A favorite lullaby?
3. Using your infant's eyes, look around the room. What is the object in the room that your infant wants to touch the most? (If it is safe, imagine the child touches it.)
4. Ask your infant to tell you about his or her pain and fear of being abandoned, feeling unsafe, unprotected, and afraid.
5. What does this child need most from you?
6. How does this child feel about you? Does it feel abandoned or ignored by you? Why? Does the infant understand what it means to be reclaimed by you? If not, explain that it means he or she will no longer be alone again; you will make sure that the basic needs are met. Your infant self will be able to develop trust in you as the inner adult to keep it safe and protected.
7. Does your baby like to be held? Is it hungry or tired or wet?
8. Is there anything your infant wants to know about you?
9. What joys does this child want to offer you and what prevents this from happening?

Closing

What did you learn about your infant self from the above exercise? How do you feel about what you learned? Answer those questions in your journal, and move to the next exercise when you feel ready.

EXERCISE THREE: TALKING IN THE MIRROR TO YOUR INFANT WITHIN

Purpose and Directions

This exercise uses mirror work to help you see your child within as a separate, distinct part of you. Mirror work is one of the most effective ways to experience the separate parts of yourself. Holding a teddy bear in your arms will enhance the sensations of holding your younger inner children.

Guidelines and Pacesetters

Most people feel awkward looking at themselves in the mirror. Don't be surprised if you notice how many freckles you have, or that your nose is not quite straight, and God forbid, you should do something different with your hair! Quiet these voices, they are the thoughts of the critics within. In the next exercise you will be working with these guys. Cuddle the teddy bear and imagine it is your young child within. Imagine the teddy bear answering, or answer yourself as the voice of the infant with baby sounds or baby talk. (The responses should be appropriate for each age.)

Allow yourself to go back and forth between the two parts within you. For instance, at one moment you may start to cry as you draw a picture representing your inner child's pain, and in the next moment, be speaking as the adult self to the crying child. You are able to do this without thinking of yourself as crazy.

Just see what happens. Observe any changes in your facial expressions as you switch roles between the adult and the infant. The mirror will help you see this. Do not worry if there is no change. Don't worry if you think this is strange—you're in good company. I have not yet met a person who can do mirror work with ease until they've tried it a few times.

If you feel crazy or weird, or simply cannot make it work for you, try changing positions. Sometimes having two chairs, one that represents your inner child and one that represents your adult self, is helpful. Switch chairs when you switch roles. If this does not work, try having a professional therapist guide you through the interaction. Later, you will have a point of reference from which to draw, and you will probably be able to do the exercise alone.

Preparation

You need some private time, a teddy bear, a mirror, your journal and pen, and some courage to try something new.

Exercise

Sit in front of the mirror. If you have a teddy bear, hold it close to you. Start rocking. You may want to close your eyes at first. You may want to hum or sing a lullaby. When you feel a connection with the feelings of your infant within, ask it what is needed, what it wants to say. Listen for the response. Then open your eyes and respond to what you heard. Interact for as long as you feel comfortable. (Come on, you can last for more than three seconds! Try at least five minutes. Go longer if you wish.)

Closing

Record this in your journal. Try writing with your least dominant hand as you let your infant self describe its feelings. Switch to your dominant hand when you let your adult self record its feelings.

EXERCISE FOUR: CREATING YOUR PROTECTOR

Purpose and Directions

Each inner child needs to have its own protector, sometimes more than one. Start by letting your child within first create the one it needs the most. This protector is the character you bring in to provide special care that the adult self is unable to provide. Creating a protector is a way to insure that your inner children will never be alone. It is as if this protector is assigned to your inner child and will always be there to care, even when your adult self is occupied in your day-to-day affairs. There are no guidelines and pacesetters for this—let your inner children run the show.

Preparation

Have crayons and drawing materials handy so that your inner child can draw the protector it wants.

Exercise

1. Ask the infant within to tell you about the person or character for whom it feels the most trust. If your infant could select anyone in the world, real or imagined, to be there always, who would it choose? (It can be Superman, an angel, or God. It can be a relative, movie star, or friend.)
2. Ask your infant within to create a picture that represents this protector.
3. Assure your infant self that this protector will be available any time he or she wants.

Closing

Keep this picture where you do your internal work, and keep it stored in your imagination, too. Always call in this character for support in your work with your infant. This character will care for, protect, and entertain your infant. It is this image that will meet the needs of your infant and heal the gaps left from childhood. Complete this exercise by acknowledging a partnership between this protector and the adult self. Call in your Higher Power as well, if this seems appropriate, because these three are the team that will heal the infant within. Record your responses in your journal.

EXERCISE FIVE: DETECTING THE CRITICAL VOICE

Purpose

This exercise helps you give a form to the critical voices you hear inside your head, so that your adult self and Higher Power can confront and challenge the negativity. The critical voice for the infant is the voice that shamed or humiliated you for having needs, for being afraid to trust, for not feeling safe enough to care. This voice carries the negative statements you hear when you are putting yourself down.

Guidelines and Pacesetters

This voice can be very poisonous, and can take on many shapes and forms. Its messages are usually very easy to hear, and can be very damaging to your children within. When working with this critical voice, get support from your Higher Power. Most of your inner children will have a specific voice that haunts them and from which they will need to be protected.

Preparation

Go to your quiet place with your pen and journal, and drawing materials. I suggest the protection of the Light.

Exercise

Respond to the following questions in your journal.

1. What negative statements do you make to yourself about your ability to care?
2. What negative statements do you make to yourself about your lovability?
3. What negative statements do you make to yourself about your capacity to trust?
4. What negative statements do you make to yourself about your trustworthiness?
5. Where have you heard those statements before? Whose voice is this? Is it the voice of a parent, relative, or teacher, a minister, priest, or coach? Are these statements you have heard from society? Is the voice imagined or real?
6. Imagine that you, as the inner adult, speak to this voice. Ask this voice what it wants. What is its intention? Is it trying to protect or to harm?
7. Using your least dominant hand, let your infant self draw a picture of this critical voice. (It may see the voice as a monster.) Know that this picture represents fears, terror and judgments created by the monster within.
8. When you finish the picture, go back to the original negative statements. Rewrite them in your journal. Next to each negative statement, write a positive affirmation.

Negative Statement	Positive Affirmation
I am so terrible I do not deserve to be loved by anyone.	I am lovable just the way I am and deserve all the love in the world.

Use these affirmations whenever you hear these wounding words. They will help dissolve the negativity and replace them with statements that are kind.

Closing

Have your adult self and Higher Power interact with this critic whenever it appears. When necessary, imagine that your Higher Power sends it away by surrounding it in a bubble of Light and releasing the bubble back into the universe.

Reassure your inner child that the critic will no longer go unchallenged. Then write in your journal and prepare for the final exercise of this step.

EXERCISE SIX: CHANGING YOUR INNER CHILD'S EXPERIENCE OF CHILDHOOD

Purpose and Directions

Using guided imagery, this exercise helps you transform the painful experiences of childhood. You will review the profile from each inner child's pain and select an issue upon which to focus. As you reflect on a recent interaction when you felt the pain of this issue, you are led back to the time in your childhood when the original trauma occurred. Bring in the support of your Higher Power and your inner child's protector to restage this scene and transform it so you can begin to heal the pain. (Each issue from each inner child's profile of pain can be reworked in this way.)

Guidelines and Pacesetters

If you react strongly to an interaction with someone, it is usually a sign that an old issue has been triggered. If as a child you were told you never did anything right, then as an adult, when that message is inferred, it will bring up the pain of the past. If in your current relationship you find yourself forever haunted with the fear that your partner will leave you, you may be reacting to an old experience where one of your parents left the other or left you. In other words, if you've been hurt in a similar way before, the hurt from the past as well as the present will emerge. If you find that no matter what you do you have a recurring reaction to a specific issue, it is most likely related to your childhood.

Numerous examples could be given, but it is most important to understand that you react strongly to people, places, and things for a reason. When you find that reason, and heal the circumstances that created it, you are then free to respond to your present interactions, not *react* to them because of the past. By using this exercise repeatedly you can truly rewrite your past. You may not be able to change the facts of your past, but you can change the way you relate to those facts.

You may have to rework each scene many times. The repetition will alter the experience, and each time your children within are rescued, they have more trust for you. The more trust they feel for you, the less they will influence and sabotage your adult life.

Preparation

Select the issue upon which to focus. Have your pen and journal ready. When writing as the younger selves, use your least dominant hand. This imagery is quite lengthy, so allow yourself at least an hour or more. Prepare your room in the way that it is the most conducive to your work. If you feel resistance to some of the directions, you may need professional guidance.

Exercise

1. Begin by taking several deep breaths, all the way down to the center of your being. (Most people imagine a spot about three inches above their belly button.) But simply follow your breath and it will take you to your personal center. Then imagine yourself surrounded by and filled with a beautiful, protective Light.

2. In your journal, describe the issue upon which you wish to focus. Describe a recent occasion that you felt this issue came up. Use the information from Step one to assist you. Note who was involved, what was said or done, and how you felt.

3. Once you are in touch with that feeling, pause for a moment and bring your focus to the place in your body where you feel that tension.

4. In your journal, describe this tension and where it was located in your body. How does this discovery relate to the information you obtained when you interviewed your body in Step two?

5. Staying aware of that tension in your body, pause for a moment, and slowly count backward from ten to one.

6. When you are finished counting and are more relaxed, ask yourself how this tension relates to this inner child's pain.

7. Let your mind go back to this time in your childhood. Allow a scene to emerge, trying not to censor or analyze. What you cannot remember, imagine. Describe that scene in your journal.

8. Who was involved in this scene? How old were you? What was happening? What were you feeling at the time?

9. Reread what you have written. How do you feel about what you wrote?

10. Ask your child self what it feels, what it needs from you, what it wants you to do.

11. Develop a strategy to alter that scene. Use the information from your research to help you intervene. For instance, do you need to get help for your parents? Do you need to remove the inner child from that scene? Should you intervene to that your child is safe to confront the parent causing the pain?

12. How can you use the protector and Higher Power to help you carry out your plan?

13. Now, use your imagination to confront your situation and to rewrite the scene. Describe the new scene in detail.

14. How does your inner child feel now that you have rewritten the scene?

15. When you feel complete and satisfied, focus on the present situation that provoked this issue.

16. Replay the recent scene. What has changed now that the original scene has been healed?

17. Make a note in your journal of any other thoughts or feelings.

Closing

You have initiated the process of transforming your infant's pain. Rework this exercise with as many issues as you choose and continue to use it whenever the issues of your infant self emerge. It will help change the reference point for your infant self's pain. Confronting the negative self-dialogue as you did in Exercise five will help you respond rather than react in your day-to-day life, but this exercise enables you to transform the original experience.

As you begin to feel less paralyzed by fears of abandonment, and as you begin to feel more comfort with touching and being touched, you will know this part of you is healing. You also will begin to trust, and to know those times when it is wise to be distrustful.

These abilities emerge as your infant self begins to trust you not to abandon it. As long as you are in contact with your infant self, he or she cannot be abandoned. Only when you collapse into painful feelings from infancy do you leave your infant as isolated, as unprotected, and as unnurtured as you were when you were that age. As you begin to take responsibility for your own safety and develop the ability to assess and respond to situations in which you might be at risk of getting hurt, you will experience a deepening of trust between you and your infant within.

When you feel ready to help your inner child begin to grieve, proceed to Step five.

෯

STEP FIVE: GRIEVING YOUR INFANT SELF'S PAIN

You cannot hope to learn how to trust, to nurture and be nurtured, or how to feel safe in the world until your infant grieves the pain. One aspect of this grief is to be truthful about what your infancy was like. Another aspect is grieving whatever you missed because of your caretaker's inabilities.

EXERCISE ONE: THE FIRST FOUR STAGES OF GRIEF

Purpose and Directions

You have gathered a great deal of information from the previous four steps. Now it is time to express the emotions attached to it. Stage by stage, step by step, you will take your inner children through their grief. Perhaps for the first time, there is someone to comfort them in this loss. You will also assess whether each inner child carries grief for a specific event and if this grief has been generalized to incorporate the grief of others who have experienced a similar event. Read through each exercise before you prepare to begin.

Guidelines and Pacesetters

Some steps in the grieving process are done by you as the adult, and some are done by you as the inner child. When responding as the younger inner child, use your least dominant hand. This will help keep their feelings less restrained or inhibited. This exercise also requires you to switch back and forth between your two selves. If you have a difficult time trading roles, then try using two chairs and physically change positions to help facilitate the switch. If this doesn't work, then seek professional guidance.

Preparation

Prepare the room so you will be comfortable. Allow several hours to complete this exercise. It is best, once you start, to continue until you are through. I suggest you call in the support of your Higher Power and the child's protector and surround yourself with Light. You will need your journal, pen, drawing materials, and separate sheets of paper. Do these exercises on the loose sheets of paper—not in your journal.

Exercise

1. In your mind's eye see your inner child before you. Talk to your child within about the panic he or she may have felt in response to the issues of this age. Explain to your inner child that the restlessness he or she feels is connected to these issues. Once your inner child is familiar with what the panic is, ask him or her to talk to you about it. Determine if this panic is related to any specific event and if you are experiencing a generalized grief in response to this event. If so, write about this in your journal.

2. Now ask your inner child to draw a picture representing the panic and fear he or she has carried all these years. It may help if you reflect on a time you felt this panic.

3. Now, as your adult self, think back to the times you tried to control situations in your life so you wouldn't have to feel this panic or loss. List these bargaining behaviors. Then ask your inner infant to list how he or she tried to bargain and control in an attempt to get its needs met.

4. Explain to your child within that it was not his or her fault that these needs were not met. Share with your inner self the information from your research. Emphasize that the problems in the family were not caused by him or her. Share with your child any anger you have about the quality of care it received. Tell your child within that it has a right to be angry, too—it was not fair that it went without—and assure it that it is safe to express this anger now.

5. Imagine you are your child within. Let your child self express the rage that was felt when its needs were ignored and not met. Stomp your feet, beat on pillows, break pencils—do whatever is needed to discharge the pain of those years. When you have exhausted yourself in the anger, let yourself drop into the feeling of despair.

6. Help your child self write a letter to your parents about how painful it is to let go, how hard he or she tried, and the anger that is present because it did not receive the kind of parenting he or she so desperately needed. Let this letter express all the stages of grief that your child within feels. When the letter is done, comfort your inner child in its despair. (You might want to use the teddy bear and rocker to facilitate this experience for the younger ages.)

7. When you feel ready to continue, write a letter to your child self stating how you feel about the care he or she received. Tell your child within what you are willing to provide for him or her at this time. Imagine that you read your letter to your inner child. When you have finished, imagine that you again comfort your child within.

8. As you are comforting your child self, imagine that your parents come into the room. Have your adult self tell your parents that you will be taking responsibility for this child's needs. Thank them for what they did, but assure them their job is finished.

9. Have your child within tell your parents goodbye. Your parents respond and then leave.

10. Conclude this grieving process by closing your eyes and surrounding you and your child self with Light. In the next step, all the pain that has been expressed will be released and all the wounds that have been opened will be healed. Take a cleansing breath and bring your focus back to the center of the Light. Thank the protector and your Higher Power, then open your eyes when it feels comfortable to do so.

Closing

Gather all the drawings and writings that you and your infant self completed during this grieving process. You will be using them in the final step of healing your infant self and in reclaiming its joy.

෬ඁ

STEP SIX: HEALING YOUR PAIN, RECLAIMING YOUR JOY

Purpose and Directions

This exercise lets your inner child release the pain emotionally, physically, and spiritually through the use of ritual. It is the final stage of grief and the final step of the formula for each of your inner children. You are provided with tools that can be used repeatedly to heal your childhood pain and reclaim the joy your children within have to share. (The modifications necessary to make the ceremonies age appropriate will be listed with each stage.)

Guidelines and Pacesetters

This process is a suggestion, not a command. If any part of this ritual feels uncomfortable to you, modify or discard any or all of that section. Devise your own way of releasing these feelings that better suits you.

The same is true if you feel any of the directions are premature. If you do not feel ready to let go of the pain around a certain issue, then release only the amount of pain you are ready to release. If you feel it's too early to bring your inner child home and have him or her melt back into your physical form, then wait to do that part of this ritual when it feels right. I do encourage you, however, to release your feelings in some way. Remember, a ritual is a ceremony of completion, but the depth of your completion will increase as your healing progresses.

Preparation

For the emotional release, you will need the following items: a pen, your journal, all your drawings and writings from step five, a copy of the picture of your inner child, a bundle of sacred plants such as sage or juniper, matches, a nonflammable bowl, and rock salt or sea salt crystals. Frankincense contains the properties of purification and protection, and it is a good choice to use in all your ceremonies. Cloves were once used to protect infants from harm and illness. You also may want to purchase a candle or a jar of whole cloves and let the scent filter through the air as you work with your infant self.

For the physical release, you will need a bathtub or shower, bath oil or beads, a body brush, a pumice stick, a face cloth or brush, and shampoo. You may want to purchase a bath oil or body lotion scented with rose. Its properties are associated with love and balance and would add a soothing agent to your body ritual for this age. An herb that could be used in your bath is rosemary, associated with releasing memories and often used to purify.

Gather the items for your emotional release and place them in the room where you do your internal work. Gather what you will need for your physical release and place them near the tub. If you want to do your body ritual in a stream, ocean or river, modify the instructions accordingly.

Allow an entire morning, afternoon, or evening for this ceremony, because it could last from two to four hours. You may either do each ritual, one right after the other, or if it feels better to you, do them one at a time. I suggest you prerecord the guided imagery on tape.

Emotional Release

1. First, use the sage stick to cleanse the room, by lighting it and waving it in each corner of the room. The smoke will absorb any residual tension or

unwanted feelings that have been released in this room during your work with your child self. Have a window open as you burn the sage.

2. Light incense if you choose.

3. Set up your bowl, candle, matches, and sea salt. Take all the drawings, writings, and letters that you prepared in step five. Decide which of these you are willing to release in this ritual fire. Also, have the copy of the picture of this child within.

4. Imagine that the entire room is filled with healing Light. Imagine the Light within you and around you as well. In your mind's eye, bring in your child self. Hold him or her in your arms, or comfortably settle your inner child somewhere in the room. You may want to use a teddy bear to symbolize the younger children within. Focus on what feelings you will be releasing. Review the work you have done with your inner child, the issues you have discovered, the healing you have experienced. Then silently ask your inner child if he or she is ready to let go of its pain.

5. When both of you are ready, light your candle. Take one of the drawings, letters, or pieces of writing and ceremoniously release it by setting fire to it and dropping it into your bowl. Imagine the emotions represented on that piece of paper are released into the flame and carried by its smoke back to the Light for transformation and purification. Release your inner child's drawing that represents the panic and fear, the list of bargaining behaviors, the anger and despair, and the letters. Burn one piece of paper at a time, so you are able to focus on the contents of that page.

6. When you have burned all the papers, use your sage stick again to purify yourself and the room.

7. Now imagine your inner child is with you and that the two of you take the cooled ashes outside and bury them in a special place in the earth. Affirm that the pain you have carried from this stage is released back to the earth for purification and transformation. Return to the place you do your internal work.

Physical Release

Before you begin, purify the bath area with your sage stick or incense. I usually play soothing music and burn candles. Once you have purified the area, run your bath, adding bath beads or oils and a handful of rock salt or sea salt.

Take a moment before you step into the tub to focus on what you plan to release. Remember that you are releasing the pain your infant self carries. The fear that he or she has about being unloved, or about being deserted, and any other issue you have uncovered can now be released from the cells of your body that hold onto that pain. Hold that intention in your mind and slowly submerge yourself in the cleansing water. Relax for a moment as you pray, meditate, or reflect on what you will release. (The issues and pain you release for each child will vary.)

Take a pumice stick, soap, and water, and gently scrub the soles and heels of your feet. Imagine as you do this that you are releasing any pain that your inner child has carried for you. Then take the body brush and gently brush over the tops of your feet, ankles, calves, and thighs. Again, imagine as you do this that you are releasing any fear or doubt or anger this inner child has carried for you. Experience the blocks to that pain being released.

Stand up, and use the body brush on your buttocks, stomach, midriff, chest, and back while you continue to release your inner child's pain. Then sit down in the tub. Use the body brush to cleanse your arms and hands. Affirm that your arms and hands will now be free to assist you in manifesting what you want or need. They will be free to touch, to love, to care.

Exchange the body brush for your face cloth and gently cleanse your face. Complete the cleansing by washing your hair.

Once you have finished, drain the water from the tub while, at the same time, you proceed with the final phase of this ritual—releasing the residual pain of each child within from your every cell. As you sit in the tub, reflect on the information you gathered when you researched your body about your inner child's pain. Focus on those areas of your body and imagine that the tension that has accumulated dissolves and is released into the water. Release only what is for your highest and best purpose to release at this time. As you develop new ways of being, your body posture will accommodate this new you, but it will take time for this to unfold. For now, release the fears releated to this time in your life . . . imagine the energy from these fears dissolves and is carried back to the earth as the water is drained from the tub.

When all the water has drained, rinse yourself in the shower. Turn to the east, the spiritual direction of new beginnings, and imagine that your whole body is flooded by beautiful, brilliant white Light. As you stand facing the east, take several cleansing breaths. Fill any places within you left empty by this release with the essence of your Highest Self.

Complete this ritual by drying off and rubbing yourself with body lotion, starting with your feet and moving up. Gently acknowledge each area of your body as you bring this ritual to a close.

Spiritual Release

Once you have physically released, return to the place where you do your internal work: the spiritual release will be done through guided imagery. Try to have prerecorded the imagery.

Take a few deep breaths. Now, see, sense or feel a cylinder of Light all around you. Take a moment to absorb the warmth of this Light. Imagine that a beam of Light extends from the bottom of your cylinder of Light and that this beam is fastened into the center or core of the earth. Then look up into the Light and see a beam extending clear to the center of the universe, securely fastened into its core. This is a cylinder of protection.

Imagine that you are holding your inner child in your arms or that your inner child stands beside you in the cylinder. Feel the essence of his or her energy as you take a deep breath. Reflect on all the pain this inner child has carried for you.

Look up into the Light. See your Higher Power descending from the Light. Imagine that your Higher Power reaches out his or her hand and asks that you and your inner child follow. As you grasp the hand of your Higher Power, you and your child self within begin to ascend into the Light. Imagine that your Higher Power takes you to the very center of the Light.

As you stand in the center, your Higher Power reaches for your inner child and takes him or her by the hand. Your Higher Power then directs your inner child into the Light and he or she is wrapped in this beautiful healing glow. Cloaked in this Light, your child within is healed of all the pain and hurt and fear.

Your Higher Power then blesses you and your child within and the two of you begin your descent. Your inner child is still with you, you can know that he or she has been healed. Spend time with your inner child, reclaim the joy and the newness he or she has to share. What it is like to spend time with this part of you that no longer carries pain? What activities do you want to engage in with this younger self? Imagine that you and your child within experience all that was missed when you were this age. Imagine basking in the joy of this younger part of self.

These are the basic instructions for healing the children. In later chapters, the instructions will be modified somewhat to be more age-specific, but still will be based on the previous Steps and Exercises. To complete the ritual for your infant self, continue with the guidelines below. Return to the respective chapters to complete the closing for the rest of your children within.

Closing

Explain to your inner child that you now want to bring it home, reintegrated into your total being. Your child will be protected and loved and feel safe. If it does not feel right to have your infant self melt back into your physical being yet, then create a safe place for the child to stay. Imagine that the protector stays with your infant within so that he or she will always feel safe. One client, for example, created a beautiful crystal palace where her inner child would feel safe. She had several protectors stay with the little girl so she would not be alone and afraid.

Ask your infant within to select the place within your physical form where it would feel the most safe. Then imagine that your youngest inner child melts into that part of your body. This merging will enhance, not drain, your life. You have resolved much of the pain and you now have tools to deal with the pain that remains. This child within has much joy and comfort to offer you once the trust is there that you will meet his or her needs. Know that if the pain of this younger self gets triggered that you will once again be able to separate from the pain and respond accordingly. But you want to reclaim the inner child and carry him or her within you where it will be safe.

Your fears of being loved and your caution about trusting others will never completely disappear. It would not even be desirable for them to be gone. It is important to be able to determine when it is safe and appropriate to trust and love as well as when it is not. But, you will now be able to recognize the fears your infant carries and have the tools with which you can respond to those fears with care.

REVISING THE GARDEN OF YOUR PAST

Complete your work with your infant within by returning to the garden of your past. Ask your infant within how it would like to contribute to this garden. Imagine that the two of you make these contributions so that this inner child will be represented in the garden of growth. If you are fortunate and have a garden or place where you can grow things, plant a seed that will represent this inner child's growth.

You have concluded your work with your infant within. Remember that you can use these exercises anytime to continue your work. Also, the exercises in chapter 9 will continue to develop your relationship with your young inner child. When you feel ready to continue your internal development, proceed to chapter 3.

3

THE TODDLER SELF

From Dependency to Autonomy

The toddler years were the first time in our development that we were mobile enough to walk away from our caretaker and verbal enough to refuse and protest. This was when we began the transition from dependency to autonomy. It is a process that continues throughout our lives, but learning how to establish and maintain personal boundaries early was essential if we were to successfully establish a sense of self. Boundaries are emotional and physical separations from our caretaker.

To gain autonomy, we needed to feel we had some control over ourselves and our environment, and learning to say "no" gave us this sense of control. As we were learning skills we also learned that we could refuse to do something. Just because our caretaker told us to do something didn't mean we had to do it. They could say "Put your coat on" and we could say "No." They could say "Eat your peas," and we could say "No." Saying "no" established a boundary. It gave us a way to declare our separateness, our autonomy. We also learned we could agree, and being able to choose gave us a further sense of autonomy and independence.

Hearing no from the adults in our lives also helped us learn about boundaries. It gave us clear limits, an idea of what was to be expected of us. It also gave us a way to experience separateness from our environment. Being told that we could not touch the stove because it was hot helped us gain knowledge of our limits. Being told not to play rough with a playmate taught us about the boundaries of others. In saying no and hearing no, we could experiment with complying and being dependent or defying and being independent.

This developmental stage is often casually referred to as the "terrible twos" because the battles between caretaker and toddler, although crucial for a child's growth, can be exhausting for the parent. Engaging in these battles, however, was essential if you were to begin this very important transition. You needed the encouragement to vacillate between dependency and autonomy. You needed to be able to both act like a grown-up or be dependent. You needed praise when you dressed or fed yourself and understanding when you chose not to. You needed to know it was acceptable to say "no" without being punished and encouraged to hear "no" when it was for your safety and protection.

Few of us received this encouragement because it required our caretaker's willingness to let go. Most often, they were ambivalent about letting go and, therefore, gave us mixed messages about acting independently. Confused about their own boundaries, they were unable to help us learn how to establish and maintain our own. The ambivalence and confusion stemmed from their need to either keep you close and dependent or to push you away and force you to be more independent. Some parents dealt with this subtly; others more aggressively. The manner in which they dealt with their confusion greatly influenced the success you had at mastering developmental tasks.

If, for instance, every time you said no, your caretaker broke into tears, feeling rejection or loss of authority, you would have most likely been unsuccessful at mastering these tasks. Having learned that you could not express your independence without causing suffering to others, you would have learned to suppress your individuality and do as others expected. The message you received was that your caretaker's needs were more important than your own. Learning to meet another's needs at the sacrifice of your own is a pattern that would follow you into your adult life and into every intimate relationship you encountered.

If, when you attempted to be independent, you were ridiculed, beaten or abandoned, you may have responded by retreating, rebelling, or throwing a tantrum. This would have led to further humiliation, abandonment, or discipline. In adulthood, your need to be independent would most likely carry those same fears. But to remain dependent would result in your feeling unfulfilled and smothered.

On the other hand, if your caretaker was anxious for you to be independent, you may have had to separate before *you* were ready to let go. The trauma in either scenario would have been just as great.

Case History: Tom

Tommy was about two when his father came back from the war. Since his birth, Tommy and his mother had been alone. He was the center of her life, and he received most of her attention. Then, suddenly, with his father back in the house, he had to sleep alone, was left with baby-sitters, and was ignored when he wept and felt lonely at night. Tommy was not ready to give up his dependence on his mother.

At age forty-two, he still was not ready. When Tom talked about his intimate relationships he complained continually about being deserted. Having been forced into independence before he was ready, he was forever trying to find women who would not push him away. However, he was constantly attracted to women who did exactly that—they pushed him away. He recreated in his adult life what he had experienced with his mother.

In therapy, Tom was able to identify his need to remain dependent as the source of his pain in his relationships with women. Once this issue was identified, his research of this stage in his life gave him the information he needed to understand how his childhood transition from dependence to independence had resulted in this pattern.

Tom began to understand that his choice in women was related to his inner toddler's fear of being ignored. Using guided imagery, he contacted his toddler self. He imagined that he assured the little boy that he would never again be alone and he explained to his little boy that he had not been ignored because he had done something wrong. His Mom's focus had simply shifted from him to his father. He promised his little boy that his dependency would not be ignored again.

I asked Tom to imagine himself and the little boy creating a protector, a nurturing maternal figure who would always be available to satisfy his inner child's needs. Tom called this imagery anytime he felt fears of being ignored or pushed away. By giving little Tommy the attention and security he needed, Tom could pursue a more mature form of love.

STEP ONE: IDENTIFYING YOUR PAIN

Whatever you experienced as a child when it was time to begin to be separate, you will repeat in your adult life, as Tom did. Whatever problems you had saying no or hearing no as a child, and whatever problems you had being separate and independent, you will repeat in similar situations when you grow up. Boundaries are very hard to create if you did not have permission to be independent or the freedom to say no. Establishing and maintaining your boundaries make you feel you have a right to be here and a right to expect privacy and consideration. If, as a child, your boundaries were constantly violated, then now you will either have loose boundaries (difficulty determining if another's behavior is a violation), or you will have rigid boundaries (many interactions are intrusive).

It may also be difficult for you to honor another's boundaries. The need for privacy may not mean much to you now because it did not concern others when you were a child. This is called "enmeshment." Enmeshment means that there is no clearly defined boundary between you and others. You don't know where you end and another begins, an awareness that springs from your ability to establish and maintain both emotional and physical boundaries.

If you and your caretaker's emotions were merged—or enmeshed—it will be difficult for you to know what feelings are yours and what feelings belong to someone else. For instance, if your mother's happiness seemed to depend on your being good all the time, then you might grow up feeling overly responsible for other people's needs.

Without boundaries, you could not have begun to separate right from wrong, good from bad. Boundaries and saying no provided you with the independence you need to relate and respond to others. You could not have begun to learn about good and bad behavior if you could not relate to others; it is from your interactions with others that you learn what about you is acceptable and unacceptable.

What did you need to become independent? You needed to feel safe enough to be both separate and dependent. It is not unusual for a toddler to jump up on mother's lap and snuggle for a moment, then jump off again to go explore the world. Checking in with your caretakers to make sure you're still loved gives you the safety to explore your world, trusting that when you return, the source of your love will still be available. Testing how much you can participate in the outside world and still be loved is a dynamic you carry into every relationship.

The degree of success you have in comfortably moving between dependence and independence is directly related to the degree of safety you felt when moving in and out of the dependent relationship with your mother or your caretaker. The first step in working with your toddler within is to identify the discomfort you carried into your adult life from this stage of development.

EXERCISE ONE: HOW YOU RESPOND TODAY

Do not be alarmed if the following statements indicate that you are carrying many issues from this stage. Most of us do. We grew up with caretakers who were ambivalent about our becoming independent. Unconscious of this ambivalence, it was expressed in their reactions to our attempts to be separate. You now have the chance to help your toddler within through this stage by giving the message that the toddler's need to be autonomous is acceptable.

Allow approximately thirty minutes for this exercise. Have your pen and journal ready. Read each statement slowly. Take a deep breath, and then check the option that most accurately indicates how often you feel or behave this way. Remember that either extreme can indicate a need for repair, except for "nevers" on asterisked statements. To review the general instructions for this exercise, please refer to pages 39–40.

Saying No	Always	Often	Sometimes	Rarely	Never
I find it difficult to say no to people.	——	——	——	——	——
When I do say no, I say it abruptly or stubbornly because I fear their reaction.	——	——	——	——	——
I feel guilty when someone asks me to do something and I say no.	——	——	——	——	——
I do not say no to close friends because I want to be liked.	——	——	——	——	——
When making plans with friends, I tend to agree with whatever they suggest that we do.	——	——	——	——	——

Being Told No					
If I ask someone to do something for me and am told no, I feel ashamed that I even asked.*	——	——	——	——	——

	Always	Often	Sometimes	Rarely	Never
I do not ask my friends to do favors for me because I do not want to feel rejected if they say no.	_____	_____	_____	_____	_____
I am afraid to assert myself at work. I may get fired or my boss might say no.	_____	_____	_____	_____	_____
I do not tell my mate or partner what I need. I would be too humiliated if he or she did not respond positively.	_____	_____	_____	_____	_____

Boundaries

	Always	Often	Sometimes	Rarely	Never
If my partner or roommate comes home angry, I assume I have done something wrong.	_____	_____	_____	_____	_____
I feel embarrassed if I am with someone who makes a scene in public. I assume others will think less of me.	_____	_____	_____	_____	_____
I feel panicky if someone I care about gets too needy and wants me to fill those needs.	_____	_____	_____	_____	_____
I feel smothered if someone gets too close.	_____	_____	_____	_____	_____
If a friend calls and is feeling low, I feel inadequate if I cannot do something to cheer my friend.	_____	_____	_____	_____	_____

Honoring Your Boundaries	Always	Often	Sometimes	Rarely	Never
I do not say anything if a roommate or friend uses something of mine that I do not want him or her to use.	_____	_____	_____	_____	_____
If a friend from out of town calls and wants to stay at my house, I say yes even if it is inconvenient.	_____	_____	_____	_____	_____
If I need a quiet evening at home and a friend calls in need of company, I will still agree to get together.	_____	_____	_____	_____	_____
If my boss asks me to work late, I say yes, even if I have other plans.	_____	_____	_____	_____	_____

Honoring the Boundaries of Others					
If I ask a friend to go to a movie with me, I try to talk my friend into it, even if I am told no.	_____	_____	_____	_____	_____
I feel offended if, when my hour is up, my therapist won't address one more problem.	_____	_____	_____	_____	_____

	Always	Often	Sometimes	Rarely	Never
Even if my roommate has said he or she does not want me to borrow a certain item, I still assume that once is okay.	_____	_____	_____	_____	_____
If I ask someone to do something for me and I am refused, I feel resentful.	_____	_____	_____	_____	_____

Closing

Look over your responses. What do your answers reveal to you about your comfort with boundaries and setting limits? If you checked always or never repeatedly, then those are the issues of your toddler within that you will want to address. Record your impressions in your journal.

EXERCISE TWO: HOW YOU CARRY THESE ISSUES IN YOUR LIFE TODAY

Take a few moments to reflect on each question. Then write about whatever feelings emerge. If you work longer than forty-five minutes, take a stretch break. To review the general instructions for this exercise, please see page 42.

1. Think of three recent occasions when you wanted to say no, but did not. Describe each situation and write about how that feels. What do these experiences suggest to you about what happened when your toddler said no?

2. Think of three recent times when someone said no to you. How did you feel? Describe the situation. What does that say to you about the experience you had with this as a toddler?

3. What feelings get triggered when you are around someone who is emotionally upset? How do you respond? Do you feel overly responsible for their feelings? if so, how? What does that tell you about how you responded to your caretaker's feelings as a child?

4. Think about the people with whom you spend the most time. How do you feel after you've seen them? If that person is depressed, do you feel depressed? If that person is exhilarated, do you feel exhilarated? What does this say about your enmeshment with this other person? Did this happen to you as a child with your caretaker?

5. Are you more comfortable being close or do you feel more secure being distant? What does this tell you about your boundaries and fears of being engulfed or abandoned?

6. In romantic relationships, do you become preoccupied with your partner's needs and tend to lose sight of your own? If so, list examples of this behavior and write down your thoughts about this.

Closing

Review your responses to the above. Combine the information from both of these exercises and compile a list of issues you have identified that your toddler self carries. Below are some examples of potential issues.

Potential Issues from This Developmental Stage

- Inability to say no to friends because you are afraid they will reject you
- Inability to set limits with your boss because you fear you might get fired
- Difficulty stating how you feel because you fear you will be humiliated or rejected
- Feeling smothered if someone tries to get too close
- Feeling inadequate if a friend is upset and you cannot make that friend feel better

These exercises should have identified both the problems as well as the strengths you carried from this stage. If your caretaker pushed you toward independence, you may have been wounded by rejection, but you also developed clear boundaries in your adult life: this is an example of a strength. Record in your journal how your experiences at this stage may have contributed positively to your development.

❧

STEP TWO: RESEARCHING YOUR INNER TODDLER'S PAIN

The exercise in Step one helped you identify any pain you have with autonomy. Now you will research the circumstances that influenced your caretaker's ability to help you become autonomous. This will help you understand why your present attempts to be independent may have been thwarted or inappropriately encouraged.

EXERCISE ONE: INTERVIEWING YOURSELF

Some people have vivid memories of their early childhood, while others do not. Since your vocabulary was developing, you may recall sensations or symbolic images more than verbal experiences—impressions rather than visual memories. You may recall smells or textures or colors, but have no images that are concrete. In this exercise, simply write down whatever comes to you; its relevance will later become clear. To review the general instructions for this exercise, see pages 45.

1. Record the facts you can recall. Where did you live? Did your family move? Did you go to daycare? Were there significant caretakers other than your parents involved in your life? Did you have siblings or grandparents who lived in the home? When did you learn to walk, talk, etc.?

2. Next, record in your journal any images, impressions, or sensations you uncover from this period in your life. Is there a symbolic image that expresses how you felt? Do you remember any stories?

Closing

Record your thoughts on how your caretakers responded to your needs to be independent and autonomous. How did these experiences influence the person you are today?

EXERCISE TWO: INTERVIEWING YOUR BODY

This exercise will determine where in your body the needs and feelings of your toddler are stored and will assess what those needs and feelings are. To review the general instructions for this exercise, refer to page 45.

1. Close your eyes and surround yourself with healing white Light. As you are imagining this white Light surrounding you, breathe deeply, relax, and allow your breathing to bring you more and more deeply in touch with the center of your being. When you feel relaxed, continue.

2. Let your focus travel freely through your body. Now either look directly into a mirror or, if you prefer, imagine that you are. Look at your body. (Try to see it without judging it.) Acknowledge your body as though you were saying hello to an old friend.

3. Where do you feel tense? Is this tension connected in any way to your inner toddler's pain? Be quiet and listen. Record in your journal any response you feel.

4. Think of a recent time you had to say no. Did you feel fear or pride? Where in your body do you hold that experience? Write about it. How is that experience related to your struggle for autonomy?

5. Now think of a recent time that you felt your boundaries were violated, or when you may have violated another person's boundaries. What was your experience and where did you hold those feelings in your body? Write down your responses in your journal.

6. Next, think of a recent time when someone said no to a request you made of them. Find where that experience is stored in your body. What does that

experience tell you about your inner toddler's pain? Record your findings in your journal.

Closing

When you have completed each question, use deep breathing to help bring your focus back to the center of your being. Surround yourself with Light. Open your eyes when it feels comfortable to do so. How do you feel about the information you received? Record your discoveries.

EXERCISE THREE: HOW YOU TREAT YOUR BODY

Setting compassionate limits with your body and responding to what your body needs is directly related to how you experienced these needs being met by your caretaker when you were a toddler. Do you find yourself being either restrictive or permissive with your physical needs? Admitting that you may treat yourself as badly as you were treated is difficult. Are you ambivalent about sex . . . afraid to say yes or no? These issues may be related to what you experienced as a toddler. Dialoguing with your body should help you understand. Go slowly, and remember, you cannot change a characteristic that you won't acknowledge. Answer the following questions in your journal. To review the general instructions for this exercise, refer to pages 47–48.

1. Are you aware of your body's limitations? If so, do you respect them? For example, do you know which foods make you overactive, put on weight, or feel depressed? Do you eat these foods anyway? If so, how do you feel about that?

2. If you imagine a person moving toward you, how close can the person get before you feel uncomfortable? What do you do when that boundary is crossed? Do you allow the violation to happen? Or do you step back and protect yourself? Or do you angrily berate the other person for getting too close? What are your thoughts about your response?

3. Are you able to say no to activities that are harmful to you? For example, can you say no to sex when you do not want to have sex? Can you turn down a piece of cake that you really do not want, even if it is offered to you by a friend?

4. Do you spend any private time with your body during the day to focus on its needs? For instance, do you take a quiet bath, do yoga, or go for a run? Or do you ignore your body, assuming it will take care of itself?

Closing

Write down any last thoughts or feelings you have about the way you treat your body. Reflect on how these ways of behaving relate to the way you were treated when you were a toddler.

EXERCISE FOUR: INTERVIEWING FAMILY MEMBERS, RELATIVES, AND FRIENDS

Return to pages 48–50 to review the general instructions for your interviews. Then, repeat the same steps you used when you conducted your research for your infancy. Specific questions relating to the toddler years are listed below. Make sure you have the support of a friend or a professional so you can check in with him or her before and after each interview. Be as comprehensive as possible. Use your journal to record your thoughts and feelings.

Guidelines and Sample Questions

Ask what that person remembers about your learning to say no. How did your parents respond to your newfound independence? Were you left with babysitters, nannies, or at daycare? If so, how did this affect your autonomy? Was there anyone in your life who may have felt apprehensive or overenthusiastic about your independence? Did you have siblings? If so, how did you get along with them? Did you share a room or have your own?

Modify these questions or add your own. Remember to ask about specifics, too. Continue your interviews by asking about social or political events that may have affected the quality of your care.

Closing

Once you have completed your interviews, take a few moments to comment in your journal about the information you received. What assumptions can you make about your caretaking? To complete this step, take the issues you listed at the end of Step one and write them down in one column. In a second column, indicate the circumstances that led to those issues and, in a third column, record how that issue is evident in the way that you treat your body. This will give you a profile of your toddler's pain. Following is an example.

Issue	Circumstances	Evidenced in the way I treat my body
I have difficulty saying no to those close to me because I am afraid they will get mad and desert me.	My father did this. He was very strict. "Talking back" was not allowed. If we did say no, we were sent to our rooms for the night, and he refused to talk to us for several days.	Unable to stay on a diet and say no to any food that is offered to me by another. I feel disgusted with myself and get depressed.

Closing

Developing this structure will help you construct the profile of your inner toddler's pain. It will also arm you with the information to help your toddler heal.

ᐯᐱ

STEP THREE: REGRESSING TO THE FEELINGS OF THE TODDLER WITHIN

What was it like to be a toddler, to learn about boundaries, saying and hearing no? Were you comfortable with the limits that were set for you? Did you feel comfortable experimenting with independence and freedom? When you reexperience your transition into independence, you will be able to determine more accurately how in your current life you might sabotage your efforts to be independent. Often people experience rage or anger when they begin to acknowledge how much their move toward independence was blocked or pushed. If your feelings become unmanageable, take a break and get the personal or professional support that you need.

EXERCISE ONE: ACTIVITIES THAT ENHANCE YOUR REGRESSION

Allow approximately thirty minutes for each activity. Review the general instructions for this exercise on page 52. Record your reactions in your journal.

1. For ten minutes, crawl around the floor on your knees. (Come on, you can do it! Pick a time when no one else is around.) Try to reach for things. Pretend it is the first time you have ever seen these objects. Taste things, touch things, and smell things. After ten minutes, write about your experience.

2. Get a bed sheet and put it on the floor. Take a bowl of applesauce and a bowl of mashed potatoes and sit in the middle of the sheet. Take a spoon and feed yourself with your least dominant hand. Record your experience.

3. Throw a tantrum. Stomp your feet, pound your fists, and whine like a toddler. Does this come easily to you, or do you feel restrained? Write about your experience.

4. Run a warm bath. Get some children's bath toys and take a bath with your playmates. Let yourself splash around in the water and play.

5. Have a friend read you a bedtime story, or buy a taped story and listen to it before you take a nap or go to bed. Later, record what you felt. Does it provoke a longing for something you never had? Does it trigger a memory from a long, long time ago?

6. Finger paint, color, or draw a picture with your least dominant hand. Paste it in your journal.

7. Buy some modeling clay. Mold it and play with it. Then create a form that represents your identity at two years old.

8. Pick an hour, an afternoon, or a day and say *no* to everything asked of you.

9. If possible, spend an afternoon with a toddler. What was it like to be a toddler? Notice what this child does and how he or she responds to the environment and to you.

10. Use your imagination to create any other activities that pertain to this age. When you feel you are familiar with the sensations and feelings you had as a toddler, record any last thoughts in your journal.

Closing

The toddler self carries pain, but it also carries joy and a sense of exploration and separateness. Having completed these activities, you probably have a better awareness of both. What have you learned about who you were as a toddler? Write in your journal any thoughts or feelings this question provokes. This overview will lead you into the next step—objectifying the feelings of your toddler within.

લ

STEP FOUR: OBJECTIFYING YOUR TODDLER SELF'S PAIN

Objectifying the toddler self's pain means separating from your fear of abandonment because you set boundaries and say no to others. Only then can you begin to see this fear as that of your toddler within. In fact, all the feelings carried from this stage will be objectified and seen as belonging to the toddler self. This frees the adult self to respond to the needs of the younger self. You can establish the part of you who fears autonomy (the toddler self) and the part of you who can support your autonomy and sense of independence (the adult self).

EXERCISE ONE: MEETING YOUR TODDLER WITHIN

Choose the method you want to use for this guided imagery. To review the general instructions for this exercise, refer to page 54. When you are ready to begin, make sure you are in your safe place, and that you will not be interrupted for at least thirty minutes.

Begin by closing your eyes and surrounding yourself with the protective Light. Use deep breathing to relax and focus. Imagine you are walking down a path in a beautiful meadow. You continue down this path, noticing the smells and the colors of the meadow. Then you see something else nearby. As you get closer you realize it is a playground. In this playground there is a playpen. In this playpen is a young child. You look closer at this child and you realize it is the toddler within you. How do you feel? Notice the child's vulnerability. What is your toddler doing? Is it sleeping, crying, playing, exploring, quietly waiting for someone to appear? Touch your inner child. How does the child respond? See if you can determine what this child self needs. Tell your toddler self that you are its future. You are proof that it survived. Tell the toddler within that you will help it heal. You have come back to its rescue. You have come back to heal the fear of abandonment that comes from the attempt to be independent and autonomous, to heal the pain involved in saying or hearing no, and to heal all the issues of boundaries or privacy that it so faithfully carried for you. Spend a few minutes with your toddler self. Notice how the two of you relate. When you feel you have spent enough time with your toddler within for now, assure your toddler self that your work with the pain will now begin. The hurt is over. The child will not be abused or abandoned for wanting to explore and be free. When you feel ready to conclude, bring your focus back to your breathing and to the Light that surrounds you. Take several cleansing breaths, and then open your eyes when it feels comfortable to do so.

Closing

Meeting the part of you who carries your independence and your fears about being autonomous can be emotional. Let those feelings be present as you continue to the next exercise. Record in your journal any feelings you had to meeting your toddler within. Complete this experience by asking your toddler to help you find its photo or to locate a picture from a magazine that looks like it. Paste that picture in your journal so you can reflect on it as you begin to ask more in-depth questions. Record in your journal any thoughts or feelings you have about this picture, then prepare to move on.

EXERCISE TWO: CREATING A DIALOGUE WITH YOUR TODDLER SELF

Toddlers use very few words, or no words at all. You may simply intuit what this inner child needs and feels. Just observe and listen and the responses will become clear. Allow at least thirty minutes for this exercise. Make sure you will not be interrupted. Write the question down in your journal using your dominant hand. Then use your least dominant hand when writing your inner toddler's response.

    1. Ask what your toddler's favorite color is.

    2. What is your toddler's favorite bedtime story? Favorite toy?

    3. What activity does your toddler self most enjoy?

    4. Ask your toddler within to tell you about its fear of being left because of misbehavior, or fear of hearing or saying no.

    5. What does this inner child need most from you?

    6. Ask your toddler within if you parent him or her the way your parents did you. If so, how does this feel?

7. How does your toddler feel about you? Does your toddler self understand what it means to be reclaimed by you? If not, explain that it means you will listen to this part of self when it feels a boundary has been crossed and it needs you to set a limit.

8. Does your toddler within feel comfortable with your setting limits and saying no?

9. Is there anything your toddler self wants to know about you? Does it trust you to protect its boundaries and to respond to its needs?

10. What joys does this inner child want to offer you and what prevents this from happening?

Closing

What did you learn about your toddler self from the above exercise? How do you feel about what you learned? Answer those questions in your journal.

EXERCISE THREE: TALKING IN THE MIRROR TO YOUR TODDLER WITHIN

To review the general instructions for mirror work, see pages 56–57. Then take a few moments to get settled as you look at yourself in the mirror. Think about the times you may hold back because you are afraid you will not be loved or accepted. Start to rock gently back and forth. Close your eyes and hum a lullaby or pretend you are rocking your toddler self, preparing it for a nap. When you feel a connection with your toddler within, ask what it needs from you to feel safe hearing and saying no, setting boundaries, and exploring and being independent without the fear of being abandoned or engulfed. Listen for the responses, open your eyes, and respond out loud to what you heard. Continue as long as you feel comfortable.

Closing

Record your experience in your journal. Use your least dominant hand and let your toddler within be expressive. Switch to your dominant hand and let your adult self record your experience.

EXERCISE FOUR: CREATING YOUR PROTECTOR

Toddlers are very tactile. They like to explore textures, tastes, and smells. Have your drawing materials handy—perhaps adding scented magic markers—for your toddler self to draw the protector. To review the general instructions for this exercise, see page 58.

1. With whom does your toddler feel most safe?

2. If your toddler self could select anyone, real or imagined, as a protector, who would it be? It could be Superman, an angel, God, or someone more familiar.

3. Ask your toddler self to draw a picture representing this protector and assure your toddler that this protector will be there any time it wants.

Closing

Keep this new drawing where you do your internal work, and keep this image stored in your imagination as well. In your work with your toddler self, you can always call in this character for support; it is this image that will meet the needs of your toddler self and help heal the gaps left from childhood. Acknowledge a partnership between this protector and your adult self. If you wish, call in your Higher Power as well. This team will heal the toddler within you. Record your responses in your journal.

EXERCISE FIVE: DETECTING THE CRITICAL VOICE

The critical voice for the toddler self ridicules you for saying no, shames you when someone says no to you, and convinces you that you have no right to be autonomous and independent. It is the voice that suggests that you ignore other people's boundaries and disregard them when they say no. Once you know who in your past criticized you, or have a symbolic form for this inner voice, your adult self and your Higher Power can challenge its negativity. Respond to the following questions in your journal. To review the general instructions for this exercise, see pages 59.

1. What negative statements do you make to yourself when you say or hear no?
2. What negative statements do you make to yourself when you set boundaries or attempt to be autonomous?
3. What negative statements do you make to yourself when you are acting spontaneous and self-confident?
4. What negative statements do you make to yourself when you want to stop feeling engulfed or rejected by someone you like?
5. Where have you heard those statements before? Whose voice is this? Is it the voice of a parent, a babysitter, a teacher, a minister, or coach? Is it a voice you have heard from society? Is the voice imagined or real?
6. Imagine that you, as the adult, speak to this voice. What does the voice want? What is the intent—to protect or to harm?
7. Using your least dominant hand, let your toddler self draw a picture of this voice. This picture represents fear, terror, and judgments created by this critic within.
8. Now go back to the original negative statements. Next to each negative statement write a positive affirmation, as demonstrated in the example below.

Negative Statement	Positive Affirmation
I am such a whimp. I can never say no to anybody. I am too afraid I won't be liked.	I have a right to say no to others even if they don't like it.

Use these affirmations any time you hear the wounding words. They will help dissolve the negativity and replace it with statements that are kind.

Closing

Have your adult self interact with this critic, and when necessary, imagine that your Higher Power sends it away by surrounding it in a bubble of protective Light and releasing the bubble into the universe.

Assure your inner child that the critic will no longer go unchallenged. Then write about this experience in your journal.

EXERCISE SIX: CHANGING YOUR INNER TODDLER'S EXPERIENCE OF CHILDHOOD

To heal this part of self, you will need to create an *internal support system* that guards you and says no. Sometimes I picture a metal barrel around my body that protects me from taking in another's pain. Some clients imagine movie characters of great strength as their bodyguards, while others call in their Higher Power.

If you were violated at this age, you will want to picture the violation stopped. Remember to bring in an adult figure, your protector, and Higher Power to help set this limit. A toddler cannot stand up to his alcoholic mother and tell her to stop hitting him. A toddler cannot tell her father to stop molesting her. To try to do so could mean greater pain, or worse. Many people get stuck trying to work with the toddler issues; they expect to be able to say no when, emotionally, they still feel like a child. It is absolutely essential to bring into your mind's eye those characters who can rescue and protect the toddler within. If you get bogged down, it may be a sign that you need professional support. If so, seek that support and ask the professional to use this exercise as a guide. To review the general instructions for this exercise, see pages 60–61.

Review the profile of this inner child's pain and select the issue upon which to focus. Then use the guided imagery provided on page 61 to rework and transform the painful scenes from this time.

Closing

This exercise began transforming your toddler self's pain. Rework this exercise with as many issues as you choose. You will know that your toddler self is healing when you can say no with ease (or at least without a lot of discomfort). The more you develop a sense of self, the more you will be able to determine what feelings are yours and what feelings belong to others. Remember that if you were never allowed to say no—never allowed your own separateness—then you should bring in your adult self to set that boundary. As that boundary is set, your toddler within will begin to feel safe, and will stop sabotaging your need to be autonomous. When you feel ready to let go, help your toddler self grieve.

ↄ

STEP FIVE: GRIEVING YOUR INNER TODDLER'S PAIN

You cannot begin to learn how to say and hear no, establish and maintain boundaries, or develop a sense of separateness until your toddler self grieves its pain about its caretaking.

EXERCISE ONE: THE FIRST FOUR STAGES OF GRIEF

In the following exercise you will help your toddler self experience those stages of loss that go along with giving up hope that things will change. You will switch between your adult and toddler selves, so you might want to set up chairs or pillows to represent the two parts within you.

Allow several hours to complete this exercise. Set up the room so you will be comfortable. I suggest that you call in the support of your Higher Power, the inner toddler's protector, and surround yourself with light. You will need your journal, pen, and drawing materials. To review the general instructions for this exercise, and to obtain the guidelines needed to assist you in this process, please refer to pages 63–65.

Closing

Gather all the drawings and writings that you and your toddler completed during this grieving process. You will be using them in the final step of healing this inner child's pain and reclaiming his or her joy.

ↄ

STEP SIX: HEALING YOUR PAIN, RECLAIMING YOUR JOY

Note: Read the modifications below, then see pages 65–69. Repeat the ceremony for healing the inner child. The issues you will focus on during your emotional, physical, and spiritual release are: your fears of being abandoned after saying no or becoming independent, and the difficulties you may have had with establishing and maintaining boundaries.

The fragrance of lavender or roses is excellent for healing this age. You can purchase them as incense, bath oils, or lotions, or use scented potpourri. Their properties are associated with love, protection, purification, balance, and healing.

Closing

When you feel ready to conclude this ritual, explain that you are bringing your toddler home, integrating this part of self back into your total being. It can feel safe in knowing that you will say no, set limits, and respond if it feels violated by another's actions.

Ask your toddler self to select the place within your body where it would feel the most protected from any potential violation. Then imagine the toddler melting into that part of your body. This merging with your toddler within will help you say no and set limits.

You are now familiar with your toddler's reactions to being violated, therefore you will be able to respond more effectively to its cues. If this inner child's issues get triggered, then use the tools you have learned to objectify these feelings so you can resolve them. When the issue is resolved, and if it feels safe, bring your toddler self back home.

If it does not feel appropriate to have your toddler self melt back into your physical being, then create a safe place where it can reside. Imagine that the protector stays with your toddler within so that it will always feel safe.

Your need to say no—to establish and maintain boundaries—will never completely disappear. Boundaries are often tested and the need to say no is always an option. Now, however, you will be able to recognize the needs your toddler within carries and will know that you have the tools to respond to them with care.

REVISING THE GARDEN OF YOUR PAST

Complete your work with this inner child by returning to the garden you created at the beginning of your work. How would your toddler within like to contribute to this garden? Imagine that you both do the work, so that this inner child is represented in the garden of growth. If you are fortunate enough to have a garden or a place where you can grow things, plant a seed to represent this inner child's growth.

This concludes your work with your toddler within. Remember that any of the exercises in this chapter can be used repeatedly to continue your work. Also, the exercises in chapter 9 will continue development of your relationship with your toddler self.

4

T H R E E   T O   S I X   Y E A R S

THE YOUNG INNER CHILD

Confronting the Good, the Bad, and the Ugly

How you feel about yourself and your body, and how you deal with and respect the positive and negative qualities in yourself and others, are related to how you experienced these issues when you were between the ages of three and six. This period was when you began to learn the difference between good and bad behavior. When you were good (acting like the adults in your life expected and wanted you to act), you were rewarded. When you were bad (acting in ways that were unacceptable to these adults), you were punished. The rewards may have been in the form of praise or you may have been given special food, toys or outings. Punishment may have been emotional: you may have been humiliated or teased, or your parents may have ignored you. Or it may have been physical: you were spanked or slapped or sent to your room. Fearing the punishments and desiring the rewards, you quickly learned what was acceptable and what was not.

Three to six was a very tender time. It was when the foundation for self-worth was being laid. If you were taught that you were basically good, but that sometimes you did bad things, you probably would have developed a solid foundation on which to build your self-worth. You would, as an adult, be able to make mistakes without feeling that you were bad, the way a child would.

On the other hand, if as a child you were constantly told how bad you were, your self-worth would have suffered terribly. You might well have grown up believing that you always would be bad. As an

90

adult, you would most likely fear making a mistake because each mistake would further confirm these feelings and this lack of self-worth. This faulty sense of self-worth becomes the core of your shame. You feel shame when you feel you are not good enough, or are unworthy of love. I believe we develop shame in response to fear. You fear that you will be abandoned because you are unlovable.

By the age of three, you are figuring out how to relate to other people. You know what to do to get what you need. Unfortunately, if you were raised in an alcoholic or dysfunctional home, your needs were probably ignored or could not have been met. In fact, you might have been ridiculed or been the object of anger for even having needs. The words you heard others use to describe you would have become the foundation for the way in which you saw yourself. If you were told you were bad, you would have begun to believe that you were bad. If you were told you were stupid, you would begin to believe that you were stupid.

Many of the negative messages you give yourself as an adult originate in this time of life. The feelings of shame, the need for perfection, the criticism you feel of yourself and others, and your black-and-white thinking all originate in this developmental stage. This is demonstrated in the story of Cindy, who worked as a secretary.

Case History: Cindy

Cindy fidgeted as she began to speak. She didn't understand, she said. No matter what she did at her job, she didn't seem to be good enough; her boss always wanted something more. She felt that her whole day was rated as a success or failure based on her boss's reaction to her work. If he praised her, she felt good. If he had a complaint or even just a suggestion, she felt she had failed. As an example, she told me about a time when she had typed some letters for him, but then had mailed them without their enclosures. He had asked her, very nicely, to fax the enclosures. Cindy did but felt so embarrassed and incompetent that she called in sick the next day.

Her response clearly seemed out of line. I asked Cindy to close her eyes and try to sense exactly who her boss resembled. She recalled a scene from her childhood. She had been playing on the floor when her father had yelled to her to get him a beer. Startled, she had run into the kitchen and grabbed the beer, but as she was taking it to him, she fell. The beer spilled all over the floor. Then an ominous figure was standing over her, screaming that she never did anything right. She had cowered, terrified, on the floor.

I had Cindy freeze the scene while we talked. I asked her to see her adult self walk into the scene and speak with that frightened child within. I had her adult self explain to the child that she was her future self. She was proof that she had grown up and survived. Cindy talked to her inner child at length about how her father was no longer a threat. She explained that her boss was a different man. He did not hit her or humiliate her when she made a mistake. For several sessions we worked with this frightened little girl. Cindy was slowly able to separate from her child within. And once she did, she was able to respond to her boss's suggestions without feeling incompetent.

Cindy was confronting her feelings of shame, rooted in a lack of self-worth and poor self-esteem. Around age three we begin to care enough about others to be concerned with how they are feeling about us. If the people we most care about accept us for all that we are, then we will learn to accept ourselves as well. However, whatever our caretakers do not like, we attempt to disown. We are too young to stay true to ourselves at the expense of losing their love. This dynamic follows us into adulthood and becomes, perhaps, the greatest factor in our people-pleasing and codependent behavior.

Cindy's story illustrates another issue that can also originate from this developmental stage—being overly responsible. Cindy's father expected her to fetch his beer and wait on him. She was too young for such a grown-up responsibility, yet she was shamed when she was unable to succeed. Many children at this age are expected to behave in ways that surpass their capabilities. A three-year-old child does become more aware of the family pain and does attempt to play "little adult" to make the pain go away. But if children are held responsible for making mommy feel better, or for keeping the house clean so daddy doesn't get angry, or for taking care of their sick grandmother, they will grow up to feel responsible for many things that are beyond control, but when their attempts to control fail, they will feel shame.

Being held responsible for situations that are beyond one's control can also inhibit activities that are appropriate for this age, such as developing one's curiosity. The words *why* and *what's this* seem to be a three-year-old's favorites. They help the child explore and begin to understand the world.

This curiosity extends to the discovery of the body, and the child asks questions about everything. The answers received will greatly affect the child's relationship to its body. This is especially true of sexuality because it is also roughly at this age that a child begins to experience the physical pleasure of genital stimulation and becomes curious about the private parts of others. It is common for a child this age to touch their genital area. If it is excessive it may indicate a problem, but for most children it is simple exploration. It is also common for a child to ask pointed questions about genitalia. The questions are a source of interest and the sensations a source of comfort. How the caretakers respond to this curiosity can have a long-lasting effect on the child's development. If they shame or tease the child, this age-appropriate act of physical discovery can become a source of shame and guilt and the natural discovery of the body can be thwarted.

The parent's awareness of their sexual feelings about their children is crucial—otherwise the child won't feel safe and won't explore their own sexuality. Both mothers and fathers need to realize that sexual feelings are normal—it is taking *action* on these feelings that is not acceptable. Women, through breast-feeding and giving birth, can better understand that sexual feelings exist in response to their children. They see it as an extension of the physical intimacy between mother and child. This is not to say that mothers do not overrespond and exploit their children, but it is less common.

However, when children at this developmental stage begin climbing on their father, and wanting to kiss them on the mouth, it can be a little disconcerting. If the father is unaware of his own sexuality and does not realize that experiencing erotic feelings towards his children is normal, he may either overreact or overrespond. Frightened by their own impulses, they overreact by completely withdrawing from all physical contact with their children. This is the most common response. Less common, but also prevalent in our society, is the father who overresponds to the child's exploration and exploits the child's sexual curiosity. The result is incest. The intent is to molest, and the child is violated. If it occurs, the child grows up feeling disconnected from their body and may develop a pattern of sexualizing needs because, as a child, the needs were responded to in a sexual manner. In adulthood, love can get confused with sex; "being loved" can become confused with "putting out." The wounds from incest run deep. If you are a victim, it is important that you be gentle with yourself and that you seek the support you need in order to heal.

STEP ONE: IDENTIFYING YOUR PAIN

This developmental stage was perhaps the most critical growth period in your life. The level of self-worth you developed was the basis for the insecurities that followed you into adulthood. Your need to be perfect and to ward off your shame originated from this age, as did your inability to succeed and your ability to master the tasks from later stages. The following exercises will help you assess the issues you carried into your adult life, and will help you determine the wounds that are to be healed.

EXERCISE ONE: HOW YOU RESPOND TODAY

The following statements help you identify your issues with self-criticism, criticizing others, shame, self-esteem, all-or-nothing thinking, body image, sexuality, and curiosity. They also may reveal the criteria you use to judge others, since what you do not like in yourself gets projected onto those around you. How often you feel in the ways described below will indicate the degree of repair that is necessary.

Allow approximately thirty minutes for this exercise. Begin by reading each statement carefully. Take a deep breath and then check the response that best suits how frequently you feel this way. Remember that either extreme can indicate a need for repair. (This is not the case for some of the five statements if your response is "never." These have been marked by an asterisk.) To review the general instructions for this exercise, see pages 39–40.

Self-Criticism	Always	Often	Sometimes	Rarely	Never
I focus on things about myself that I do not like.	_____	_____	_____	_____	_____
If I do one thing wrong at work, I obsess about that mistake and discount any achievements I have made that day.	_____	_____	_____	_____	_____
I spend a great deal of time worrying about what others think of me.*	_____	_____	_____	_____	_____

	Always	Often	Sometimes	Rarely	Never
My internal dialogue is made up of self-deprecating statements.*	_____	_____	_____	_____	_____

Criticism of Others

I am very judgmental of others.	_____	_____	_____	_____	_____
I have a hard time accepting the imperfections of my friends.	_____	_____	_____	_____	_____
I dislike people who are too fat or too skinny.	_____	_____	_____	_____	_____
If I'm at a party, I feel more secure if I feel that I look better than most of the people there.	_____	_____	_____	_____	_____

Shame and Unworthiness

If something goes wrong at work, I assume I am responsible.	_____	_____	_____	_____	_____
If a store clerk is rude to me, I assume I must have done something wrong.	_____	_____	_____	_____	_____
I feel angry and embarrassed if I offer my services to someone and my help is refused.	_____	_____	_____	_____	_____
I believe it is conceited to say positive things about myself.	_____	_____	_____	_____	_____

All-or-Nothing Thinking

	Always	Often	Sometimes	Rarely	Never
If a friend says he or she will meet me and is late, I refuse to make plans with that person again.	_____	_____	_____	_____	_____
If I make a mistake while participating in a new activity, I never engage in that activity again.	_____	_____	_____	_____	_____
If I ask someone to do me a favor and am refused, I never ask again.	_____	_____	_____	_____	_____
When I first meet new people, I either really like or really dislike them.*	_____	_____	_____	_____	_____

Body Image and Sexuality

When I look in a mirror at my body, I focus on what I want to change.	_____	_____	_____	_____	_____
I wear baggy clothes so my body is not so noticeable.*	_____	_____	_____	_____	_____
I think masturbation is sick and dirty.	_____	_____	_____	_____	_____
I have sex with someone because I do not know any other way to feel close.	_____	_____	_____	_____	_____

	Always	Often	Sometimes	Rarely	Never
I have sex because I am angry or sad and I want to get away from what I feel.	_____	_____	_____	_____	_____

Being Overly Responsible

	Always	Often	Sometimes	Rarely	Never
I am afraid to relax and let someone else be in charge, because I fear something will go wrong and I will be at fault.	_____	_____	_____	_____	_____
It is easier to do a task myself than to ask someone else to do it. He or she would not do it the way I want it to be done anyway.	_____	_____	_____	_____	_____
I am overly cautious about things like making sure the doors are locked, the iron is unplugged, and everything is safe.	_____	_____	_____	_____	_____
I feel that if I don't do it, no one will.	_____	_____	_____	_____	_____

Curiosity

	Always	Often	Sometimes	Rarely	Never
I am afraid to ask about something I don't understand because I am afraid others will think I am stupid.	_____	_____	_____	_____	_____
I dislike it when others ask irrelevant questions.	_____	_____	_____	_____	_____

	Always	Often	Sometimes	Rarely	Never
I have to understand how to do something immediately or else I lose interest.	_____	_____	_____	_____	_____
I refrain from asking other people questions that are too personal.	_____	_____	_____	_____	_____

Closing

Look over your responses. What do they tell you about your young inner child and the issues of this stage? How have you carried these unresolved issues into your adulthood? For instance, if your responses reveal that you judge others often, but rarely yourself, then you may be projecting your negative qualities. You may have a distorted view of yourself as well as them.

The more rigid your responses, the more rigidity you experienced as a child. The more judgments you have of yourself and others, the more severely you were judged as a child. The less curiosity you exhibit, the less your curiosity was welcomed when you were a child. Record in your journal any thoughts or feelings that have been provoked by this exercise.

EXERCISE TWO: HOW YOU CARRY THESE ISSUES IN YOUR LIFE TODAY

In this exercise you continue to explore the issues of the young inner child: good and bad, self-criticism, criticism of others, curiosity, and sexuality. You may feel part of self when you feel your need to be right, when you have no tolerance for your humanness or the humanness of others, or when you feel guilt or shame at failing in what you feel are your responsibilities.

Read each question, then take a few moments to recall a time when you may have encountered such circumstances. Record your thoughts in your journal. If you work longer than forty-five minutes, take a stretch break and then continue. To review the general instructions for this exercise, refer to page 42.

1. Think of a recent time when you felt critical of someone else. How did you deal with that feeling? Did you express it, repress it, or deny it?

2. What does your criticism of this other person reveal about you? What emotional reaction did this behavior trigger in you?

3. What do you do when you begin to see things in other people that you do not like?

4. Define what shame means to you. Think of a time when you felt shame. Describe the incident. What element of the experience triggered those feelings of shame?

5. What areas of your life are affected by your shame? Does it get in the way of how you relate to your body or the amount of money you make? Does it influence your sexuality, creativity, or intellectual abilities? Write about the influence your shame has on these areas.

6. Define guilt. Do you experience guilt differently than shame? How?

7. Think of a situation where you experienced guilt. If you had not felt guilt at that time, what would you have felt?

8. How do you use sexuality in relationships? Do you focus on sex too much or not enough?

9. Are you curious? Are you comfortable asking questions even if you feel you'll appear stupid?

Closing

Combine this information with that from Exercise one and make a list of the issues you have carried into your adult life. (Some examples are listed below.)

Potential Issues That Result From This Developmental Stage

- Feeling awkward about your body
- Being highly critical of yourself—full of shame
- Using sex as the only way to feel close
- Being a perfectionist
- Having no tolerance for another's behavior

Your Young Inner Child's Strengths

These exercises helped you identify some of wounds, but also suggested strengths. As you think back over the years between three and six, reflect on what strengths you may have gained from your experience. For instance, you may have been wounded if your caretakers were critical of you, but you could have also developed a sensitivity to criticism and may try not to be critical with others. Record in your journal how these years may have contributed positively to your development.

℃℈

STEP TWO: RESEARCHING YOUR YOUNG INNER CHILD'S PAIN

A great deal of the pain from this stage of development has been inherited by mimicking your caretakers' attitudes about themselves, their bodies, and others. If they felt shame about their bodies, you may have picked up that shame. If they were highly critical of others, you may well have learned that behavior. No matter how offensive some of your parents' behavior was to you, there is some part of you that internalized that behavior. Often, this is rooted in your young inner child. During these years you developed your attitudes about relating to yourself and others.

Your caretakers may have inherited their shame or judgmental character from *their* parents. Or these attitudes may have been responses to things that happened to your caretakers during this period of your life. For instance, if the primary earner in your home lost a job, he or she may have been angry and bitter, and perhaps blamed everyone else. Perhaps you were even the target of this blame. If so, you may have carried that blame and shame into your adult life and could be projecting these feelings onto others, just as they were projected onto you.

Researching the attitudes your caretakers had will help you understand the attitudes you may have inherited. Researching the events that occurred in their lives during this stage will help you understand if these events influenced your acceptance of your positive and negative qualities, and your sense of self worth.

EXERICISE ONE: INTERVIEWING YOURSELF

Allow at least forty-five minutes for this exercise. If you need more time, take a stretch break. To review the general instructions, see page 45.

1. Record what facts you know about this period in your life. Where did you live? Did you go to daycare or preschool? Did you have babysitters or nannies? Did you have siblings or grandparents who lived in the home? Describe what your living situation was like when you were this age.

2. Record in your journal any images, impressions or sensations that seem particularly strong in your memory of this time. Is there a symbolic image that expresses how you felt?

3. Try to recall what you were told about your body and about sex. Write down what you recall. Who told you these things? What do you think were their intentions?

4. What were you told about your worth as a human being? By whom? What did you feel?

Closing

How do you think the experiences that you have recalled have influenced the person you are today? Record your impressions.

EXERCISE TWO: INTERVIEWING YOUR BODY

Use this exercise to help you determine where in your body the judgment, shame or overresponsibility of your young child within are stored. To review the general instructions for this exercise, refer to page 45.

1. Close your eyes. As you imagine this white Light surrounding you, begin to breathe deeply, into the very center of your being. When you feel relaxed, continue.

2. Let your focus travel through your body. Look directly into a mirror or pretend you are looking into a mirror at your body. Acknowledge your body as though you were saying hello to an old friend.

3. Scan your body to see where you feel tense. Ask this tension if it has something to say about the judgment or shame of your three-to-six-year-old within. Be quiet and listen. Record any response you receive.

4. Think of a time you felt shame. Where in your body do you hold that? Ask your body how that experience relates to your childhood. Answer the same questions, substituting guilt for shame.

5. Go through the same process for times that you felt judgmental, judged, or overly responsible.

6. Think of a time you felt criticized. Where is that experience stored in your body? What does that experience tell you about your young inner child's pain? Record your findings in your journal.

7. Think of a time that you felt excitement or joy. Where in your body do you carry those feelings? What does that tell you about your childhood? Answer the same questions, substituting feelings of inner peace and serenity.

Closing

When you have completed each question, bring your focus back to the center of your being. In your imagination, surround yourself with Light. Open your eyes when it feels comfortable to do so. All of us carry some feelings of shame and judgment. It can be painful to locate the places in our bodies that hold the tension of these negative feelings. Reflect on your experiences in your journal.

EXERCISE THREE: HOW YOU TREAT YOUR BODY

Much of how you treat your body is rooted in this developmental stage. You become the wounding parent who neglects, abuses, or molests your body as you recreate the way you were treated as a child. It is as if your body becomes the bad child you try to control, mold, and protect. The questions that follow will help you discover how your attitudes toward your body originated from this stage. Record your responses in your journal. To review the general instructions for this exercise, refer to pages 47–48.

1. Do you praise yourself when you are the "ideal" size and berate yourself because you put on a pound or two?

2. If you overindulge in one food, do you use it as an excuse to binge?

3. Is your body the primary souce of your self-esteem, or a reason for low self-esteem?

4. Do you try not to look at your body in a mirror because you feel it is not ideal? If you do look in the mirror, do you concentrate on what you need to change or can you appreciate the positive qualities you do see in your body?

5. Do you find that you are highly critical of the bodies of others?

6. Do you obsessively compare your shape and size to others?

7. How do you feel about your sexuality? Do you feel shame or guilt?

8. Do you abuse your body by overwhelming or overstimulating it with coffee, drugs, food, or drama?

9. Do you molest your body by binging, purging, taking laxatives, fasting, overexercising, or practicing unsafe or detached sex?

Closing

Write down any other thoughts or feelings you have about the way you treat your body. Remember that the way you relate to your body is indicative of how you were treated at this age. What assumptions can you make about that treatment based on this information? How does that make you feel? Record your responses in your journal.

EXERCISE FOUR: INTERVIEWING FAMILY MEMBERS, RELATIVES, AND FRIENDS

In this last exercise, you will research the circumstances of your years from age three to age six. You need to gather as much information as possible about what may have influenced your acceptance of your positive and negative characteristics. Prepare your interview sheets using the same format as on pages 50–51.

Guidelines and Sample Questions

Who was involved in your life at that time? How did your mother or main caretaker relate to you? Critically or supportively? Did you receive the attention and direction you needed or was your caretaker's focus elsewhere? Did your parents get along? Were there any rifts between them or among any family members? Did you spend any time away from your parents? Did you have babysitters, nannies, or daycare? How did these people relate to you? Were they critical or judgmental? Did they shame you or encourage you? Obtain as much information as possible about the emotional climate at that time. Does anyone remember how you responded? How were your relations with siblings or peers? Remember, this is when you begin to relate to others and can shame and be shamed, criticize and be criticized, judge and be judged. Continue your interviews by asking about world events, political scandals, or similar events that may have affected the quality of your care.

To get a profile of your young inner child's pain, do the following. Take the issues from Step one and put them in one column. To the right, list the circumstances that may have caused this issue. Now, in a third column, indicate how that issue is demonstrated in the way that you treat your body. An example is below.

Issue	Circumstances	Evidenced in the way I treat my body
I am very critical about the emphasis people put on the way they dress and the amount of money they have.	My father divorced my mother when I was four. He said he couldn't bear the way she took care of herself. He shamed her for the way she dressed me as well. Mom felt she was not good enough for Dad. She always felt ashamed of herself after that.	I am highly critical of my attire and never seem to comfortable or secure the way I am dressed.

Closing

Developing this structure will help you begin to construct the profile of your young child's pain. It will also arm you with the information you will need to help him or her heal.

Once you have this information, proceed to Step three, which will help you reexperience the feelings and sensations of this age.

❧

STEP THREE: REGRESSING TO THE FEELINGS OF YOUR YOUNG INNER CHILD

What were you like between the ages of three and six? What judgments and feelings did you pick up from those around you? Was it safe to ask questions, to explore your body, and to act "good" and "bad"? Did you become overly responsible, or take the role of the little adult?

EXERCISE ONE: ACTIVITIES THAT ENHANCE YOUR REGRESSION

These activities help you get in touch with your feelings as a three-to six-year-old child and thereby determine what you missed or witnessed at this age. They will also help you understand what your young inner child needs from you now. Once you can assess and respond to your inner child's needs, you will be able to experience greater joy.

Allow at least thirty minutes for each activity. Write in your journal about your reactions. I recommend you review the general instructions for this step on page 52.

1. If possible, spend an afternoon with a three-to-six-year-old. Gather information about what it is like to be this age. Notice what this child does and how he or she responds to the environment and to you. Record your experience in your journal.

2. With finger paints, paint a picture for your scrapbook. Use only your least dominant hand. Do you worry about making a mess?

3. Go where there is a lot of activity. Spend fifteen minutes writing many "why" questions?

4. Rent a child's video or go to a child's movie at the theater and make believe you are no older than six. What is it like to see the film through a child's eyes?

5. Pick one day and make at least five intentional mistakes—dial a wrong number, drop an ice cream cone, give a store clerk the wrong amount of money for a purchase. Write in your journal how that feels.

6. Make a list of five things you like about yourself and five things you dislike. Then spend an hour, an afternoon, or a day pretending as if the exact opposite were true. For example, pretend that you like that your nose is large and that you dislike that your hair is shiny and thick.

7. Make an "I hate _____ " list. Write as many things down as you can. Keep this in your journal for later use.

8. Pick a language in which you are interested. Learn twenty-five simple words or phrases, and speak that language for an hour, an afternoon, or a day using only those few words or phrases. Experience what it is like to have a very limited vocabulary.

9. Record any sensations or feelings you had in response to these exercises.

Closing

Your young inner child carries pain, but he also carries your positive traits—a sense of curiosity and a connection to your sexuality. Now you might have a greater awareness of the traits of your three-to-six-year-old within. What have you learned about who you were when you were three to six years old and how do you continue to carry those traits? Write down the thoughts or feelings this question provokes. This overview will lead you into the next step, which is separating from and objectifying the feelings of your three-to-six-year-old within.

☙

STEP FOUR: OBJECTIFYING THE PAIN OF YOUR THREE-TO-SIX-YEAR-OLD WITHIN

Objectifying the young inner child's pain means that you separate from your shame, guilt, and rigid all-or-nothing thinking. It means you objectify your need to compare, judge, criticize, and be overly responsible. All the feelings that are carried by your young child within will be objectified and seen as this part of you. This will free you as the adult to respond to the needs of this younger self. It will allow you to establish the part of you who feels these negative feelings (the young child) and the part of you who can challenge the negative ways of behaving (the adult self).

EXERCISE ONE: MEETING YOUR YOUNG INNER CHILD

Go to your safe place when you will not be interrupted for at least thirty minutes. This will give you ample time to meet your three-to-six-year-old within and to relate to this younger self before you interact with his or her pain. To review the general instructions for this exercise, see pages 54.

Close your eyes and surround yourself with the protective Light. Use deep breathing to relax and focus. Now imagine that you are once again walking down a path in a beautiful meadow. You continue down this path, noticing the smells and the colors of the meadow. You see a playground. You go to it. Now you see a sandbox to your right. As you look closer, you realize that the child playing in the sandbox is the three-to-six-year-old within you. What is your inner child doing? What is he or she making in the sand? Gently touch your inner child. How does he or she respond? See if you can determine what this child needs. Speak with this inner child and explain that you are proof that it survived. Tell this child within you that you have returned to help it heal. All your needs to judge and compare are carried by this child who sits before you.

Spend a few minutes with this inner child. How do the two of you relate? When you feel you have spent enough time with this young child within you, assure it that your work with the pain will now begin. The hurt is over. The pain can now be healed. To conclude, bring your focus back to your breathing and to the Light that surrounds you. Take several cleansing breaths, and open your eyes when it feels comfortable to do so.

Closing

Your three-to-six-year-old within will be more talkative than the infant and toddler. It will have more words, more questions, more defined needs. End by asking this inner child to help you find its photo or picture from a magazine. Paste that picture in your journal so you can reflect on it as you begin to ask more in-depth questions. Record in your journal any feelings you have about meeting this inner child and about this picture.

self, and the negative, judgmental thoughts you have about others. This exercise helps you detect that voice. Once you know who it is and have a form for that critical voice, the adult self and the protector can challenge the negativity. Respond to the following questions in your journal. To review the general instructions for this exercise, see page 59.

1. What negative statements do you make about yourself?

2. What criticism do you most make of others?

3. What words do you most often use when you blame yourself for something that goes wrong? What words do you most often use to blame others?

4. What negative statements do you make to yourself about your body and your sexuality?

5. Where have you heard those statements before? Whose voice is this? Is it a parent, a teacher, a priest, or coach? Are these statements you have heard from society? Is the voice imagined or real?

6. Imagine that you, as the adult self, speak to this voice. Ask this voice what it wants. What is the intent? Is it trying to protect or to harm?

7. Using your least dominant hand, let your young inner child draw a picture of this voice within. This picture represents the shame, criticism, over-responsibility, and rigidity carried from childhood.

8. When you have completed the picture, go back to the original negative statements. Rewrite them in your journal. Next to each negative statement write a positive affirmation, such as the one below.

Negative Statement	Positive Affirmation
I could never be as good as that person.	I am fine just the way I am.

Use affirmations any time you hear the wounding words. They will help dissolve the negative words and replace them with kind statements.

Closing

Have your adult self interact with this critic, and when necessary, imagine that your Higher Power sends it away by surrounding it in a bubble of protective Light and releasing the bubble into the universe.

To conclude this exercise, assure your inner child that the critic will no longer go unchallenged. Write about this experience in your journal.

EXERCISE SIX: CHANGING YOUR THREE-TO-SIX-YEAR-OLD'S EXPERIENCE OF CHILDHOOD

Negativity that evolves from this stage can be devastating. Under all of this negativity is shame. This is the key feeling that this inner child carries. We can learn how to work with the negativity by dealing with this shame. It does take practice and it does take work, but it can be done by reworking a scene from the past.

The more you rework the moments you feel shameful, critical, or judgmental, the more you will be able to move through these painful feelings and heal that wounded child within. Each time you have an experience such as this, you give your inner child a new reference point. The child learns that you will not abandon it by collapsing into fear. By separating from the fear, you can interact with it and therefore heal it.

Review the profile of this inner child's pain and select the issue upon which you want to focus. Then use the guided imagery to rework and transform this pain from your past. You may rework each scene many times; it is the repetition that alters the experience. Each time your child is rescued, that child builds more trust in you. (To review the guided imagery, see pages 60–61.)

Closing

This guided imagery helps you transform your three-to-six-year-old child's pain. It should be used whenever you feel your shame or judgments emerging, but rework this exercise with as many issues as you choose. It will help you change the reference point for this inner child's pain.

You will know this part of you is healing when you begin to have more compassion for yourself and others. As you develop options for responding to yourself and to those around you, you will challenge your three-to-six-year-old's all-or-nothing way of relating to the world. As you learn to tolerate or dissolve the discomfort of shame, as you learn to accept that it is human to make mistakes, and as you develop a trusting and supportive relationship to your body and your sexuality, you will be repairing the wounds of this inner child. When you feel ready to let go, proceed to helping your child grieve.

☙

STEP FIVE: GRIEVING YOUR THREE-TO-SIX-YEAR-OLD CHILD'S PAIN

You cannot begin to heal the shame or dissolve the judgment, criticism, and overresponsibility this child feels unless you can help this inner child grieve. This young inner child needs your help to let go of that pain. Every statement of blame you make is a reflection of the blame you endured as a child. Every critical comment you make is a reflection of the criticism you received as a child. And every judgment you feel toward others is a reflection of the judgments you felt when you were young. The depth of this pain will depend upon the degree of shame, blame and judgment you received. It also will depend upon the amount of responsibility you took on for the pain in your family. Both will determine the depth of your grief.

EXERCISE ONE: THE FIRST FOUR STAGES OF GRIEF

The following exercise helps your young inner child grieve. It will experience the panic, the need to bargain, anger, and despair. Every time you challenge your negativity you will feel your three-to-six-year-old's grief. Each time you move towards health you move away from the pain of this inner child. This move demands that this inner child grieve. Go gently and maintain respect for the healing process in which you are engaged. To review the general instructions for this exercise, see page 63.

Allow several hours to complete this exercise. I suggest you call in the support of your Higher Power and your inner child's protector and, in your imagination, surround yourself with Light. You will need your journal, your pen and drawing materials.

Closing

Gather all the drawings and writings that you and your three-to-six-year-old within completed during this grieving process. You will be using them in the final step of healing your inner child's pain and reclaiming its joy.

෴

STEP SIX: HEALING YOUR PAIN, RECLAIMING YOUR JOY

Read the modifications below and then return to pages 65–69 and repeat the ceremony for healing the inner child. The issues from this stage are your criticism of self and others, negative feelings about your body and sexuality, and any fears you have about being curious and inquisitive.

Herbs appropriate for this stage are chamomile, yarrow, and star anise. Chamomile can be used in your bath or brewed as tea, and is associated with protection, healing, and love. Yarrow is associated with dealing with negativity, and is excellent with this age because you are focusing on healing the positive and negative qualities within you. Star anise is associated with negotiation between opposites. (This would be an asset for any of these ceremonious rituals.) Choose the herb that best suits you.

Closing

When you feel ready to conclude this ritual, explain to your child within that you now want to bring him or her home, that it is time to integrate this part of self back into your total being, so that child can feel protected from being blamed, shamed, judged, or criticized. If it does not feel appropriate to have this self melt back into your physical being, then create a safe place where he or she can reside. Imagine that the protector stays there too, so that the child will always feel safe.

If it feels comfortable, ask your young inner child to select the place within your physical form where he or she would feel the most protected from this abuse. Imagine that this inner child melts into that part of your body. This merging will enhance your ability to accept the positive and negative within yourself and others and will enable you to exhibit your curiosity and to relate to your body with less shame. Imagine basking in the joy of this younger part of self.

If this inner child's issues get triggered, then, once again, use the tools you have learned to objectify these feelings so you can interact with and resolve them. But when the issue is resolved, and if it feels safe, bring your three-to-six-year-old back home.

Your fears of being shamed, judged, and blamed, and your caution about being judgmental, blaming, and critical will never completely disappear. Your need to be overly responsible will not either. But you will now be able to recognize these feelings, and have the tools with which you can respond to those feelings with care.

REVISING THE GARDEN OF YOUR PAST

Complete your work with this inner child by returning to the garden of your past. How would your child like to contribute to this garden? Imagine that you do this work together so that this inner child will be represented in the garden of growth. If you are fortunate enough to have a garden or a place where you can grow things, plant a seed to represent this inner child's growth.

This concludes the work with your three-to-six-year-old within. Remember that you can use these exercises repeatedly to continue your work. Also, the exercises in chapter 9 will contribute to continuing the development of the relationship with your young inner child.

THE GRADE-SCHOOL CHILD WITHIN

Judgment by One's Peers

How well you fit into your social groups, the degree of comfort you feel with your co-workers and close friends, the degree of self-confidence or self-consciousness you feel when you have to perform or compete, and the success you experience in a career or at starting and completing projects are all related to how well you mastered these tasks when you were between the ages of six and twelve. These years are called the middle years because they span the time between the rapid physical and psychological growth of the first six years and the marked changes that arise with puberty. The focus was on mastering tasks of a social rather than a psychological nature. Although this growth most often took place by developing relationships with your peers, there was also a new emphasis on establishing relationships with adults outside of your family.

Fitting In

This period was the first time we move into a social structure outside of the home. Being part of the group, trying to be the same as everyone else, and not standing out were primary concerns. We began to focus on "fitting in" and not "looking like a fool!" Being included meant that we were accepted by our peers. Being excluded meant that we were not. It was a time in our lives when best friends could change as quickly as the wind. One minute we could be included in the core group, the next we could be out. One minute we could be laughed at, the next we were included or ignored. Every time we had to answer a question or present something in front of the class, we risked humiliation, rejection or shame. We were on trial and the jury was made up of our peers. How well you survived this "peer review" is usually demonstrated by how much self-confidence you feel as an adult. If you failed to develop these kinds of social skills in this developmental stage, you may often now, as an adult feel painfully awkward when thrown into group situations where you suddenly feel you may be accepted or rejected based on what you do or say. Many of us have this kind of fear about public speaking: suddenly we find ourselves alone, facing a group, fearing humiliation. We are at their mercy, just as we used to feel in front of our grade school classes. Sally's story illustrates this very well.

Case History: Sally

As a child, Sally had a rather low and husky voice. Every time she spoke, someone in her class laughed because it seemed so strange for such a deep voice to come from the throat of such a small girl. She hated it when she had to read in front of the class. Many times she would refuse.

In adulthood, Sally still felt this fear keenly. Her job demanded that she participate in staff meetings and contribute to client discussions. Every time she had to speak, her palms began to sweat and her heart seemed to beat as loud as a drum.

I asked Sally to close her eyes and see that frightened, humiliated fourth grader standing in front of the class. I had her picture her inner adult talking to this child about her voice and her humiliation. I asked her to comfort her and tell her it would soon be okay. Sally explained to her little girl that those days were gone. Her body had grown into her voice; the laughter of others had been replaced by their interest in what she had to say.

When the inner child realized that she was no longer stuck in that classroom, she began to let go of her fear. She was free to talk to Sally about how awful these childhood events had been, and Sally was able to listen and assure her that all that was over now. Little Sally's feelings began to dissipate and dissolve. Slowly, Sally began to feel comfortable when she had to speak publicly. It took repeated dialogues with her inner child before this progress occurred, and there are still times when Sally feels nervous before she speaks. But she is no longer paralyzed by her fear. She is able to work with her little girl and remind her that the past is gone. She doesn't have to be afraid of being laughed at or teased anymore.

If you identify with Sally's story, then perhaps you also have an inner child who was traumatized in a similar manner. Identifying this child will help you challenge your fear.

Completing Tasks and Assignments

Another task that needs to be mastered at this age is the ability to complete projects or assignments. Starting and completing these assignments were skills that needed to be learned. If there was no one there to teach them, you probably didn't learn them. If there was no one to provide an external structure and teach you the discipline of sitting down and focusing on your homework, you probably would not have been able to develop your own internal structure and sense of discipline. In adulthood, if you are unable to complete tasks, you may assume that you are lazy or are a procrastinator. Perhaps the real issue is that you simply never had the opportunity to internalize a sense of discipline and structure at the appropriate age.

Often this failure to learn the skills related to task completion can express itself in your adult life as professional or personal self-sabotage. It appears as an inability to progress professionally and to define personal goals effectively. You may sabotage financial gains because you do not want to surpass your parents. You can even sabotage yourself physically, recreating the same health patterns your parents had, as a way to remain loyal to them. Each of you will have your own unique way of sabotaging yourself, but often the underlying motive is to avoid surpassing your parents.

If this idea of professional or personal self-sabotage feels like something you are doing to yourself, then you will probably discover that something occurred in this six-to-twelve-year-old stage of development that thwarted your ability to develop the self-confidence and the skills you needed to progress. For instance, when you were between six and twelve, your parents or family may have experienced some great crisis. The wage earner may have lost a job, the caretaker may have become ill, there may have been physical or sexual abuse. If you had to remain focused on your family, then you may have had little time or energy to develop your skills. In fact, you may have felt that pursuing them would be disloyal to your parents or family because it would have taken your energy away from the crisis at hand.

In addition, if succeeding means surpassing one or both parents, then this inner child may interfere. As children, you need to think of your parents as "all-knowing" even when you know they are not. It makes you feel safe and protected, especially when you begin to go out into the larger world. Even though your parents were not all-knowing, even if they were not reliable, you never really lose our emotional, irrational need for them to be so. Surpassing them, learning to do things your parents were unable to do, taking risks your parents were unable to take, means moving beyond them. To do this can feel disloyal.

You can surpass your parents and step into the person you were meant to be only when you give up the illusion that they know what is best for you. Your inability to give up this illusion can be seen in any behavior that results in professional or personal self-sabotage. Many people hold themselves back at work because they would surpass what their parents did.

The common belief is that, as children, you are supposed to surpass your parents. In fact, most of your parents want you to be more successful than they were, but not so successful that you no longer need them. You may be afraid to become more successful, because the minute you surpass them you become expert of your life. This deprives your parents of one of their primary parenting tasks, but it also deprives you of others you can mimic and strive to become. Both situations trigger grief.

To ward off this grief, many of us find mentors whom we can admire and emulate. This is an important step in professional growth. Just as the six-to-twleve-year-old needed to bond with an adult outside of the family, in our work we need to have superiors we respect and from whom we can learn. When we deal with our need to have someone else tell what is best for us, then we can step into our own power. As long as you are caught in that need to place someone above you, you cannot claim your own unique expertise.

This need is carried by your six-to-twelve-year-old within. Respond to this need by helping your inner child transfer the adulation from others to the adult within you. This will involve grief. The adult self will have to help the six-to-twelve-year-old grieve the surpassing of the parents, and grieve the illusion that the parents know more than your inner adult. Grief related to your parents inability to teach you also may be triggered.

STEP ONE: IDENTIFYING YOUR PAIN

Even though these years were quiet psychologically, they were very active socially. If you have any problems with fitting in, with looking like a fool, or performing in public, or difficulty completing professional or personal tasks, you will have at least one and perhaps more than one inner child from this stage who will need healing.

Remember these years established the foundation on which your adolescence was built. If you were unable to fit in, the awkwardness you would have experienced as a young teen would have been that much more devastating. If you were unable to master the task of completing projects, your study habits and acceptance of structure in adolescence would have been poor. If you never established a comfortable identity within your peer group, during adolescence you would have found it difficult to establish an identity. You needed to identify with and be accepted by those of the same age. When the second stage of declaring your independence surfaces in adolescence, you need a strong connection with your peers so that you can successfully separate. If that connection never occurred, your adolescent development suffered.

In the following two exercises you will assess the damage that was done during these years. Identifying the pain carried into your adult life will give the information you need to begin your work.

EXERCISE ONE: HOW YOU RESPOND TODAY

The list of statements below will help you determine what problems you may have with relationships with peers, public speaking, beginning and completing projects, and your comfort with competition. You may find that you often feel the ways described below, but have no memory of discomfort from this age. If this is the case, do not be alarmed. It is common for the effects of these unmastered tasks to go unnoticed until a situation brings them into view. For instance, you may have been able to get by in school even though you were not able to complete tasks efficiently because your school system was negligent in monitoring your progress. Your problem may not have become apparent until later, when you flunked out of college because of poor study habits or lost a job because you were unable to meet deadlines. The original issue will still relate back to this time, however, and it will also still be this inner child who will need help developing the self-discipline and internal structure needed to succeed.

Read each statement carefully, then respond accordingly. Record any thoughts or feelings in your journal. Allow approximately thirty minutes for this exercise. Unless marked by an asterisk, a response of either extreme can indicate a need for repair. To review see general instructions for this exercise, see pages 39–40.

Acceptance of and by Peers	Always	Often	Sometimes	Rarely	Never
I feel unaccepted by most of my peers.	_____	_____	_____	_____	_____
I feel judged by most people my age or by those in my profession.	_____	_____	_____	_____	_____
I feel I have little in common with people my own age, or those in my profession.	_____	_____	_____	_____	_____
I feel excluded from the activities of others.	_____	_____	_____	_____	_____

Fitting in Socially

	Always	Often	Sometimes	Rarely	Never
I do not belong to organizations because I feel self-conscious.	_____	_____	_____	_____	_____
When I go to social gatherings, I feel out of place.	_____	_____	_____	_____	_____
I am more comfortable being alone than with a group of friends.	_____	_____	_____	_____	_____
The groups I have participated in feel closed, and I have not felt a part of the "clique."	_____	_____	_____	_____	_____

Public Speaking

	Always	Often	Sometimes	Rarely	Never
I avoid certain professional positions because I would have to talk in front of others.	_____	_____	_____	_____	_____

	Always	Often	Sometimes	Rarely	Never
I get physical symptoms of anxiety (palm sweating, rapid heartbeat, cracking of voice) whenever I am faced with speaking before a group.	_____	_____	_____	_____	_____
I am unable to speak spontaneously in front of others. I plan exactly what I want to say before it is my turn.	_____	_____	_____	_____	_____
Even if I feel strongly about a subject, I will not speak up in public because I get too tongue-tied.*	_____	_____	_____	_____	_____
When I speak in public, I am not aware of anyone else in the room. I do not feel nervous, but I do seem to be disconnected from myself and others.*	_____	_____	_____	_____	_____

Task Completion and Self-Discipline

	Always	Often	Sometimes	Rarely	Never
I describe myself as a procrastinator and feel lazy when it comes to getting things done.	_____	_____	_____	_____	_____
I worry about going into business for myself, for fear that I do not have the self-discipline to succeed.	_____	_____	_____	_____	_____

	Always	Often	Sometimes	Rarely	Never
I have sabotaged my professional advancement because of my inability to meet deadlines.*	——	——	——	——	——
I experience problems in my relationships because I promise to take care of things and then fail to do so.	——	——	——	——	——
Physical Competition Skills	*Always*	*Often*	*Sometimes*	*Rarely*	*Never*
I feel clumsy participating in any sport.	——	——	——	——	——
In team sports, I fear being chosen last.	——	——	——	——	——
I refuse to participate in a sports activity in which I feel self-conscious.*	——	——	——	——	——
I love to dance, but I only do so in the privacy of my own home.	——	——	——	——	——

Closing

What are your thoughts after having responded to these statements? What do your responses tell you about the issues you may carry from this stage? Were there any categories to which you responded with either extreme. Remember, an extreme response to an asterisked statement does not indicate a need for repair.

EXERCISE TWO: HOW YOU CARRY THESE ISSUES IN YOUR LIFE TODAY

As you reflect on these questions, remember that the issues of this inner child are fitting in, learning how to complete tasks, and succeeding in self-determined goals. Record your responses in your journal. To review the general instructions for this exercise, see page 42.

1. Do you worry about being accepted by your peers? Can you think of a time when this was the case? Describe it in your journal. What does it feel like to review that situation now that you have more information about this stage of your development?

2. Have there been times when you have worried about standing out? If so, when? Describe one of those times.

3. Have there been times when you were in the "in group" and have been aware of someone who was excluded? How did you feel? What, if anything, did you do?

4. Make a list of similarities and differences you see in yourself and three of your closest friends. How do you feel about this?

5. List your professional goals. Do you feel satisfied with your achievements? If not, why?

6. List the emotional, social, and physical characteristics of your parents. Next, make a list of their professional and financial achievements. How do you compare to them? What does this say about your need to remain loyal, or your capacity to surpass your parents?

7. Whose opinion do you value more than your own? About which subjects? Why do you not trust your own opinion in this area? How do you feel about this? How does this affect your belief in yourself and your abilities?

8. Think of a situation where your inability to complete something jeopardized your career or a relationship. Describe this situation and comment on it now.

9. When you participate in a social event, do you feel energized or drained? What does this response tell you?

Closing

Now take the information from Exercise one and combine it with your responses to this exercise. Make a list of issues you have carried into your adult life from this developmental stage. Some examples are listed below.

Potential Issues from This Developmental Stage

- Feeling self-conscious in social gatherings
- Inability to complete something you have started
- Not being able to attain professional goals
- Keeping yourself in debt so you never achieve financial stability
- Fear of public speaking

Your Grade-School Child's Strengths

These exercises not only identified your issues, but they should also have suggested strengths that were carried from this stage. As you think back, reflect on the strengths that you may have acquired based on your experiences. For instance, you may once have felt ostracized from a group. Although this would have been wounding, you may have become more sensitive to others when they feel left out. Record in your journal how the experiences during these years may have contributed positively to your development.

∽

STEP TWO: RESEARCHING YOUR GRADE-SCHOOL CHILD'S PAIN

You now need to gather information about the events that took place and the atmosphere that prevailed when you first began school. Your objective is to explore why you may have difficulty fitting into groups, feeling accepted by your peers in adult life, or beginning and completing tasks. You need to find out as much as you can about the people who influenced your life at the time, including those who may have helped and those who may have hindered your growth: your peers, teachers, scout and church leaders, babysitters, siblings, and other relatives.

As you conduct these interviews, remember that many of the qualities you developed regarding work, relationships, sports, and public speaking originated from this developmental period. You have already listed the specific issues that relate to this stage. In your interviews, you need to discover the circumstances that caused these issues. To review the general instructions, see pages 45.

EXERCISE ONE: INTERVIEWING YOURSELF

Use this exercise to determine what you remember. You should have some vivid memories from this stage, since you had both the mental capacity to record events and the vocabulary to describe them. If you recall little, it may be a sign that something traumatic happened, causing you to shut down emotionally. If so, the memories may surface later when you are ready to deal with them. Allow at least forty-five minutes to respond to these questions.

1. Record the factual information you know from this period: where you lived, where you went to school, who your friends were, your extracurricular activities, adults who made a lasting impression on you, what you remember about your family, and your relationships to each member. Were there significant caretakers other than your parents involved in your life? Did you have siblings or grandparents who lived in the home?

2. Record in your journal any images, impressions, or sensations that linger from this time. Is there a symbolic image that expresses how you felt? Can you remember any stories of your grade-school years?

Closing

How do you think these experiences affected the person you are today? Record your thoughts.

EXERCISE TWO: INTERVIEWING YOUR BODY

Where in your body do you hold the tension from this time? If you had a traumatic event, it is stored somewhere in your body. If you were unable to learn what you needed to learn, that is also tension held somewhere in your body. Use the following guided imagery to help discover where in your body you carry your child's pain. To review the general instructions for this exercise, refer to page 45. Record your responses in your journal.

1. Close your eyes and surround yourself with healing white Light. As you imagine this white Light surrounding you, use deep breathing to relax and to bring your focus to the very center of your being. When you feel relaxed, continue.

2. Let your focus travel freely through your body. Try to establish contact with each body part in turn. Now look directly into a mirror or if you prefer, imagine that you are. Look at your body. Attempt to see it without judging it. Acknowledge your body as though were saying hello to an old friend.

3. Where do you feel tense? Does this tension indicate something about your inner child's pain? Be quiet and listen. Record any response you feel.

4. Think of a recent experience in which you had to fit into a new group. Where in your body do you hold that experience? Write about that experience. How is that experience related to your childhood?

5. Go through the same steps for any recent time that you felt afraid to speak in public or physically compete, afraid to try something new, or afraid you would not be accepted.

6. Think of a recent time you had a project due. Did you complete it? If so, how did that feel? Where in your body did you sense joy and accomplishment? If you did not complete that project, where did you store your disappointment and shame? Record your findings in your journal.

Closing

When you have completed each question, use deep breathing to help bring your focus back to the center of your being. Surround yourself with Light. Open your eyes when it feels comfortable to do so. How do you feel about what your body told you? How does this information relate to the way you carry yourself and present yourself to the world? Record your responses in your journal.

EXERCISE THREE: HOW YOU TREAT YOUR BODY

Do you start diets or exercise programs only to drop out of them? Do you obsessively worry about your appearance when you are in front of a crowd? Are you afraid your body does not fit into the norm? Do you make self-deprecating remarks about your body? Do you sometimes judge your body as you were judged by your peers?

No one is more belittling than cocky grade-school kids. They have not learned the skills of compassion. Often, you relate to your body with this same lack of care. Try to be candid when responding to the questions below, so you can detect this pattern.

Answer the following questions in your journal. To review the general instructions of this exercise, see pages 47–48.

1. Do you make fun of the way you look or ridicule yourself when you look in a mirror?
2. Do you refer to yourself as a fat slob, a skinny runt, or another self-deprecating name when you look at yourself in a mirror?
3. Do you feel comfortable in your body?
4. Do you compare your appearance with that of others and have mood swings based on whether you feel you look better or worse than they?
5. How do your parents take care of their bodies? How are you different or the same?
6. Write down any other thoughts or feelings you have about the way you treat your body. How does your relationship to your body mirror the way you felt when you were between six and twelve? How does this make you feel? What do you want to change? Record your responses in your journal.

Closing

When you have finished your writing, surround yourself with healing Light. Thank your Higher Power. Be silent for a moment and say whatever you need to say to your body before you close.

Just as you were tried before a jury of your peers, your body is sometimes tried before a jury of the judgmental parts of you. Determining the maladaptive ways you relate to your body will enable you to choose more gentle, effective ways to relate to your physical self. Just as you responded to kindness and compliments when you were a child, so, too, will your body respond when you treat it with loving and tender care. Your body is not the enemy. Your internalized judgments are the enemy, and you have the capacity to change them once you are aware of them.

EXERCISE FOUR: INTERVIEWING FAMILY MEMBERS, RELATIVES, AND FRIENDS

In these interviews you will be determining the circumstances and attitudes that hindered or enhanced your development between the ages of six and twelve. Carefully select the people you want to interview. Return to pages 46–50 and repeat the steps you used to prepare for your previous interviews. If you begin to feel overwhelmed or unsafe, take a break or discontinue the interviews for awhile. Seek professional or personal support if you feel the need.

Guidelines and Sample Questions

If you are interviewing a relative or family friend, ask about how you interacted with family members. Ask what that person remembers about you and your parents' relationship. Were there special activities that you shared with any family member? Were you particularly close to one parent or the other? Ask if that person can describe how your parents dealt with the issues relevant to this stage. Did either of them fear public speaking, feel socially self-conscious, have trouble with self-discipline, etc.?

If you are interviewing a parent, ask if you were involved in extracurricular activities. If so, what does that parent remember about your participation? Did you do well in school? Did you have a lot of friends, or play alone? How did you and your brothers and sisters get along when you were this age? What does your parent remember now about the relationship with you? Does this person remember any traumatic events that may have happened to you in school or at home?

Obtain as much information as possible. If you are interviewing a coach or an adult who was especially important to you, decide if there are relevant questions that you feel comfortable asking that involve your family.

In concluding this step, take the issues you listed from Step one and list them in a column to the left. Next list the circumstances that caused this issue. In a third column, indicate how that issue is evident in the way you related to your body. This combination will give you the pain profile of your grade-school child within.

Issue	Circumstances	Evidenced in the way I treat my body
I can begin projects but never seem to complete them. I have things all around the house that I have started and never finished.	My mother was an alcoholic who had projects all over the house that she never completed. I had no one to teach me the skills needed to do this.	I dress in a sloppy manner, and often look like I didn't have the time to finish dressing.

Closing

Developing this structure will help you begin to construct the profile of your inner child's pain. It will also supply you with the information you will need to help that child heal. Once you have this information move to Step three.

STEP THREE: REGRESSING TO THE FEELINGS OF THE SIX-TO-TWELVE-YEAR-OLD WITHIN

What was it like to be in grade school, to be on trial by a jury of your peers? How did it feel to try new tasks, to compete in athletic events, and to speak in front of class? In this next set of exercises you will be regressing to the feelings you had when you were in grade school. You may discover shame, fear, competitiveness, insecurity. Let these feelings emerge. If they are not already in your awareness, they are buried somewhere inside. Flush them out so you can heal them.

EXERCISE ONE: ACTIVITIES THAT ENHANCE YOUR REGRESSION

Some of the following activities can be done in your home, others require that you participate in activities away from home. I also highly recommend that you review the general instructions for this exercise. Please refer to page 52. Record your reactions to each activity in your journal.

1. Go to a social meeting or a new Twelve Step meeting alone and see what it feels like to make acquaintances, perhaps to feel uncomfortable or left out. (If this exercise feels too uncomfortable, don't do it.)
2. To experience the sensations of physical awkwardness and the challenge of physical mastery, try a physical activity you have never tried before. Ride a bike, go skating, try exercise equipment that is new to you, play tennis or squash, or go for a swim. Notice how you feel, which muscles you use.
3. Play a team game with other people—such as a board game, a physical game—and try to work with others toward a common goal.
4. Go to the zoo with a friend. Pick out the animal that most reminds you of yourself. Describe this animal and yourself.
5. Build something, bake something, create something you have never before created. Start from beginning to end, then share the results with at least one other person.
6. If possible, spend an afternoon with someone between six and twelve. Use this time to gather information about what it is like to be this age. Notice what this child does and how he or she responds to the environment and to you.

7. Record any other sensations or feelings you had in response to these exercises.

Closing

You carry pain from the time you were in grade school, but you also carry the joy and excitement of learning something new. Now you may have a better awareness of both. In the exercises you have done so far, what have you learned about what you were like when you were between six and twelve? Write down the feelings this question provokes.

ᑫᓛ

STEP FOUR: OBJECTIFYING YOUR PAIN OF YOUR GRADE-SCHOOL INNER CHILD

Objectifying the pain you felt means that you must separate from the fear you feel when you are around peers, the anxiety you feel when you have projects to complete, are asked to speak in public, or physically compete. It also means that you begin to see your inability to succeed as being related to this inner child's need to remain connected to your parents. All the feelings carried by this inner child will be objectified and projected onto this part of you. This frees your adult self to respond to the needs of this younger self. It allows you to establish the part of you who feels the fear, anxiety, and loyalty (grade-school self), and the part of you who can respond to this discomfort (the adult self).

EXERCISE ONE: MEETING YOUR GRADE-SCHOOL CHILD

Choose how you want to do this guided imagery. To review the general instructions, see pages 54. When you feel ready to begin, make sure you are in your safe place, and that you will not be interrupted for at least thirty minutes.

Begin by closing your eyes. Surround yourself with the protective Light. Breathe deeply. Now, imagine you are walking down a path in a beautiful park. In this park there is a clump of trees and a very special treehouse. In this treehouse you see your grade-school child. How do you feel when you gaze up at this inner child? What is this inner child doing? Is the child willing to come down and spend some time with you? Gently touch this child self. How does the child respond? See if you can determine what this inner child needs. Talk with your grade-school child. Tell it that you are its future. You are proof that it survived. Let your inner child know you have come back to heal the loneliness and fear. All your fears about being judged, all your shame for not fitting in, and all your worries of being exposed and looking like a fool are carried by this child who stands before you. Spend a few minutes with your child within. Notice how the two of you relate. When you feel you have spent enough time with this inner child, assure it that your work with the pain will now begin. The hurt is over. The child will not be left alone again. When you feel ready to conclude, bring your focus back to your breathing and back to the Light that surrounds you. Take several cleansing breaths, then open your eyes when it feels comfortable to do so.

Closing

Record in your journal any responses you had in meeting this inner child. End this experience by asking this inner child to help you find its photo or to locate a picture from a magazine that looks or feels right. Paste that picture in your journal so you can reflect on it as you begin to ask more in-depth questions. Record in your journal any thoughts or feelings that this picture provokes.

EXERCISE TWO: CREATING A DIALOGUE WITH YOUR SIX-TO-TWELVE-YEAR-OLD WITHIN

Children between six and twelve often have a lot to say. If yours is shy or afraid, it is because of the depth of the wounds. Be gentle and give this inner child time to feel trust.

Allow at least thirty minutes for this exercise. Write the question down in your journal using your dominant hand. Use your least dominant hand when writing your inner child's response.

1. Ask your inner child what its favorite game is.
2. What about a favorite subject in school? Or a best friend?
3. Does this child have an imaginary friend? If so, who is it?
4. How does this child like its brothers or sisters? Do they get along?
5. Ask this inner child to tell you about its pain.
6. What does the child need most from you?
7. How does this child feel about you? Does this inner child understand what it means to be reclaimed by you? If not, explain that it means the child will no longer be alone when faced by its peers. It means you will be there when the child fears speaking in public or gets concerned that a project won't get done.
8. Does your grade-school inner child need help with homework, a project, or a problem with a friend? Ask what the child needs from you the most.
9. Is there anything this inner child wants to know about you?
10. What joys does this child want to offer you and what prevents this from happening?

Closing

What did you learn about your grade-school child from the above exercise? How do you feel about what you learned? Answer those questions in your journal.

EXERCISE THREE: TALKING IN THE MIRROR TO YOUR SIX-TO-TWELVE-YEAR-OLD WITHIN

To review the general instructions for this exercise, refer to pages 56–57.

Sit in front of the mirror. Start rocking. Close your eyes and reflect on all that you have discovered about this part of you. Think of the issues you listed in Step one. When you feel a connection ask the child what is needed, what is felt, what he or she wants to say. Listen for the response and then open your eyes and respond to what you heard. Try to visualize your six-to-twelve-year-old sitting in front of you or looking back at you out of the mirror. Stay with this dialogue as long as you feel comfortable.

Closing

Record your experience in your journal. Use your least dominant hand to let your child write. Then switch back to your dominant hand and let your adult respond.

EXERCISE FOUR: CREATING YOUR PROTECTOR

Your inner child will most likely need to have more than one protector. For instance, you may create a protector to be with the child while speaking in public, and another one who helps when a project is due. (As I was writing this book, I created a character who helped keep me organized and on track. He was a high school teacher whom I had especially trusted. Whenever I would get behind schedule I would imagine him gently nudging me ahead.) Use your imagination and draw on the creativity of your inner child as well. Have your crayons and drawing materials nearby so that the two of you can create and draw the protector you need. To review the general instructions for this exercise, see pages 58.

1. Choose the issue you'd like to address.
2. If your inner child could select anyone in the world, real or imagined, to help them with this issue, who would that character be? The character might be a teacher, a coach, an angel, or God. He or she can be a relative, movie star or friend.
3. Imagine that you and your child draw a picture or find a symbol that represents this protector.
4. Tell your inner child that this protector will be there any time he or she wants.
5. Repeat these steps for each protector.

Closing

Keep these pictures or symbols in the place you do your internal work and stored in your imagination as well. In your work with your six-to-twelve-year-old, call in these characters for support. They will help heal the wounds and fill the gaps left from this developmental stage. Complete this exercise by acknowledging a partnership between this protector and the adult self. Call in your Higher Power as well if this seems appropriate because this is the team that will heal this child within you. Record your responses in your journal.

EXERCISE FIVE: DETECTING THE CRITICAL VOICE

The critical voice between six and twelve is the voice that carries the haunting statements you heard at home and at school. This voice will tell you that you cannot succeed, that you will make a fool out of yourself and that you should not even try. This voice will terrorize you when you have to appear in public, tell you that you will never fit in, or that you look too fat, too ugly, or too thin. The following exercise will help you detect this character. Once you know who it is and have a form for that critical voice, the adult self and the protector can challenge the negativity. Respond to the following questions in your journal. To review the general instructions for this exercise, refer to page 59.

1. What negative statements do you make to yourself when you have to appear in public or be around a crowd of strangers?
2. What negative statements do you make to yourself about your ability to succeed, or finish what you have started?
3. What negative statements do you make to yourself when you could do something new or to compete physically?
4. What negative statements do you make to yourself when you begin to succeed or move ahead?
5. Where have you heard those statements before? Whose voice is this? Is it the voice of a parent, a teacher, priest, or coach? Are these statements you have heard from society? Is the voice imagined or real?
6. Imagine that you, as the inner adult, speak to this voice. Ask this voice what it is that it wants. Is its intent to protect or to harm?
7. Let your six-to-twelve-year-old within draw a picture of this voice. This picture represents fears, terror, and judgments created by the critic within.
8. When you have completed the picture, go back to the original wounding and negative statements. Rewrite them in your journal. Next to the negative statement write a positive affirmation, like the example below.

Negative Statement	Positive Affirmation
I should have known better than to try and do that.	It is fine to try new things even if I do not succeed.

Use these affirmations whenever you hear your critic trying to put you down. They will help dissolve the negative statements and replace them with statements that are kind.

Closing

Have your adult self interact with this critic, and when necessary, imagine that your Higher Power sends it away by surrounding it in a bubble of protective Light and releasing the bubble into the universe. Assure your inner child that the critic will no longer go unchallenged. Then write about this in your journal.

EXERCISE SIX: CHANGING YOUR GRADE-SCHOOL CHILD'S EXPERIENCE OF CHILDHOOD

This exercise leads you through guided imagery that enables you to transform the experiences you had in grade school. Review the profile of this inner child's pain. Select one of the issues and think of a current situation in which you felt this way. When you have the issue and the situation in mind, use the guided imagery from pages 61–62 to rework and transform these painful scenes.

Closing

Many issues come from this time in your life. Use the exercises in chapter 9 to confront them in the moment as they arise in your adult life. The previous imagery can be used to transform your earlier experiences so this inner child no longer has to carry this pain.

As you develop and nurture the part of you who can succeed, you help this inner child resolve the outdated loyalty to its parents. As you learn the skills necessary to complete tasks, as you learn how to tolerate discomfort and fear from trying something new, you will be responding to this inner child's fears. When your inner child trusts that you will not abandon it to face these tasks alone, it will have no need to sabotage your efforts to excel and succeed.

This step began transforming this inner child's pain. Rework these exercises as often as you choose. Then get ready to help your inner child grieve.

❦

STEP FIVE: GRIEVING THE PAIN OF YOUR GRADE-SCHOOL INNER CHILD

Grieving will be a major part of the healing for this inner child. This inner child sabotages your efforts to succeed in order not to look like a fool or so it can remain loyal to your parents.

EXERCISE ONE: THE FIRST FOUR STAGES OF GRIEF

This exercise will help your six-to-twelve-year-old within begin to let go, and consists of activities, guided imagery, drawing and writing in your journal. Each will contribute to your helping your pre-adolescent self experience its grief.

Allow several hours to complete this exercise. I suggest you call in the support of your Higher Power and this child's protector, and surround yourself with Light. You will need your journal, your pen, and drawing materials. To review the general instructions for this exercise, see pages 63–64.

Closing

Gather all the drawings and writings that you and your inner child completed during this grieving process. You will be using them in the final step of healing this inner child's pain and reclaiming his or her joy.

℘

STEP SIX: HEALING YOUR PAIN, RECLAIMING YOUR JOY

Read the modifications below and then return to pages 65–69 and repeat the ceremony for healing the inner child. The issues that you will be focusing on during your emotional, physical, and spiritual release are your discomfort with fitting in, fear of public speaking, and inability to begin or complete projects.

Peppermint, known for its protective qualities, can be used in your bath. Thyme is appropriate for this stage because its properties are associated with courage and ambition, and it enhances your ability to engage in childlike fun. If you want to burn incense, I suggest frankincense for its cleansing and protective qualities.

Closing

When you feel ready to conclude, explain to your inner child that you now want to bring him or her home. It is time to integrate this part of self back into your total being. That child can feel comfortable with peers and feel secure that it knows how to begin and complete a project. This integration also will enable this child to speak in public with less fear and to progress professionally and personally.

Ask your six-to-twelve-year-old to select the place within your body where it would feel most protected from pain. Then imagine that this inner child melts into that part of your body. Merging will allow you to accomplish the tasks associated with this age with more ease. Your child within will signal you when you are at risk. As the child begins to trust that you will respond, it will have less need to sabotage your efforts to succeed.

If this inner child's issues get triggered, then, once again, use the tools you have learned to objectify these feelings so you can interact with and resolve them. But when the issue is resolved, and if it feels safe, bring your six-to-twelve-year-old self back home.

If it does not feel appropriate to have your child self melt back into your body, then create a safe place where it can reside. Imagine that the protector stays with your middle-aged child within so that he or she will always feel safe.

The issues you carry from this time in your life will never completely disappear. However, now you will be able to recognize the feelings of your six-to-twelve-year-old self and respond to those feelings with care.

REVISING THE GARDEN OF YOUR PAST

Complete your work with this inner child by returning to the garden of your past. Ask your child within how it would like to contribute to this garden. Imagine that both of you make these contributions so that this inner child is represented in the garden of growth. If you have a garden or a place where you can grow things, plant a seed that will represent this inner child's growth.

This concludes your work with your grade-school child. Remember that you can do these exercises repeatedly to continue your work. Also, the exercises in chapter 9 will continue the development of the relationship with your grade-school self.

6

THE YOUNG TEEN WITHIN

Getting Comfortable With Discomfort

Puberty marked the beginning of our transition into adulthood. We made this shift physically much more quickly than we did mentally or socially. We spent most of our adolescence trying to settle in. All of the tasks mastered up to this point in our development paved the way for this transition. The bonding and trust we learned as infants provided the security we needed as we risked relating to the opposite sex. The ability to set limits and to say no provided us with the foundation needed to establish sexual boundaries. The sexual exploration and the confrontation with the good and bad qualities within prepared us for the comparisons that so ruthlessly occurred among teens. The social and educational skills mastered in grade school set the tone for the academic and social adventures that were ahead.

Whatever you were unable to master before you turned twelve became a major stumbling block. Even under the best of circumstances, the move into adolescence is usually awkward. Discomfort with the sexual attraction you felt toward others and your struggles with social awkwardness and isolation became key issues. The need for peer approval became even greater because your entire self-image rested in the judgments of those around you.

Between twelve and fifteen years, teens are primarily involved in same-sex activities. When sexual interest did begin to spark, however, few knew what to do with it, because this new interest was accompanied by the rapid physical changes. The teen years are a time of acne and baby fat and voices that crack. Emotions and the body are at odds.

It is a time when a person is, perhaps, the most self-conscious physically, and yet the most compelled to take emotional risks. The tension between the emotional and the physical was what made us feel so hopelessly awkward.

To deal with the awkwardness you may have acted manly and disinterested, or you may have giggled a lot as you got your best friend to ask the object of your interest if he or she had an interest in you. But whatever you did you most likely experienced "addictive love." The songs supported it, the movies supported it, the media supported it, so it must have been love. You were either interested in quantity and went steady with someone new every other day, or you were too shy to go steady at all. Or you may have stumbled through this stage in extreme isolation. If you were confused about your sexuality, or found yourself interested in the same sex, your sense of isolation could have been even greater. If you started using drugs or alcohol and never encountered these emotions in the first place, you may first begin to address them now.

No matter how old you are, there is no way through these feelings of awkwardness, but to realize them! The awkwardness is lessened if you can talk about your discomfort, but learning to cope with the awkwardness is definitely a developmental task that is important to your growth. It is directly connected to your self-esteem and to your fears of not being accepted. It is also directly connected to your sexuality. Since this is a time when you once again engage in sexual exploration, your judgment and your shame related to sexual activity is often reactivated at this time.

There were numerous anxieties that accompanied this age. Many of you responded by withdrawing. Ill-equipped to deal with these anxieties, you turned to alcohol or drugs to avoid the pain. How awkward you felt then usually reflects the degree of success you had in mastering the earlier tasks because they provided the foundation that enabled you to tolerate and cope with these anxieties. Johnnie's story illustrates this very well.

Case History: Johnny

I first saw him after he had been in recovery from drugs for nine months. Finally, the fog in his head was clearing. He was beginning to feel like his old self. Unfortunately, feeling like his old self resulted in his feeling uncomfortable, anxious, moody and depressed. These emotions are common for someone in the first year of recovery, but they are also common for someone in the first year of adolescence. I asked Johnny to give me a history of his drug use. He had started smoking marijuana around the age of twelve. For the next twenty-three years, he had used it almost daily.

Johnny had used drugs to cope with the anxieties of adolescence. Now he had to experience those feelings straight. He said he felt like a damn kid again. I told him that, emotionally, he was. Johnny was still an adolescent at thirty-six. He had an adult body and adult responsibilities, but emotionally he was about twelve. In helping Johnny piece together his childhood history, it was clear that the traumas he had suffered before age twelve had so grossly impaired his emotional development that he did not have the tools to deal with the onslaught of anxieties at adolescence. Johnny had coped with these anxieties by avoiding them through drug use.

Johnny's therapy involved more than just reworking his teen years. It involved going through the previous developmental stages as well, and, together, we reworked major scenes from his childhood. We did not repair a faulty foundation, but slowly constructed a completely new emotional foundation from which he could challenge his adolescent anxieties successfully. Johnny would not have been able to resolve these issues if he had not stopped using drugs to cope. He needed a solid and viable recovery program to be able to sustain abstinence while he worked on his painful past. Johnny also could not have done this alone. He could not have become his own internal parent until he had been parented by someone else. I became this parent, whom Johnny was later able to emulate and internalize.

STEP ONE: IDENTIFYING YOUR PAIN

If you are working with this program sequentially, by the time you get to your teens, you should have cleared up the emotional gaps from the earlier developmental stages. As you work with your young teen, it will be important to reassure that teen that the awkwardness and need for approval from others does subside. The anxieties lessen, and you are proof that your teen did survive. This age benefits greatly from a protector because what many teens need is someone to coach them through these awkward times. It is also a stage that cannot be reworked if you are actively using drugs or alcohol. You must learn to cope with awkwardness non-addictively.

Besides the social and sexual awkwardness and the need for approval from others, these young teen years are often when incest or molestation occurs. Because a young teenage body is developing, it can suddenly be exploited by others. If you are a victim of incest that occurred at this time, these issues might emerge now as well. It is necessary to heal that violated part of self in order to learn how to set limits and feel safe.

In the following exercises, you will need to identify the adolescent anxieties you are still experiencing. These anxieties may not be apparent in your adult life because they are most active in times of transition. Perhaps you will identify previous times when you were in transition and you were faced with such issues. Focus on these times to see how well you coped with awkwardness.

EXERCISE ONE: HOW YOU RESPOND TODAY

These statements will help you assess the degree of awkwardness, both social and sexual, you have carried into your adult life. They also will help you determine how much your self-image is rooted in the opinions of others. There are also statements that will help you see if you are dependent on drugs, alcohol, addictive behaviors, and whether you are a victim of molestation.

Most people are quick to identify the extent of their social and sexual awkwardness. In fact, for most, it is a relief to have these feelings identified. It is more challenging, however, to be honest about the emphasis you put on the opinions of others. Remember, it is difficult to reclaim your power to determine who you want to be if you continuously project that responsibility onto others. Try to be as honest as possible with yourself.

It is difficult to reclaim your power if you continue to use drugs, alcohol, or addictive behaviors to cope with life. Unfortunately, one aspect of addiction is denial, and it may be difficult for you to be honest about your behaviors. If you suspect that you may be addicted to alcohol, drugs, or certain dysfunctional behaviors, I encourage you to seek the help that you need. References can be found in the Appendix.

It is also painful to confront being an incest survivor. The ramifications of that assessment far surpass the scope of this book. If you feel uneasy answering that section, it could be an indication that there is something to be explored.

I believe this is especially true for women. We live in a society that exploits us sexually, emotionally, and physically. Regardless of whether we were actual victims of incest, we could still have been victims of sexual harassment or assault. Separating the *reality* from the *possibility,* however, is paramount to your healing. All of us live with the possibility of sexual assault, but those who have to heal from the reality of sexual molestation need a more comprehensive healing than I can provide in this book. Again, draw on your support system and seek professional help if your reaction to any of these exercises becomes unmanageable.

Find time to be quiet and set the tone in the room in which you do your internal work. Allow approximately thirty minutes to complete this exercise. Have your journal ready.

Read the following statements and check the response that best indicates how often you feel this way. Unless noted with an asterisk, a response at either extreme can indicate a need for repair. To review general instructions for this exercise, refer to pages 39–40.

Social Awkwardness

	Always	Often	Sometimes	Rarely	Never
I have difficulty going to social functions by myself because I feel so nervous.	_____	_____	_____	_____	_____
I get tongue-tied if I run into an acquaintance unexpectedly.	_____	_____	_____	_____	_____
If I go to a party, I tend to stay pretty close to the person I came with. I feel too shy to talk to new people.	_____	_____	_____	_____	_____
I am uncomfortable in public. I feel self-conscious, as if people are watching me.	_____	_____	_____	_____	_____

Physical and Sexual Awkwardness

I feel uncomfortable with my body; it is too fat, too thin, too short, too long, too different.	_____	_____	_____	_____	_____

	Always	Often	Sometimes	Rarely	Never
I tend to feel clumsy and non-athletic.*	_____	_____	_____	_____	_____
I am sexually inhibited.	_____	_____	_____	_____	_____
I like the lights off when I am having sex.	_____	_____	_____	_____	_____
I feel uncomfortable when I am around a person to whom I feel attracted.	_____	_____	_____	_____	_____

Dependency on Approval from Others

	Always	Often	Sometimes	Rarely	Never
I need a second opinion on the decisions I make.	_____	_____	_____	_____	_____
If I am wearing an accessory I like and someone makes an unflattering comment, I take it off.	_____	_____	_____	_____	_____
If I am in a group of people, I notice the one person who does not seem to like me.	_____	_____	_____	_____	_____
I have a hard time trusting my own judgments, so I rely on those close to me to determine what is appropriate and essential.	_____	_____	_____	_____	_____

Dependency on alcohol, drugs or addictive behavior

	Always	Often	Sometimes	Rarely	Never
I smoke, do drugs, or drink alcohol excessively.*	_____	_____	_____	_____	_____

	Always	Often	Sometimes	Rarely	Never
Whenever I am nervous, I respond by putting something in my mouth, like food, drugs, or cigarettes.*	_____	_____	_____	_____	_____
When I receive news that is hard to handle, I behave in a way that later results in negative consequences.	_____	_____	_____	_____	_____
Whenever life gets tough, I bury myself in my work.	_____	_____	_____	_____	_____
Whenever I am upset, sex is the only activity that settles me down. It doesn't matter with whom, I just know that I need that release.*	_____	_____	_____	_____	_____
When I feel panic, I seek relief with alcohol, drugs, cigarettes, shopping, gambling, etc.	_____	_____	_____	_____	_____
I engage in destructive activity that has severe consequences on my finances, relationships or my health.	_____	_____	_____	_____	_____

Signs of being an incest survivor

	Always	Often	Sometimes	Rarely	Never
I feel a sense of impending doom.	_____	_____	_____	_____	_____
I have nightmares about big monsters engulfing me.	_____	_____	_____	_____	_____

	Always	Often	Sometimes	Rarely	Never
There are times when, for no reason at all, I have an anxiety attack.	_____	_____	_____	_____	_____
I have or have had a history of urinary tract infections.*	_____	_____	_____	_____	_____
Sex is repulsive to me.*	_____	_____	_____	_____	_____
I worry about my child being sexually abused.	_____	_____	_____	_____	_____
When people get too close or cover my face, I feel claustrophobic and nauseous.	_____	_____	_____	_____	_____
Certain odors terrify me, but I don't know why.*	_____	_____	_____	_____	_____

Closing

The information about your social, physical, and sexual awkwardness should be self-explanatory. If you do not remember specific situations, memories may become clearer as you work with the rest of the formula.

The information you get about your dependency on approval from others can be a little more complicated. It is important to feel you can ask someone what they think. We all need feedback. Dependency is when you completely lose sight of what you wanted to do because you value another's opinion so greatly. You are dependent when you feel you have to poll all your friends before you make a move. Depending on another for guidance is directly indicative of the degree to which you trust yourself. This may vary for different areas of your life. One of the tasks of adolescence is obtaining information from others to help you define a sense of self. Staying dependent on, and continuing to gather information about the same situations over and over again is evidence that you have work to do on this issue.

However, this is not the case if you are in early recovery from an addiction. By the time you reach recovery, your addicted self has been running your life to such a degree that you do not have a responsible part of yourself to trust. Twelve Step programs, proven to be the most effective treatment for addictions, are built on the concept of powerlessness and a need to trust in a power greater than self. You must have a long period of abstinence from your addictive behavior before your trust in self is restored.

The category about addictive behavior may help you determine if you have a problem. If it is, get help. As I said in the introduction, this material is not appropriate for those of you who are in early recovery, especially from chemicals. It is too compelling, and can threaten your abstinence. If you feel you have an addictive problem, refer to the resources at the end of the book for further help. Likewise, if your answers to the category on molestation indicate that you may be a victim, then I strongly suggest that you seek the help you deserve.

EXERCISE TWO: HOW YOU CARRY THESE ISSUES IN YOUR LIFE TODAY

As you reflect on these questions, remember that the task of this inner child is to learn how to cope with its feelings of social and physical awkwardness. Remember too, to look for how certain strengths may also have emerged from the challenges of this period. Record your responses in your journal. To review the general instructions for this exercise, refer to page 42.

1. With which aspects of your sexuality do you feel comfortable?
2. With which aspects of your sexuality do you feel uncomfortable?
3. How do you reach decisions about love-making? Is this comfortable for you? If not, why not?
4. When did you attend your last social function? Who did you go with? How did you feel?
5. Do you use any drugs or alcohol? Do you feel you have a problem with chemical use? Do you have to "use" something before you go on a date, attend a social event, or have sex?
6. In what areas of your life do you feel the most confident trusting your own judgment? Why?
7. Have you ever thought you may be an incest survivor? Have you ever discussed this with anyone? Do you feel it is necessary to explore this possibility now? If so, what do you plan to do?

Closing

Take the information you obtained from Exercise one and combine it with the insights you gained from this exercise. From this combination, construct a list of issues that have been carried into your adult life by your young inner teen. Below are some examples. Write your reactions to these issues in your journal.

Potential Issues that Result from this Developmental Stage

- Being sexually shy or inhibited
- Having an inappropriate need for other's approval

- Using substances or destructive behavior to cope with discomfort of life
- Feeling socially inadequate
- Feeling overly self-conscious about physical appearance

Your Young Inner Teen's Strengths

Although these exercises have identified your issues, they should have also suggested possible strengths that were carried from this stage. As you think back over the ages of twelve to fifteen, reflect on the strengths that you may have acquired. For instance, you may have experienced an awkward situation with a boyfriend or girlfriend, but, having gone through this, you may have been better equipped to deal with awkwardness. Write about the possibility of having developed strengths at this age. On the other hand, do not be alarmed if you have difficulty finding such strengths.

☙

STEP TWO: RESEARCHING YOUR YOUNG INNER TEEN'S PAIN

The transition into the teen years was a challenging one for your parents as well as for you. Suddenly, a docile prepubescent child transformed into a person who was at odds with everything; a demanding "know it all." On the other hand, you also wanted assurance and protection, guidance, and love.

As if this were not enough stress, the situation was exacerbated by the awkwardness felt with peers. Unfortunately, the peer group was the main source of support, but because of shyness and lack of interpersonal skills, few of you knew how to make use of this support.

Caught between pulling away from your parents and not knowing how to connect with your peers is the root of much of the awkwardness and isolation that is so prevalent in this stage. How successfully you were able to manage this isolation, loneliness and awkwardness depends on what was going on around you at that time. The task of this stage, however, was not to be relieved of this awkwardness and isolation, but simply to be allowed to learn how to cope with the discomfort. If there were other problems in your home or within you, then your opportunity to learn how to cope with this discomfort would have been greatly impaired.

Researching the events of this time will help you determine how much you were able to learn how to cope with the discomfort of change. These feelings reemerge anytime you confront a change. If you never learned how to cope with discomfort as a teen, you will not have the skills needed to cope with it as an adult.

To help you recall this time I suggest you research the music that was popular and try to recall your favorite song. If you had a favorite movie, you may want to rent it, review it and see what feelings emerge. If there was one particular activity that dominated your interests during this period—baton twirling, horseback riding, softball, playing a musical instrument—you want to try doing it again (particularly if it's something that you have long since abandoned) and see what feelings it provokes.

EXERCISE ONE: INTERVIEWING YOURSELF

Allow at least forty-five minutes to respond to these questions. To review the general instructions for this exercise, refer to page 45.

1. Record the factual information you recall, such as where you were living and what school you attended. Who were your best friends? Did you have a boyfriend or girlfriend? Did you go steady or experience puppy love? What extracurricular activities did you participate in? Were you involved in sports, pep clubs or the school band? How did you get along with your siblings and did you have very many friends? Did you start drinking or using drugs? What do you remember about your home life? Was there anything out of the ordinary that would have interfered with your mastering the tasks specific to this age?

2. Record in your journal any images, impressions or sensations that seem particularly strong in your memory of this time. Is there a symbolic image that expresses how you felt?

Closing

How well do you feel you were able to learn how to cope with your loneliness, awkwardness and isolation? Record you conclusions. When you feel ready to gather more information, prepare to proceed.

EXERCISE TWO: INTERVIEWING YOUR BODY

The purpose of this exercise is to help you determine where you store the unexpressed awkwardness and isolation in your body.

1. I suggest you begin by closing your eyes and surrounding yourself with healing white Light. As you are imagining this white Light surrounding you, begin to breathe deeply in to the very center of your being. When you feel relaxed, continue.

2. Let your focus travel through your body. Now either look directly into a mirror or pretend you are looking into a mirror at your body. Acknowledge your body as though you were saying hello to an old friend.

3. Where do you feel tense? Does this tension tell you something about your young inner teen's discomfort? Be quiet and listen. Record any response you feel.

4. Think of a recent time when you felt awkward. Where in your body do you hold that experience? Write about that experience. How is that experience related to your early teens? Record your response.

5. Go through the same process for times when you felt loneliness or isolation from your peers.

6. Think of a time you felt uneasy because you were going to be meeting someone new. Where is that experience stored in you body? What does that experience tell you about the pain from your early teens? Record your findings in your journal.

7. Now think of a time you had sex with someone new. Where in your body did you hold that excitement or tension and what does it now tell you about the residual feelings from your early teens?

Closing

When you have completed the questions, use deep breathing to help return your focus to the center of your being. Let yourself be surrounded with healing Light. Open your eyes when it feels comfortable to do so. You may be surprised at the information your body gave you. If you anesthetized your body you may have received no information at all. Don't be alarmed. Reflect on your experience.

EXERCISE THREE: HOW YOU TREAT YOUR BODY

How comfortable are you when you feel physically or sexually awkward? Do you allow yourself to experience this awkwardness? Most of you avoid situations where you might feel awkward sexually or physically, but you pay a price. You never get to move through the stage of awkwardness so you can learn to feel at ease. Use the following questions to help you determine the degree of discomfort you are willing to tolerate. To review the general instructions for this exercise, refer to pages 47–48.

1. Do you avoid physical sports because you may feel awkward or clumsy, or because you get too competitive?

2. Do you change your plans to go to a party because your hair doesn't look right or a blemish appears?

3. Do you feel comfortable with your body when you are having sex? If not, discuss the discomfort.

4. How do you deal with the times when you feel you do not look your best?

5. Do you use drugs, alcohol, nicotine, caffeine, or food to ward off feelings of awkwardness and loneliness?

6. Have you refused to go on blind dates because you feel uncomfortable with how you look? Does your degree of comfort depend on external factors or internal ones? For instance, if you are feeling great about yourself and you go to a party where everyone is dressed casually and you have on a suit, does it affect the good feeling you had about yourself?

Closing

How well are you able to deal with your physical and sexual awkwardness? Have you learned how to cope? Write down any other thoughts or feelings you have about the way you treat your body.

EXERCISE FOUR: INTERVIEWING FAMILY MEMBERS, RELATIVES, AND FRIENDS

This exercise determines how well you learned to cope with discomfort, awkwardness, isolation, and loneliness. In your interviews, you will be looking for any evidence of distractions from this goal. Family members and relatives will tell you about events in your home life. Best friends, teachers, or coaches could tell you what may have occurred at school. Be careful not to overwhelm yourself with interviews. Select three or four people and be as comprehensive with them as possible. See pages 48–50 for the guidelines on how to prepare for your interviews. Suggestions for questions are listed below. Record all your thoughts, reactions, and feelings in your journal.

Guidelines and Sample Questions

Ask what were you like at this stage. What activities were you in? Who did you date? What were you like with friends? How well did you do in school? How did you spend most of your time? How did you relate to the person you're interviewing? How did that person feel about you? Were there any concerns or complaints? If you are interviewing someone other than your parents, ask what this person remembers about your relationship to your parents. Ask about your siblings as well. Find out as many specifics as possible. Also remember to ask about world events, political scandals, or social situations that may have interfered with your development during these years.

Closing

Combine the information from your research with the issues you listed in Step one. Try to determine why you developed these ways of behaving and then explore how this behavior is extended to the way you treat your body. The following is an example.

Issue	Circumstances	Evidenced in the way I treat my body
I am terribly uncomfortable in new situations. I would rather be alone than have to confront the uneasiness I feel in strange surroundings.	My father was promoted and my family had to relocate when I was twelve. I had to leave all my old friends. After that, I never felt like I belonged or fit it.	I become very preoccupied about how I look when I have to go somewhere new. Sometimes it will take hours to get ready and I still never think I look like I fit in.

Developing this structure will help you talk to your young teen self about what influenced the ability to cope. It will also arm you with the information you will need to help this part of you heal.

ᘒ

STEP THREE: REGRESSING TO THE FEELINGS OF YOUR YOUNG INNER TEEN

Reexperiencing the awkwardness of your early adolescence is no joy. Learning how to be comfortable with being uncomfortable in some situations is a tall order. Unfortunately, that is exactly what you must do when you work with your young inner teen. On a more positive note, just think how much easier life would be if you were able to cope with your uneasiness—to be able to tolerate this discomfort, not avoid it with drugs, alcohol, destructive behaviors, or preoccupation with other people's opinions.

EXERCISE ONE: ACTIVITIES THAT ENHANCE YOUR REGRESSION

These activities help you experiment with accepting the feeling of discomfort and experience the awkwardness of your young inner teen without acting out. If the awkwardness becomes too unmanageable, then slow down the pace. Coping means tolerating comfortably, not gritting your teeth and surviving. If the activities feel too stressful or if you find yourself wanting to behave in ways that would be harmful to you, then modify them until they are manageable. Review the general instructions for this exercise on page 52. Look over the following suggestions and decide which activities you are willing to do. Each one has a particular purpose, so the more you complete, the better. Each exercise also has specific preparations, so follow them accordingly. Record your reactions to the exercises in your journal.

1. Go to a department store and try many clothes and accessories. Choose things that you would never buy. Experiment with the absurd! For instance, try on a cowboy hat, a wild pair of earrings, or a flamboyant tie; something that reflects the more outrageous you. Purchase one item and wear it in public.

2. Listen to the music that was popular when you were this age. See if you can remember your favorite song.

3. Rent movies that were popular when you were this age.

4. If you are single, go out on a blind date. What would your twelve-to-fifteen-year-old feel? If you are in a relationship, ask your partner to play "first date" with you. Go through all of the steps—the call, the pick-up, the date, and the good-bye. Try to pretend as much as possible. Let your young inner teen feel what it could not feel before.

5. Ask a same-sex friend to go to a dance or a social function with you. Pretend to be between twelve and fifteen. Notice how you cope with your feelings. Notice what you want to do to escape the awkwardness you feel. Share them with your friend. Compare notes and reactions.

6. If you used drugs and alcohol, make a chronological list of what you used, when, and what was going on in your life at the time. What experiences did you miss because of your use of chemicals?

7. If possible, spend an afternoon with someone between twelve and fifteen. Notice what they do and how they respond to the environment and to you.

Closing

Upon completing these exercises, you will have an indication of your ability to cope with awkwardness. Learning to cope comfortably opens your gateways to maturity. Once you can deal with the uneasiness of change, you are ready to move to the next adolescent task—defining the real you. Experiencing your young inner teen's uneasiness and dealing with this uneasiness are two different matters. In Step four you will learn how to objectify this uneasiness and interact with the part of you that carries it.

ꙮ

STEP FOUR: OBJECTIFYING YOUR YOUNG INNER TEEN'S PAIN

Objectifying the young inner teen's pain means separating from feelings of awkwardness and isolation. It means that you begin to see these feelings as belonging to your teen within. Your adult self can then respond to the needs of this younger self as you establish the part of you who feels the discomfort (the teen self), and the part of you who can respond to this discomfort (the adult self).

EXERCISE ONE: MEETING THE YOUNG TEEN WITHIN

This guided imagery will help you understand all that your teen self carries. You will separate from those feelings and interact to help the teen learn how to cope. Choose the method you want to use to experience this guided imagery. Allow approximately thirty minutes for this exercise. To review the general instructions for this exercise, see page 55.

Begin by closing your eyes and surrounding yourself with protective Light. Use deep breathing to relax and focus. Now imagine you are walking down a path in a beautiful meadow. You continue down this path, noticing the smells and the colors of the meadow. You see some figures nearby. As you get closer you see it is a group of teens gathered under a tree. As you look closer, you see that one of them is your teen within. What do you feel when you realize this? Can you notice your teen's vulnerability? What is he or she doing? Call your teen's name and ask this inner child to join you for a moment. Don't be surprised if this child seems awkward and shy, just notice how it does respond. Explain to your teen self that you are its future. You are proof that it survived this awkwardness and isolation. Tell your teen within that you will coach it through the uncomfortable feelings. You have come back to help cope with its isolation, awkwardness, and fear. All your fears about being isolated, all your awkwardness and shame, and all your anxieties about change are carried by this inner child who stands before you. Spend a few minutes with your teen self. Notice how you relate. Don't be alarmed if it feels awkward; with time this awkwardness will ease. When you feel you have spent enough time with your teen self, assure that self that your work with the awkwardness will now begin. The isolation is over. This inner teen will not be left alone again. When you feel ready to conclude, bring your focus back to your breathing and back to the Light that surrounds you. Take several cleansing breaths, then open your eyes when it feels comfortable to do so.

Closing

This first meeting will probably be awkward. Most of you try to avoid confronting this uneasy, awkward part of self. However, you will soon be gathering the support you need to work with this inner child's discomfort. End this experience by asking your teen self to help you find its photo or to locate a picture from a magazine. Paste this picture in your journal so you can reflect on it as you begin to ask more in-depth questions. Record in your journal any thoughts or feelings you had about meeting your child or about this picture.

EXERCISE TWO: CREATING A DIALOGUE WITH YOUR TEEN WITHIN

This inner child may have few words to say. It is up to you as the adult within to help with this awkwardness and shyness and to be able to cope with your own as well. If you have difficulty, act as if you are someone else—someone who would not be uncomfortable with this awkwardness. Allow at least thirty minutes to complete this exercise. Write the question down in your journal, then pause a moment and write your inner teen's response.

1. Ask your teen what he or she most likes to do.
2. What is your teen's favorite song, favorite pastime, favorite subject in school?
3. How does your teen get along with its family members and friends? Does your teen date, have a boyfriend or girlfriend, work or just hang out?
4. Does your inner teen understand the feeling of awkwardness? Explain the function of this awkwardness, saying it is the way that teen will learn to cope with the discomfort that accompanies change. Is your teen within willing to tell you about his or her uneasiness?
5. What does your inner teen need most from you?
6. How does your inner teen feel about you? Does your teen understand what it means to be reclaimed and coached by you? If not, explain that it means you will be there to help your teen cope with the feelings of awkwardness and discomfort.
7. Is there anything your young inner teen wants to know about you?
8. What joys does this inner child want to offer you and what prevents this from happening?

Closing

What did you learn about your teen within from the above exercise? How do you feel about what you learned? Answer in your journal.

EXERCISE THREE: TALKING IN THE MIRROR TO YOUR TEEN WITHIN

To review the general instructions for this exercise, refer to pages 56–57. Sit in front of the mirror and take a few moments to get settled. Close your eyes and think of a time when you felt awkward or lonely. When you feel a connection with these feelings, let them take the form of your teen within. Try to imagine your inner teen sitting in front of you, or looking back at you from the mirror. Ask your teen what is needed, what is felt, what your teen wants to say. Listen for the response. Then open your eyes and respond to what you heard. Continue this dialogue as long as you feel comfortable. When the exercise feels complete, record your experience in your journal.

EXERCISE FOUR: CREATING YOUR PROTECTOR

Your teen within will need a unique protector, someone who can act as a coach. This character needs to be someone you can imagine standing behind you coaching you through the feelings of discomfort. This protector will become the voice inside your head who says you will survive feeling awkward or clumsy or out of place. If you can't think of any real character who could have played this role, then invent the coach that your inner teen needs. Your teen may want to draw this character or find a picture in a magazine that represents that coach. If the character is real, try to find a photo of this person. To review the general instructions for this exercise, refer to page 58.

1. Ask your teen self if he or she could select anyone in the world, real or imagined, to be the coach, who would that character be?
2. Ask your inner teen if it has a picture, wants to draw a picture, or wants to find a picture in a magazine that represents this character. Once you have the picture, tell your inner teen that this coach will be available any time he or she wants.

Closing

Store this picture where you do your internal work and hold this image in your imagination as well. In your work with your teen within always call in this character for support to help him or her through the discomfort of change. It is this image that will meet the needs of your teen within and will heal the gaps left from this stage. Complete this exercise by acknowledging a partnership between this protector and the adult self. Call in your Higher Power as well, if this seems appropriate, because this is the team that will heal the young teen within you. Record your responses in your journal.

EXERCISE FIVE: DETECTING THE CRITICAL VOICE

The critical voice for the inner teen is the voice that shames or humiliates you for feeling awkward. This voice tries to convince you that you are the only one feeling like a "geek." This voice carries the negative statements you hear when you are putting yourself down. This exercise helps you detect this character so the adult and coach can challenge this negativity. Respond to the questions in your journal. To review the general instructions, refer to page 59.

1. What negative statements do you make to yourself when you feel awkward and afraid?
2. What negative statements do you make to yourself when you feel alone and like you are the only one who feels out of place?
3. What negative statements do you make to yourself when you go out on a date with someone new?
4. What negative statements do you make to yourself when you are faced with change or a new experience?
5. Where have you heard those statements before? Whose voice is this? Is it the voice of a parent, a teacher, priest, or coach? Are these statements you have heard from society? Is the voice imagined or real?

6. Imagine that you, as the adult, speak to this voice. Ask this voice what it is that he or she (or it) wants. What is the intent? Is it trying to protect or to harm?

7. Let your teen within draw or locate a picture of this critical voice within. This picture represents fear, terror, and judgment—responses to your awkwardness and isolation.

8. When you have the picture, go back to the original wounding and negative statements. Ask your coach to help you rewrite them. Next to each negative statement, write a positive affirmation.

Negative Statement	Positive Affirmation
I am such a klutz. I hate that I act like such a geek.	The way I act is fine. It's okay to feel uncomfortable at times.

Use these affirmations any time you hear these wounding words. They will help dissolve the negativity and replace it with statements that are kind.

Closing

Have your adult self interact with this critic, and when necessary, imagine that your Higher Power sends it away by surrounding it in a bubble of protective Light and releasing the bubble into the universe. To conclude this exercise, assure your inner child that the critic will no longer go unchallenged. Write about this experience in your journal.

EXERCISE SIX: CHANGING YOUR INNER TEEN'S EXPERIENCE OF CHILDHOOD

Remember that the goal in intervention is not to keep your inner teen from feeling awkward, but to develop the coping skills to tolerate this discomfort. Bringing in the coach and the Higher Power is what will enable your teen self to tolerate the uneasiness. Using this support whenever you feel discomfort will eventually help this part of you feel comfortable with the uneasiness of change.

Review the profile of this inner child's pain and select the issue upon which to focus. Review the general instructions on pages 60–61. Then use the guided imagery to rework and transform the painful scenes from this time. Have your pen and journal ready as you prepare to complete this writing exercise. Prepare your room in the way that is the most conducive to your work. Allow approximately one hour for this exercise.

Closing

This exercise should begin helping your awkward self learn how to cope with the discomfort of change. This part of you is healing when you can cope with change without addictively acting out and when you can feel comfortable even though you feel discomfort.

ℰℐ

STEP FIVE: GRIEVING YOUR INNER TEEN'S PAIN

Your young teen within will grieve the time wasted because you did not learn how to cope. If you were a victim of incest at this age, however, the grieving process will be much more extensive. You will want to draw on resources that deal with the specifics of incest in much more detail than I am able to present in this book.

EXERCISE ONE: THE FIRST FOUR STAGES OF GRIEF

The following exercise will help your inner teen grieve the pain of all the time that has been missed by not knowing how to cope with discomfort. Allow several hours to complete this exercise. Set the room up so you will be comfortable. Call in the support of your Higher Power and your protector and surround yourself with Light. You will need your journal, your pen and drawing materials. To review the general directions for this exercise and to obtain the guidelines needed to assist you in this process, please refer to pages 63–65.

Closing

Gather all the drawings and writings that you and your inner teen completed during this grieving process. You will be using them to release your inner teen's pain and claiming his or her ability to tolerate discomfort.

ℰℐ

STEP SIX: HEALING YOUR PAIN, RECLAIMING YOUR JOY

Read the modifications below and then return to pages 65–69 and repeat the ceremony for healing the inner child. The issue on which you will focus during your emotional, physical, and spiritual release is learning to accept discomfort.

Hyssop, cinnamon, and calendula (also know as marigold) are excellent herbs for the ceremonial release of your teen's pain. Cinnamon can be used as an herb tea, as a candle, or in the bath. Its properties are associated with healing and soothing your fears, and with increasing concentration. Hyssop helps ward off negativity, and calendula can be used to purify and protect. If you decide to burn incense, frankincense or cinnamon are best.

When you feel ready to conclude this ritual, explain to your young inner teen that you now want to bring him or her home. It is time to integrate this part of self back into your total being, so your teen can be supported as you master the task of feeling awkward.

Ask your twelve-to-fifteen-year-old to select the place in your body where he or she would feel the most supported when faced with an awkward situation. Then imagine that your young inner teen melts into that part of your body. By merging with this inner child you will be able to cope more effectively with any feelings of awkwardness you may face. If this inner child's issues get triggered, use the tools you have learned to objectify these feelings so you can interact with and resolve them. But when the issue is resolved, and it feels safe, bring your young teen self back home.

If it does not yet feel right to have your young teen self melt back into your body, then create a safe place where your teen can reside. Imagine that the protector stays with your inner teen within so that it will always feel safe.

Your fear of being alone and awkward and the need to be able to cope will most likely continue to be a challenge. You will now, however, be able to recognize those feelings as the feelings of your inner teen, and know that you have the tools in your possession with which you can supportively respond to those fears.

REVISING THE GARDEN OF YOUR PAST

Complete your work with this inner child by returning to your garden of the past. Ask your young inner teen how it would like to contribute to this garden. Imagine that you both do the work so that this inner child will be represented in the garden of growth. If you have a garden or a place where you can grow things, plant a seed that will represent this inner child's growth.

This concludes the work with your young teen within. Remember that you can redo these exercises to continue your work. Also, the exercises in chapter nine will contribute to continuing the development of the relationship with your inner teen self.

or programs that promote your health, it is often related to the inner adolescent's fear that things will be too different when the goals of the program are reached. Therefore, it is better to sabotage than to be disappointed, fail, or look bad. Often, you rebel against professional advancement for the same reason. You may rebel against structure because it could lead to success.

Setting limits with your inner adolescent is part of the process you need to learn. Many of you allow this rebellious self to run your life. Unable to establish a more mature form of independence, you find yourself forever caught in a state of rebellion. You rebel against everything. You may rebel against the norm, against authority figures, social and religious restrictions. You may rebel against your partner or your parents, and you will most likely rebel against yourself. Such was the case with Sarah.

Case History: Sarah

No matter how many times Sarah promised herself she would start a diet on Monday, when Monday came, it always passed without a change in the way she ate. Sarah was only fifteen pounds overweight, but her obsession with this fifteen pounds occupied most of her free time. She endlessly planned her food intake, fantasized about what her life would be like when she was thin, and mentally shopped for a new wardrobe. But nothing ever changed. Desperate, she sought help to find out why she could never succeed.

There was a battle going on in Sarah. Her inner adult wanted to stick to the food plan, but her inner adolescent rebelled. Once this inner child rebelled, the critical voice emerged, attempting to control and humiliate her into following the plan. Her critic and her rebellious adolescent self were in a power struggle, vying for control. Sarah was so overrun by this power struggle that the responsible adult part of self was nowhere to be found.

First, Sarah and I retrieved her inner adult. It was a slow process. This battle between the adolescent (who wanted to be accepted as she was) and the critic (who always thought she could be better) had been going on for years. Those two parts within Sarah struggled over *every* issue. Weight was just the most recent battleground.

As we worked with these two extremes, Sarah began to sense the presence of this power struggle in many areas of her life. She realized it had kept her from developing the career she wanted, had influenced her choice in men, and had kept her from pursuing a college degree.

Since weight was the active battleground, it was the issue we addressed. The work involved a confrontation with her critic, as well as setting limits with her adolescent self. Using guided imagery and inner dialogue, Sarah was able to mediate and negotiate with these two parts within. Once they were neutralized, Sarah was sufficiently empowered to follow her food plan because this power struggle no longer had to be externalized. Sarah did still need a food plan to help her eat a better, healthier diet, but she was able to follow this plan without feeling deprived because her inner adult was back in charge. Her inner adolescent had no need to rebel because the food plan was flexible enough to be followed.

STEP ONE: IDENTIFYING YOUR PAIN

Rebelling when you were an adolescent was essential if you were to move into the final stage of development—preparing for your place in the adult world. There may have been many reasons that this rebellion did not occur. In order to rebel, there had to be someone you cared enough about to rebel against, and there had to be a structure against which you could safely rebel. If you were raised in a dysfunctional home where the rules were so rigid you did not dare rebel, or the rules were so loose there was nothing to rebel against, you would never have been able to master this task. Instead it would have been projected onto other areas of your life, as it was with Sarah.

The need to rebel follows you into adulthood and can jeopardize your career, your relationships, and your definition of self. If you find you often feel at odds with yourself and others, then you will definitely benefit by doing some work with your rebellious teen within. If, on the other hand, you were never able to rebel, you may feel stifled, full of repressed anger and may need to examine your development with respect to how you defined your sense of self.

EXERCISE ONE: HOW YOU RESPOND TODAY

The following statements will help you identify the areas of your life where rebellion may be present. You need to determine if you have problems standing up for yourself, if you are caught in a state of active or passive rebellion, or if your critic becomes activated when you rebel and gets projected onto your lover or spouse. You also need to explore how thoroughly you have been able to create a strong sense of your own identity.

Identifying the adolescent within can be intimidating. If your adult self is timid, you may be afraid of this part of self. The odd truth about your inner adolescent is that the more afraid you are, the more destructively your adolescent will rebel. Your inner adolescent needs the security and safety of knowing that you are in charge.

Adolescence is a time to bump up against the walls that define you. This enables you to determine who you want to be. If there were no walls, there was nothing to bump up against. It is like the toddler who could not separate from the caretaker if there was not a bond with that caretaker. So it is with the adolescent. You could not rebel against a caretaker who was afraid or uninvolved. This same dynamic exists between the inner adult and the adolescent within.

You need to discover the vulnerabilities of your inner adult. Are there no walls for your inner adolescent to bump up against? Is your inner adult too afraid of its rebellious inner adolescent to provide the structure that your teenager actually longs for but would never admit? This exercise will provide the information you need to strengthen your inner adult so that the adolescent within can feel safe.

This exercise should take approximately thirty minutes. Read the following statements and indicate how often you feel or behave this way. Remember that, except when noted with an asterisk, an always or never can indicate a need for healing. To review the general instructions for this exercise, refer to pages 39–40.

Do You Stand Up For Yourself?

	Always	Often	Sometimes	Rarely	Never
If someone tries to order me around, I am unable to stand up for myself.	_____	_____	_____	_____	_____
I am in therapy and if my therapist does or says something I do not like, I say nothing.	_____	_____	_____	_____	_____
If my bank makes a mistake, I feel uncomfortable pointing it out.	_____	_____	_____	_____	_____
If my close friends criticize me or treat me in an offensive manner, I have difficulty confronting them with their abusive behavior.	_____	_____	_____	_____	_____

Are You Caught in an Active State of Rebellion?	Always	Often	Sometimes	Rarely	Never
I have lost jobs because when my bosses asked me to do something I did not want to do, I reacted hostilely or angrily.*	_____	_____	_____	_____	_____
If I am driving on the freeway and someone cuts me off, I catch up with the car and try to intimidate the driver by tailgating or yelling profanities.*	_____	_____	_____	_____	_____
If my lover or spouse acts in a way I do not like, I retaliate in a violent way.*	_____	_____	_____	_____	_____
If I am losing an argument, I storm out of the room and refuse to discuss the matter any further.*	_____	_____	_____	_____	_____

Are You Caught in a Passive State of Rebellion?

	Always	Often	Sometimes	Rarely	Never
If my boss asks me to do something I do not want to do, I will agree but then forget or fail to complete the job.	_____	_____	_____	_____	_____

	Always	Often	Sometimes	Rarely	Never
If a driver behind me flashes his lights indicating he wants me to move out of the fast lane, I ignore and slow down even more, so that the driver is forced to go around me.	____	____	____	____	____
If my lover or spouse behaves in ways I do not like, I will retaliate by spending money, not coming home, or secretly going out with someone else.*	____	____	____	____	____
If I am involved in a discussion and it is not going my way, I lose interest in the topic, or pretend I am listening when I am really thinking about something else.	____	____	____	____	____

Does Your Critic Get Projected onto Those Close to You?

I do not like the way my lover or spouse runs his life.	____	____	____	____	____
I get angry at my lover or spouse when confronted with the way I behave.	____	____	____	____	____
I like the dishes done a certain way, and I hate it when my lover or spouse does them differently.*	____	____	____	____	____

	Always	Often	Sometimes	Rarely	Never
I am very concerned with what my lover or spouse wears in public.*	_____	_____	_____	_____	_____

Have You Defined Who You Are?

I agree with the political beliefs of those close to me.	_____	_____	_____	_____	_____
Even if I do not like the styles, I buy clothes that the magazines say are the most fashionable because I want to fit in and be like everyone else.	_____	_____	_____	_____	_____
If my best friend does not like someone, I do not like that person either.	_____	_____	_____	_____	_____
I feel if you saw me in a crowd, you would not notice me because there is nothing about me that stands out.	_____	_____	_____	_____	_____

Closing

If you were able to rebel as an adolescent, you were probably able to develop the skills needed to stand up for yourself and confront a situation that violated your sense of personal identity. If, however, you were unable to rebel, then your response in the first category may indicate that you have difficulty standing up for yourself.

If you suddenly feel uneasy and irritated at someone else, or if you find yourself criticizing another person's character, it can indicate that you have felt your sense of self violated by that person, but you have failed to stand up for yourself. In the following steps, you will learn how to create a dialogue with your inner adolescent to determine the nature of that violation and the healing that needs to take place.

You tend to be actively rebellious if you have experienced a great deal of this kind of violation and have never been able to feel empowered. The anger and

5. Do you ever eat, drink, or smoke anything as a way to anger someone close to you?

6. Are you physically intimidating when you feel angry or hurt?

7. Do you withdraw physically or sexually as a way to get revenge?

8. Do you think your body is exceptional, acceptable, or does it never quite measure up?

Closing

We are often angry at our bodies and attempt to "whip" them into shape. Like an adolescent, our body will rebel. We will gain or lose weight, get sick or feel fatigued. Hopefully these questions gave you some insight about how much your body rebels. Write any last thoughts or feelings you have about the way you treat your body. If your body were an adolescent would it rebel against the way you treat it? Record your responses in your journal.

When you have finished writing, imagine the healing light filling all the empty spaces that may have been left in response to what you have acknowledged. Thank your Higher Power, and then be silent for a moment and say whatever you need to say to your body before you close.

EXERCISE FOUR: INTERVIEWING FAMILY MEMBERS, RELATIVES, AND FRIENDS

Since you are going to be talking to others about your rebellious nature, make sure you do not set yourself up to be abused. There may still be unresolved feelings between you and others. Go slowly, and if at anytime you feel uncomfortable, stop the interview and go to a place you feel is safe. Also, be prepared to hear differing opinions about your behavior at this age. Each person interviewed will have a different view, depending on whether you were rebelling against that person or with them.

Prepare your interview sheets using the same format as shown on pages 46–50.

Guidelines and Sample Questions

Ask relatives or family members how you related to them during this period. Ask if you rebelled and, if so, what you rebelled against. What do they remember about how you got along with your parents? Did you argue with them, or did you do as you were told? How did your parents get along with each other and with your siblings? If you are interviewing family members other than your parents, ask how your parents related to you when you were fifteen. How did they stand up for themselves and how did they stand up to you? Explore what you may have learned from them. If you are interviewing your friends, ask more probing questions about what you were like, what your relationship with your parents was like, and how you behaved at school. When appropriate, ask about any world events, political scandals, or social situations.

When you have completed all of your interviews, compile the information and compose the profile of your inner adolescent's pain. Take the issues you listed from Step one and put them in a column to the left. Next put the circumstances that may have caused this issue. Now, in a third column, indicate how that issue is evident in the way that you relate to your body. The following is an example.

Issue from adolescence	Circumstances	Evidenced in the way I treat my body
I have difficulty standing up for myself with friends. If something happens or is said that I don't like, I usually just withdraw and don't speak to them for awhile.	My father did not like my rebellious actions. He beat me any time I talked back. I quickly learned to stay quiet and to retreat.	I carry tension in my shoulders. I hunch over and look like I am always ready to be abused.

Closing

Developing this structure will help you begin to construct the profile of your inner adolescent's pain. It will also arm you with the information you will need to help your adolescent.

உ

STEP THREE: REGRESSING TO THE FEELINGS OF THE ADOLESCENT WITHIN

Experimenting with rebelling and breaking rules can be either fun or frightening, depending on how you experienced these feelings when you were an adolescent. If reexperiencing the emotions of your rebellious self feels too frightening, slow down the pace and find a friend who can support you in your recreating these sensations. Keep in mind that you are developing the tools to work with your angry adolescent self.

EXERCISE ONE: ACTIVITIES THAT ENHANCE YOUR REGRESSION

Read the instructions for the following activities. Do the ones that appeal to you. To review the general instructions for this exercise, see page 52.

1. Go to a department store and purchase one outrageous piece of clothing or accessory that you "would rather die than be seen in" (such as giant, bold earrings or a flamboyant tie.) Wear it in public. (It can be a place where you don't know anyone!) Record how it felt to receive certain "looks" or attention. Record how it felt if no one noticed.

2. Find a rule that is "safe" to break, and break it. For example, sneak a burrito into a theater, stay on the Stairmaster at the gym for thirty minutes instead of the allotted twenty, or make a food sculpture on your plate when you are at a restaurant, as two of my friends did. (They sculpted a sailboat out of a baked potato, chocolate mousse, a skewer, and a napkin!)

3. Look around your home, apartment, or room. What does it say about your individuality? How can you make it more *you?* Come up with a plan to achieve this.

4. Spend an afternoon playing the music that was popular when you were this age.

5. Reread your favorite novel from that time. Write down your memories.

6. Rent a video from that era. Record any memories it brings back.

7. If possible, spend an afternoon with a fifteen-to-seventeen-year-old. Notice what they do and how they respond to the environment and to you. Record that experience in your journal.

Closing

Your inner adolescent carries your anger and rebellion, but also your sense of individuality. Having completed these activities, you should have a better awareness of both. In all the exercises you have done so far, what have you learned about who you were as an adolescent? Record your answers in your journal.

ᴄ∕ꜱ

STEP FOUR: OBJECTIFYING YOUR INNER ADOLESCENT'S PAIN

Objectifying your inner child's pain means that you separate from your need to rebel or the rebellion that is still going on now within you. You begin to see your need to stand up for yourself as the need of your adolescent within. The feelings that are carried by your adolescent self need to be objectified and seen as this part of you. This will free the adult self to respond to the violations of selfhood that this inner child perceives. It will allow you to establish the part of you who feels the violation and need to rebel (the adolescent self) and the part of you who can respond (the adult self).

EXERCISE ONE: MEETING YOUR ADOLESCENT WITHIN

This guided imagery will help you get in touch with all that your adolescent self carries. You will then separate from those feelings and interact with the adolescent self so you can get to know this child within you. Allow approximately thirty minutes to complete this exercise. To review the general instructions for this exercise, refer to page 54.

Close your eyes. Surround yourself with protective Light. Use deep breathing to relax and focus. Imagine you are walking down the street on which you were raised. Notice the old familiar smells and sights. See the home in which you lived as an adolescent. How does it feel to revisit your home? Walk into the house and go to the room where your adolescent self resides. See that adolescent in the room. What is he or she doing? Studying, listening to records, talking to a friend, or watching T.V.? Make contact with this inner child and introduce yourself as the future self. How does he or she respond? Don't be alarmed if your adolescent self pulls back. Give this adolescent time to adjust. See if you can determine what this inner child needs. Tell this child that you will help deal with the anger and teach it how to rebel. Explain that you have come back to help. Know that all your need to rebel, all of your anger, and all of your fear related to your struggle to be you is carried by this child who stands before you. Spend a few minutes with your adolescent self. Notice how the two of you relate. Do you feel challenged, intimidated, or afraid? When you feel you have spent enough time with this inner child, assure your adolescent that your work together will now begin. The hurt, the rage, the isolation is over. Your teenager will not be violated and abandoned again. When you feel ready to conclude, bring your focus back to your breathing and back to the Light that surrounds you. Take several cleansing breaths, then open your eyes when it feels comfortable to do so.

Closing

This first meeting can be emotional. It can be intimidating or cold and distant. Sometimes it is like meeting a stranger or someone who doesn't like you very much. Other times it's like meeting an old friend. End this experience by asking your adolescent self to help you find its photo or to locate a picture from a magazine. Paste that picture in your journal so you can reflect on it as you begin to ask more in-depth questions. Record in your journal your thoughts or feelings you have about meeting this child or about the picture.

EXERCISE TWO: CREATING A DIALOGUE WITH YOUR ADOLESCENT SELF

Your adolescent self may feel angry and rebellious towards you. He or she may not want to talk at all. If this happens, try to be patient and not give up. Often, we treat this part of self the same way our parents treated us. In this exercise, explore how it feels to converse. Don't worry if you end up feeling stuck. Creating the protector and detecting the critic will help you deal with this part of yourself. Allow at least thirty minutes for this exercise. Write the questions in your journal and record your inner adolescent's response. To review the general instructions for this exercise, refer to pages 55–56.

7. Ask your adolescent self to draw a picture of this critic or to find a picture in a magazine. This picture will now represent the judgments you make of yourself about being you.

8. When you have the picture, go back to the original negative statements. Call in your protector and rewrite them, one at a time, in your journal. Next to each negative statement write a positive affirmation.

Negative Statement	Positive Affirmation
I do not care what he said, I'll do as I damn well please!	I can listen to what someone says and choose how I want to proceed from there.

Repeat these affirmations any time you hear these wounding words. They will dissolve the negativity and replace it with statements that are kind.

Closing

Have your adult self interact with this critic and, when necessary, imagine that your Higher Power sends it away by surrounding it in a bubble of protective Light and releasing the bubble into the universe. To conclude this exercise, assure your inner child that the critic will no longer go unchallenged. Then write about this experience in your journal.

EXERCISE SIX: CHANGING YOUR INNER ADOLESCENT'S EXPERIENCE OF CHILDHOOD

Keep in mind that part of the task of your adolescent self is to create and maintain a defined sense of self. In these interventions it will be important to help that adolescent confront anything that hinders that process. Review the profile of this inner child's pain, select the issue upon which you wish to focus, then use the following guided imagery to rework the painful scenes from this time. By reviewing this scene and bringing in the support of your Higher Power and your protector, you can create an intervention that will rework and transform this violation of selfhood. General instructions and a guided imagery for this exercise are on pages 60–61.

Closing

This will have started transforming your inner adolescent's pain by changing the reference point. Rework this exercise with as many issues as you choose and continue to use it whenever the issues of your adolescent self emerge.

You will know this part of you is healed when you feel secure in who you are and when you *respond*, as opposed to *react*, to those around you.

೦ಌ

STEP FIVE: GRIEVING YOUR INNER ADOLESCENT'S PAIN

Your inner adolescent's grief is about the time you have spent not being yourself. The pain you experience here will be related to all the times you didn't stand up for yourself, the times you felt your selfhood violated and said nothing. It will be related to the energy you expended on struggling to be you. Perhaps, most importantly, it will be related to the loss you feel at having had no one there to help you learn how to be you.

EXERCISE ONE: THE FIRST FOUR STAGES OF GRIEF

The following exercise will allow you to help inner adolescent release the pain of the attempt to define a sense of self and the pain related to too much or too little rebellion. Allow several hours to complete this exercise. Set the room up so you will be comfortable. I suggest you call in the support of your Higher Power and your protector and surround yourself with Light. You will need your journal, your pen and drawing materials. To review the general directions for this exercise, refer to pages 63–64.

Closing

Gather all the drawings and writings that you and your adolescent self completed during this grieving process. You will be using them in the final step of healing your inner adolescent's pain.

℘

STEP SIX: HEALING YOUR PAIN, RECLAIMING YOUR JOY

Read the modifications below and return to pages 65–69 and repeat the ceremony for healing the inner child. The issues you need to focus on during your emotional, physical, and spiritual release are your need to rebel and fear of being yourself. There are several herbs that could be used to enhance this release. Borage is associated with courage and fortification of the inner self. Basil elicits the inspiration needed in promoting a sense of self, and is associated with the properties of strength, love, and protection against the unknown. Horehound is used to increase mental clarity and trust while warding off outside influence. These herbs could be brewed as tea or used in your bath to enhance your physical release.

Some of you may simply have moved from the structure of your home and family to the structure of a marriage and a spouse. No matter how you moved or failed to move into adulthood, this developmental stage was greatly influenced by what you experienced at home.

Your same-sex parent would have had the most influence on you. It was from that parent that you learned how to be an adult. Fathers teach their sons how to become men, and mothers teach their daughters how to become women. It was important, therefore, to have been able to see traits in your same-sex parent that you wanted to emulate. If you did not admire this parent, the identification would have been much more problematic. You would have been confused and ambivalent if the traits were not appealing to you, but instead repulsive, abusive, or simply out-of-date. You may, even today, be expending a great deal of energy to make sure you are nothing like your same-sex parent.

The societal models you observed would also have had an impact. Our society does not teach us to become mature and responsible adults. Because of media and advertising, we are subjected to a great deal of pressure about who we need to be. We are programmed about what we should buy, how we should look, what material goods promise to ensure our success. Unlike the previous generations, we are not encouraged to save for material goods—We are encouraged to buy now and pay later! Plastic money has changed the values of our society. It has created, in many cases, individuals who are unable to delay gratification, a generation who believes that "more is better," and that *now* is all–important. As the world becomes smaller and smaller through global communication, and the threat of nuclear war, and the reality of poverty and social erosion become more clear, this attitude becomes even more prevalent. It is the lack of permanence and stability discussed in the introduction to this book. The degree to which it existed when you were preparing for adulthood would dictate the degree to which you still struggle with being responsible for yourself. It will do you little good to blame society, or even your parents, for your immaturity. The point in describing the affects of both is to help you identify the *origins* of your issues so you can begin to challenge them yourself.

What did you learn from society about becoming an adult? Was your move away from home difficult? Did you feel your family was willing to see you become independent and a respected adult? How well did each member of your family respond to your move? This was not only a difficult time for you, it was a transition that could have been difficult for anyone who lived in your home, especially your parents.

Unable to deal with their own mixed feelings about letting go of their children, many parents may unconsciously sabotage their child's efforts to move out. Or, ironically, may push their child out of the nest too soon because they are unable to deal with the inevitable pain of saying goodbye. Every time a child leaves home, the family goes through a transition and each family member is uniquely affected. Your parents, your siblings, and you each have specific needs and feelings that affect this transition.

What you needed to make this transition successfully were parents who helped you learn to be responsible, make plans for your future, and who supported your independent decisions. You also needed them to listen without judgment and to respond only when asked. What you needed from society was a structured way to become an adult, evidenced in many cultures that have rites of passage from childhood to adulthood. Our society has no such ceremony. If this kind of support and structure had been available to you before you became independent you might have been much better prepared to deal with life maturely.

Unfortunately, few of you receive this kind of family support or social structure. Fewer yet experience a ceremonial rite of passage, so many of you have issues that originated in this stage. Some of these issus are gender-related. For instance, women were much less prepared by their families in this society to be on their own. Most were trained to become caretakers and encouraged to find a mate. Some were encouraged to go to college first, but few of us were encouraged to move out on our own.

In fact, until recently it was considered normal for women to fear being on their own. Despite the general shift in attitude about this, however, there are still many good reasons for women on their own to feel afraid. Women are certainly more at risk in this society than men. The rate of rape and domestic violence all point to a higher victim rate in women than in men. It takes a great deal of courage to challenge the expectations that society and family place on us.

Men tend to make the transition into adulthood more easily, but not without need for repair. Men are not given the chance to deal with their fears of being on their own, and although they may be emotionally ill-equipped, they are expected to move out and prepare to be a major contributor to the work force. They are also trained, however, to find a good woman who will take care of their basic needs.

with the following exercises. This information is necessary if you are to fill the gaps in your young adult's development that prevent you from successfully living in the adult world.

EXERCISE ONE: HOW YOU RESPOND TODAY

The following statements will help you assess the areas in your life where you need to be more mature. They will help you determine how much you need to focus on providing for yourself, increasing your level of responsibility, improving your career, or challenging your gender-related limitations. Check the response that indicates how often you feel this way. Record any thoughts or feelings that emerge as you read each statement. Allow approximately thirty minutes to complete your work. Unless noted with an asterisk, a response at either extreme can indicate a need for repair. To review the general instructions for this exercise, see pages 39–40.

Ability to Provide For Yourself	Always	Often	Sometimes	Rarely	Never
I rely on others to pay my rent, utilities, and food.*	_____	_____	_____	_____	_____
I am irresponsible about paying monthly bills on time.	_____	_____	_____	_____	_____
I do not take care of my laundry, prepare my meals, and clean or contribute to cleaning my home.*	_____	_____	_____	_____	_____

Level of Responsibility					
When someone asks me to do something even though I agree, I do not follow through.	_____	_____	_____	_____	_____
When I get a parking or speeding ticket I do not pay it on time.	_____	_____	_____	_____	_____

	Always	Often	Sometimes	Rarely	Never
If I cannot keep an appointment, instead of calling to cancel I just do not show up.	_____	_____	_____	_____	_____
If I harm or damage something that does not belong to me, I remain quiet and hope the owner does not notice.*	_____	_____	_____	_____	_____

Career Satisfaction

I feel dissatisfied with where I am in my professional growth.	_____	_____	_____	_____	_____
I feel unmotivated to pursue the credentials I need for me to do what I want professionally.*	_____	_____	_____	_____	_____
I do not select jobs that fully reflect my professional capabilities.	_____	_____	_____	_____	_____
I am not successful in my relationships with co-workers.	_____	_____	_____	_____	_____

Gender-Induced Beliefs

I believe that women are more satisfied if they stay at home and take care of the household.	_____	_____	_____	_____	_____
I believe that men are more capable of entering the work force than women.	_____	_____	_____	_____	_____

	Always	Often	Sometimes	Rarely	Never
I believe that no matter how hard men try, they cannot rear a child as effectively as a woman.	_____	_____	_____	_____	_____
I believe that women have less physical stamina than men.	_____	_____	_____	_____	_____
My partner and I argue about how the house should be cleaned.	_____	_____	_____	_____	_____
I believe the wife should be the most responsible for the kids.	_____	_____	_____	_____	_____
I believe that a man should make more money than a woman.	_____	_____	_____	_____	_____

(If you respond with "never" to the previous statements, it may mean you are either in denial about the influence society has had on your beliefs or that you have done a great deal of work in this area.)

Closing

Review your answers. What do they tell you about the issues you need to explore? Evaluate your responses, then prepare to continue to the next exercise.

EXERCISE TWO: HOW YOU CARRY THESE ISSUES IN YOUR LIFE TODAY

As you respond to these questions, keep in mind that the issues of your young adult within are involved with how well you have moved into the world. Use the following questions to ascertain how you feel about your place in the world. Determine your successes and the areas in which you need help. Allow at least forty-five minutes. Record your responses in your journal. To review the general instructions for this exercise, refer to page 42.

1. What are your personal needs and how well do you take care of them?
2. Is there anyone else who prepares your meals or takes care of any of your basic needs? How do you feel about this?

3. Is here anyone for whom you are responsible? If so, who? How do you feel about this?

4. In what areas of your life do you feel you are responsible? In what areas do you feel irresponsible?

5. What is your professional dream?

6. Are your pursuing it? If not, why not?

7. What are your financial goals?

8. Do you have a plan for attaining those goals?

9. What are your interpersonal needs? With friends, family, a lover, or spouse?

10. Are those needs getting met?

11. What, if any, are your spiritual or religious beliefs? Do you practice them?

12. Do you feel you have gender-related limitations? How do these inhibit you from doing what you want to do and being who you want to be?

13. Has there been any activity or event or achievement that has taken place in your life this far that has served as a rite of passage into adulthood? If so, describe it.

Closing

Review your responses to the above. Combine this information with your responses to Exercise one and develop a list of issues you have identified that need your repair. Some examples of these issues are listed below.

Potential Issues That Result From This Stage

- Inability to hold a job
- Propensity to relate to opposite sex in a limiting manner
- Failure to pay bills, bad credit rating
- Continuous arguments with roommates or partner about household chores
- Frustration with professional status

Your Young Adult's Strengths

These exercises have identified your issues but they also should have suggested possible strengths that were carried from this stage. Reflect on the strengths you may have developed because of your experiences. For instance, you may have had a run-in with an employer because you could not behave responsibly at work. Even though you may have been embarrassed, this could have influenced you positively by making you take your work more seriously. Write in your journal how the experiences may have contributed positively to your development.

☙

STEP TWO: RESEARCHING YOUR YOUNG INNER ADULT'S PAIN

Exploring the situation you were in as you were learning to be an adult and examining the messages you absorbed from society in general will you better understand the reasons you may be ill-equipped to live in the adult world. If your parents did not have these skills, and there was no one who could teach them to you, you may not have learned how to provide for yourself and be responsible. What you witnessed in your home you may either have repeated or rebelled against as you prepared to move out on your own. As you research the pain of your young adult self you will focus on the attitudes and events that may have had an impact on your development.

EXERCISE ONE: INTERVIEWING YOURSELF

If you were not willing and able to learn what you needed to learn about being a responsible young adult, there were reasons. You were by no means "just lazy" or "no good." Your resistance served a purpose. Keep this in mind as you begin to reflect on these questions. Renting popular movies that depict the time you were this age or playing music from this era may help trigger old memories. Allow at least forty-five minutes to complete this exercise. To review the general instructions for this step, refer to page 45.

1. Record what factual information you know, such as where you lived, where you went to school. Did you date, go steady and, if so, with whom? What was your social life like? Did you go to your prom and graduation? Did you have plans to continue school? If so, what were they? What do you remember about your goals and aspirations when you were this age? What were your fears? What events do you recall that had a significant effect on your life at that time? When did you leave home? Did you go to college, get a job, get married? What are your memories of this transition? What thoughts do you have about it now? How did your parents and family members respond to your moving out? What did you learn from your parents about being responsible and providing for yourself? What were their attitudes about what it meant to be a man or a woman? How did they manage their money and their time? What did you learn from their behavior?

2. Then record in your journal any memories of stories you have been told or have heard about your transition into adulthood.

Closing

Are there any general feelings, sensations, or impressions that you identify with this period? Is there a symbolic image that conveys the way you felt during this stage? How do you think these attitudes and events affected your ability to become a responsible adult? Record your thoughts.

EXERICSE TWO: INTERVIEWING YOUR BODY

Your body makes the most dramatic statement about how you feel in the world. Let your body tell you what you may not be able to see. It perhaps carries more of the memory of how you really felt about leaving home and moving out into the world than your conscious mind does. Use the following exercise to determine where in your body you carry this residual tension. To review the general instructions for this exercise, refer to page 45.

1. Where do you feel tense? Does this tension have something to say about your young inner adult's pain? Be quiet and listen.
2. Think of a time when you were unable to provide for youself—you didn't have enough money for food or to pay your bills on time. Where in your body did you hold that experience? Write about that experience. How is that experience related to your young adulthood?
3. Go through the same process for a time when you felt insecure about your professional achievements or uneasy about your gender-related roles.
4. Think of a time when you felt unsure about your place in the world and find where that experience is stored in your body. What does that experience tell you about your young adult's discomfort?

Closing

When you have completed each question, bring your focus back to the center of your being. Surround yourself with Light. Open your eyes when it feels comfortable to do so. Reflect on the information your body gave you.

EXERCISE THREE: HOW YOU TREAT YOUR BODY

Whether you feel you have a right to claim your place in the world is shown in the way you treat your body. If you feel ill-at-ease with your body, it may indicate the lack of ease you feel in the world. If you feel you have no right to take up space in the world, your body may reflect this as well. You may be thin and not want to take up physical space, or you may be overweight, perhaps even obese, as your body takes up the space you are emotionally afraid to claim. Use the following questions to help you explore this connection. Keep in mind that your ability to be responsible for your body mirrors your ability to be responsible for yourself. To review the general instructions for this step, refer to pages 47–48.

1. How well do you provide for your body?
2. Do you get regular medical and dental check-ups?
3. Do your clothes reflect respect or neglect?
4. Do you regret that you have the body you have? Are you comfortable, self-conscious, or obsessed with how it looks?
5. How do you carry your body? What does this say about you?
6. How does your body reflect your masculinity or femininity?

1. Find a new interest that you want to pursue. Research the steps that would need to be taken in order to pursue that interest. Create a plan that shows how that new interest would influence your life financially, socially, intellectually, and physically.

2. Look up an old high school or college buddy. If possible, get together and reminisce about old times.

3. Make a budget for your money and time for one week. Follow it as best you can. Write about your experience.

4. Rent a video or go see a movie that was particularly meaningful to you when you were this age.

5. If possible, visit one of your old hangouts. Record what you felt.

6. Write about the ways that you still feel emotionally, socially, financially, or professionally like a young adult.

7. If possible, spend an afternoon with someone who is this age. Notice what his or her interests are. How does he or she relate to you? How do you relate to this young adult? What does this tell you about how you relate to your young adult within?

Closing

In all the exercises you have done up to this point, what have you learned about who you were as a young adult? Write in your journal about the feelings this question provokes.

℘

STEP FOUR: OBJECTIFYING YOUR YOUNG ADULT'S PAIN

Objectifying the young inner adult's pain means that you begin to view your irresponsibility as the result of what you did not learn when you were between the ages of seventeen and twenty-one. In addition, it means that you begin to view your gender-related traits as behaviors you developed at this stage of your life. The feelings that are carried by your young adult self need to be objectified and viewed as this part of you. This frees the adult self to respond to the needs of this younger self. It allows you to establish the part of you who feels irresponsible and ill-equipped to deal with the adult world (the young adult self) and the part of you who can respond to this discomfort (the adult self).

EXERCISE ONE: MEETING YOUR YOUNG ADULT WITHIN

Go to your safe place and make sure you will not be interrupted for at least thirty minutes. This will give you ample time to meet your young adult self and to relate to this inner child before you proceed to interact with him or her with respect to pain. Choose the method you want to use for this guided imagery. To review the general instructions, refer to page 54.

Begin by closing your eyes. Use deep breathing to relax and focus. Surround yourself with protective Light. Imagine you are walking down a familiar street. You notice the people walking by. Then you recognize someone. It is your young adult. He or she may look as you did when you were between seventeen and twenty-one or may symbolically represent you at that age. What do you feel when you first see him or her? Notice his or her vulnerability. Where is your young adult going? Gently touch this inner child. What is the response? See if you can determine what this younger self needs. Explain to your inner child that you are his or her future. You are proof that he or she survived. You may not have all the answers but you can help him or her grow up. You have come back to his or her rescue. You have come back to heal his or her loneliness and fear. All your fears about "making it," all your confusion about what you want to be, and all your worries of being irresponsible are carried by this young adult who stands before you. Spend a few minutes with this part of you. Notice how you relate. When you feel you have spent enough time with your young adult, assure him or her that your work with the pain will now begin. The fear is over. He will not be left unadvised and ill-equipped again. When you feel ready to conclude, bring your focus back to your breathing and the Light that surrounds you. Take several cleansing breaths, then open your eyes when it feels comfortable to do so.

Closing

This first meeting can be exasperating. Sometimes it is like meeting a stranger, sometimes it's like the same person you are today. Record in your journal any responses you had in meeting your young adult self. End by asking your inner adult to help you find a photo or a picture from a magazine that looks like him or her. Paste that picture in your journal so you can reflect on it as you begin to ask more in-depth questions. Record in your journal any thoughts or feelings that this picture provokes.

EXERCISE TWO: CREATING A DIALOGUE WITH YOUR YOUNG ADULT WITHIN

There may not be as much distinction between you and this inner child as there was for the younger inner children. If you feel like you are the same, use the young adult's perspective and imagine yourself as the responsible adult self who replies. Allow at least thirty minutes for this exercise. To review the general instructions for this step, refer to pages 55–56.

1. Ask your young adult what his or her favorite activity is.
2. What are your young adult's plans? College, a job, or marriage?

3. What are his or her dreams and aspirations? What would he or she most like to be?

4. Ask your young adult within to tell you about the fears of not knowing how to succeed in the world. Is there any confusion about what role that young adult is supposed to play?

5. What does your young adult need most from you?

6. How does he feel about you? Does the young adult self understand what it means to be reclaimed by you? If not, explain that it means you will help your young adult learn what he or she needs to learn in order to succeed in the adult world. You will take classes, read books, even hire professionals if need be, to insure the needs of this inner child are met.

7. Does your young adult self need help preparing for college, or have questions that only you can address?

8. Is there anything your young adult self wants to know about you? Are there any concerns he or she has about what you've done with your life?

9. What joys does this inner child want to offer you and what prevents this from happening?

Closing

What did you learn about your young adult self from the above exercise? How do you feel about what you learned? Answer those questions in your journal.

EXERCISE THREE: TALKING IN THE MIRROR TO YOUR YOUNG ADULT SELF

There may be even fewer observable changes as you switch between your adult self and your seventeen-to-twenty-one-year-old within. If you have difficulty feeling responsible and wise enough to be the parent, then focus, rather, on being the younger self. Imagine interacting with someone you respect and trust who could serve as a model for you as the young adult. To review the general instructions for this exercise, refer to pages 56–57.

Sit in front of the mirror. Start rocking. Close your eyes and focus on the feelings that have emerged from this stage. When you feel a connection with those feelings, begin to ask what it needs or what it wants to say. Listen for the response. Open your eyes and respond to what you heard. Continue this dialogue for as long as it feels comfortable to do so.

Closing

Record your experience in your journal.

EXERCISE FOUR: CREATING YOUR PROTECTOR

Your young inner adult will need protectors who can act as advisors for each of the adult tasks he needs to master. Review your list of issues from Step one and ask your younger self to help you create an advisor, an expert who could help with the task-mastering, or could help ease the discomfort and uneasiness. For instance, you may have never learned how to balance your checkbook. In your imagination, you would create an advisor who could help. Get watercolors, magic markers, drawing material, and magazines so your young adult self can create a picture that represents this protector. To review the general instructions for this exercise, refer to page 58.

1. Focus on the issue for which you need the advisor. Ask the young adult to tell you for whom they feel the most trust. If not, work together to create a protector. Make a list of all of the characteristics this advisor would need. Then draw or find a picture that represents this character.
2. Create a protector for each issue.
3. Assure your young adult that these advisors will be available any time.

Closing

Keep these pictures where you do your internal work. In your work with your young adult within always call in these advisors for support when appropriate. These are the characters who will help your young adult self grow up. Complete this exercise by acknowledging a partnership between these advisors and the adult self. Call in your Higher Power as well if you want. This is the team that will heal the young adult within you. Record your responses in your journal.

EXERCISE FIVE: DETECTING THE CRITICAL VOICE

Your critical voice may be so familiar to you that it could be difficult to objectify it. It is often disguised as the part of you who likes to 'make things happen,' 'gets things done,' but the nature is abusive and often motivated by shame. This exercise helps you view this voice as that of the critic within. Once you know who it is and have a form for that critical voice, the adult self and the advisors can challenge the negativity. Respond to the following questions in your journal. To review the general instructions for this exercise, refer to page 59.

1. What negative statements do you make to yourself about your ability to succeed?
2. What negative statements do you make to yourself about your ability to be responsible?
3. What negative statements do you make to yourself regarding your masculinity or femininity?

4. What negative statements do you make to yourself about the opposite sex?

5. What negative statements do you make to yourself about your professional achievements?

6. Where have you heard those statements before? Whose voice is this? Is it the voice of a parent, a teacher, priest, or coach? Are these statements you have heard from society? Is the voice imagined or real?

7. Imagine that you, as the adult self speak to this voice. Ask this voice what it is that it wants. What is the intent? Is it trying to protect or to harm?

8. Create or find a picture of this critic within. This picture represents the feeling of fear and judgment created by the messages you received that said you would not, could not, should not succeed.

9. When you have the picture, go back to the original wounding and negative statements. Rewrite them in your journal. Next to the negative statement, write a positive affirmation.

Negative Statement	Positive Affirmation
I could never be competent enough to be in charge.	I am capable of doing whatever I choose.

Use these affirmations any time you hear these wounding words. They will dissolve the negativity and replace it with statements that are kind.

Closing

Have your adult self interact with this critic, and when necessary, imagine that your Higher Power sends it away by surrounding it in a bubble of protective Light and releasing the bubble into the universe. To conclude this exercise, assure your inner child that the critic will no longer go unchallenged. Then write about this experience in your journal.

EXERCISE SIX: CHANGING YOUR YOUNG INNER ADULT'S EXPERIENCE OF CHILDHOOD

Review the profile of this inner child's pain and select the issue on which you wish to focus. Then use the guided imagery provided on pages 61–63 to rework and transform the painful scenes from this time. Repeated use of this exercise will enable you to transform the experience of your past.

Unlike the earlier ages, this process may demand that you take the information you get from this imagery and get the help you need in your real life. As was previously suggested, if you needed someone to teach you how to balance your checkbook, find a person in your real life who can do this. If you need a financial advisor, hire one. If you need to learn how to cook, take a class. The specifics of what you need to do will become more clear as you do this exercise.

Closing

You have begun to transform your young adult's pain. Rework this exercise with as many issues as you choose and continue to use it whenever the issues of your young adult self emerge. Confronting the negative self-dialogue as you did in Exercise five will help you intervene in your day-to-day life, but this exercise enables you to transform the experience you had as a young adult. You will know this part of you is beginning to get what he needs when you begin to feel you can manage your life. When you feel you can provide for yourself and be responsive to others and responsible for yourself, you will be able to contribute to another's life. You will feel more autonomous and less dependent.

ℰℐ

STEP FIVE: GRIEVING YOUR YOUNG INNER ADULT'S PAIN

You cannot hope to grow up, learn to be responsible, provide for yourself, and make a place for yourself in the world until your young adult within grieves. This involves being honest about your young adult years. It also involves grieving because you didn't get what you needed to facilitate your transition into adulthood. For this exercise, I suggest you stay focused on the issues your young adult self needs to heal the last few years at home.

EXERCISE ONE: THE FIRST FOUR STAGES OF GRIEF

Allow several hours to complete this exercise. Set up the room so you will be comfortable. Call in the support of your Higher Power and the advisors and surround yourself with light. You will need your journal, your pen and drawing materials. To review the general instructions for this exercise, see pages 63–64.

Closing

Gather all the drawings and writings that you and your young adult self completed during this grieving process. You will be using them in the final step of healing your childhood and reclaiming all of its joy.

ℰℐ

STEP SIX: HEALING YOUR PAIN, RECLAIMING YOUR JOY

Read the modifications below and then return to pages 65–69 and repeat the ceremony for healing the inner child. Your focus during the emotional, physical, and spiritual ceremonies of this stage is the issues

Arranging Your Time

It will work best if you can dedicate a whole day to completing your Right of Passage Ritual into adulthood. This will give you plenty of time to pace the exercises so they do not become too overwhelming.

I also recommend that you do these exercises alone. They are your "Rites of Passage" into your adult life. No one can make this transition with you or for you. The only exception is if you have been working with a group and your group has planned to do this ritual together. But trying to do this ritual with someone who has not gone through the same process as you will diminish its effects.

CEREMONY ONE: RETIRING YOUR CHILDHOOD JOURNAL

Purpose and Directions

When you go on trips, you probably take pictures and then put these pictures in a photo album to have a memento of the trip. So it is with your childhood journal. This book has chronicled your transition from childhood to adulthood. It is an important record and deserves to be honored. It is also a record, however, that needs to be retired. The following exercise lets you ceremoniously retire the journal of your past and christen the journal that will chronicle your journeys in adulthood.

Preparation

Take the journal in which you have made all of your entries during your work with your inner children. If you used more than one, assemble them in order and put them in a small box or something that will keep them intact. Now take the new journal that you have purchased for your new adult self. Go to the place where you do your internal work and prepare to begin the ceremony.

CEREMONY

1. Take the journal you have used to document your journey through your childhood.
2. Place this journal on your lap and put your hands on the cover.
3. Close your eyes and breathe deeply. In you imagination, surround yourself with protective Light.
4. Focus on all that you have recorded on these pages. Let the memories float through your mind like clips from the movie of your past.

5. When you feel you have reviewed your past, open your eyes. Retire your childhood journal to a special niche in the place you do your internal work.

6. Sit down again, take your *new* journal, and hold it on your lap.

7. Turn to the first page and, in the right-hand corner, record the date and time.

8. Close your journal, close your eyes, and place your hands on its cover.

9. Affirm to yourself that all of the entries that go into your new journal will be for your highest and best purpose. Affirm that these pages will serve as a record of your continued growth. There may be more entries from the children within, but there will also be entries made by your adult and future selves.

10. Open you eyes. Find the place where you want to keep your new journal and place it there.

11. Sit back down, take a cleansing breath, return your focus to the center of your being and feel the protective Light around you.

ᴄᴈ

CEREMONY TWO: INITIATION CEREMONY WITH YOUR MENTORS

Purpose and Directions

In making your transition from childhood to adulthood, it is important to acknowledge the people who have been your role models, both negative and positive. In this next exercise, you will be led through an initiation ceremony with each of the mentors who taught you what it meant to be an adult. Some of your adult traits may be in response to negative role modeling. For instance, you father might have been domineering and ruled your home with an iron fist. In response to this overbearing behavior, you could have developed traits that were just the opposite; you may be unobtrusive or passive. Even though you formed your positive trait in response to his negative one, you may still want to pay tribute to this modeling. On the other hand, you may want to experience this initiation ceremony only with those whom you admired. I encourage you to read through the ceremony and decide for yourself. After all, it is *your* initiation into adulthood that you are celebrating.

Preparation

Go to your quiet place. Have your pen and your new journal nearby. Play music. Burn incense. Light a candle. Do anything that helps create an initiatory atmosphere. Allow approximately five to ten minutes for each mentor.

CEREMONY

1. Turn back to the journal entry you made for the exercise entitled "Find Your Adult Self." Review your answers. Then take a moment to reflect on the mature traits you have acquired on your journey from childhood to adulthood. Describe these traits in your journal.

2. Take the list of adults you admired and note in your journal which of their characteristics you were able to adopt. Include each person you used to help you learn what it meant to be an adult.

3. Close your eyes and imagine one of your mentors standing in front of you. Pause for a moment and look this person directly in the eyes. Express to your mentor the gratitude you feel for the support and guidance.

4. Imagine that your mentor gives you an initiation gift. Think about what this gift might be. Let you mentor explain that this gift is a symbol representing your initiation into adulthood.

5. Imagine that you also give your mentor a gift of gratitude.

6. Extend your hand to this mentor. As your hands clasp, imagine all the traits you admire in this person transmitted to you through this handshake. Feel the essence of these traits filling every cell of your body.

7. Imagine your mentor walks away. You let go of him as your mentor.

8. Repeat the steps of this ceremony for each of your mentors.

ᴄɔ

CEREMONY THREE: CLEANSING YOUR BODY OF CHILDHOOD WAYS

Purpose and Directions

This ritual gives you a unique way of purifying your body by ridding it of its old, dead skin. It is symbolic of getting rid of the old, childish ways of behaving that no longer serve you in adulthood. This bathing ritual is slightly different than the rituals you did in the physical healing with each of your children within. By now you are probably accustomed to bathing ceremoniously. If, however, you are uncomfortable with any aspect of this exercise, then feel free to either modify or discard it. Read through the entire ritual so you can be familiar with it before you begin.

Preparation

Run your bath water and add those oils, fragrances, or herbs that you like. Prepare the bath area in a manner appropriate for the ceremony. Set up your tape deck, light candles, or burn incense.

Take approximately one cup of sea salt. (You can use table salt, too.) Make sure you have salt *granules*—not the rock salt used in the previous rituals. Mix hand lotion with the granules until it has a paste-like consistency. You will be applying this mixture to your body, but not to your face. The granules are too rough to be used for your face. You want it to be moist so you can spread it easily onto your skin. (If you have a microwave, you might consider warming up this mixture for about ten to fifteen seconds.) Take the mixture and place it by the tub. Take two towels and place one by the side of your tub and one on the floor near the tub.

CEREMONY

Sit on the side of the tub. Take a little bit of the salt and lotion mixture and rub it on your left foot and calf. Massage it on to your body. This will loosen any dead skin, leaving your skin fresh and new. Do the same for your right foot. Then place your feet in the water. Gently rinse the mixture off your feet and calves.

Next, stand up in the water. Follow the same procedure for your knees and upper thighs. Continue to apply the paste all the way to your waist. Submerge yourself in the water and gently rinse the mixture from the lower half of your body.

Now apply the mixture to your upper body and your arms and shoulders. When you have finished with your whole body and rinsed the mixture off, wash your hair and rinse your face with fresh water. Remain in the tub but drain the water and salt granules from the tub. As the water is leaving the tub, close your eyes and affirm that all of your childish ways, which interfere with your being the adult you want to be, are carried by the water out the drain, and back to the earth.

When the tub is empty, rinse it, and refill it with clean, pure warm water. Submerge yourself. Let your body remember what it was like to be in the womb. Then sit cross-legged in the tub and emerge from the tub as the adult you.

Dry yourself off. Notice how fresh the new you feels.

℅

CEREMONY FOUR: MERGING WITH YOUR ADULT SELF

Purpose and Directions

You have completed your bathing ritual and are now ready to step into the adult you are meant to be. The following ceremony to accomplish this task will help you do this, and can be used repeatedly to strengthen your experience as an adult. Remember though, that each time you complete this ceremony it will be different because the adult self is forever in a process of becoming.

Preparations

Go to your quiet place and prepare the room in any way that feels comfortable. Allow approximately fifteen to thirty minutes for this exercise.

CEREMONY

1. Sit in a meditative position. Close your eyes and bring your focus to the center of your being.
2. Imagine the adult that you want to be. See yourself as someone who has stepped into his or her power. See this self radiating confidence and love.
3. Notice how you dress when you have stepped into the true essence of who you are.
4. Now merge with this image. Become that adult you want to be. Notice how you feel, how you walk, how you greet others that you see. Spend as much time with this experience as you like. When you feel complete, bring your focus back to the center of your being, and slowly open your eyes.

Closing

Record your experience in your new journal.

☙

CEREMONY FIVE: PERFORMING YOUR POWER DANCE

Purpose and Directions

What we think in our minds and feel through our emotions is often not integrated until we experience it in our bodies. This exercise gives you a way to physically *feel* your power and a way to integrate the effects of your emotional growth into your body.

Guidelines and Pacesetters

Movement and dance can be very profound experiences. The first time in my adult life that I experienced creative movement was when I was in Hawaii on a retreat. I had not really danced since I was twelve years old. I had taken dance lessons from the age of three and I had continued to dance in my younger years. But something happened to me when I turned twelve. As my body started developing, and I was confronted with the physical and sexual awkwardness of adolescence, I shut down. I had remained that way ever since. At the retreat, however, I was experiencing many changes that were the culmination of much internal work. One day, I took a walk. I found myself in the middle of a sugar cane field, in a clearing. I stood still, looked up at the sun, and spontaneously began to dance.

At first it was painful. I began to sob. I felt self-conscious but continued to make slow, rhythmic moves. Energy started moving to places in my body that had been blocked for years. The sobbing ceased. The movements became more free. I began to feel power as I moved without restraint. I danced for perhaps fifteen minutes and then the sound of a tractor approaching brought on the familiar fear of being exposed. I stopped cold in my tracks, but I had felt this power and now knew how to tap into that source.

That night I performed in front of a circle of women. It was the first time since age twelve that I had danced in public with ease. I now use the tool of power dancing to unblock energy when I feel stuck. I have included this exercise in the Rite of Passage ritual because I believe it is essential to come back to the body if we are to become the adults we are meant to be. The body records the patterns we have learned throughout our life. If we were to change these patterns, we need to physically address them.

It can be tremendously painful to do so, especially if you are a victim of sexual or physical abuse. If the idea of a power dance is too threatening to you, hold off until you are further along in your growth. Five years earlier I could not have had the experience I had in the field. My body was not yet ready to let go. You have been conducting a dialogue with your body throughout these exercises, so take time now to ask your body if it is ready to let go. If you do not feel like dancing, then honor how you feel. Come back to this exercise when it feels comfortable for you to do so. I encourage you, however, to record in your journal how you feel. Your entry is a way to reflect on the progression of your growth when and if you return to do this dance.

Preparation

Find a private place in your home, backyard, on the beach, in the fields, anywhere that you feel safe. Allow from five minutes to two hours, depending on what you choose to express.

Exercise

1. Make a list of the family members, friends, and co-workers with whom you are closely involved.

2. Think about each person and describe in your journal any childish ways you have of relating to them.

3. Which of these behaviors enhance your relationships? Which ones hinder your relationships and need to be changed?

4. Take each behavior that you want to change and recall an interaction when you exhibited that behavior. Picture the interaction in your mind's eye and then freeze the scene.

5. Consult with your Higher Power or the appropriate protector and devise the new way you want to respond to this person—as an adult.

6. Replay the scene imagining that you act in the new mature way.

7. Write in your journal how this new behavior feels.

8. Either imagine or have a real conversation with this person explaining how your relationship to them will now be different. If necessary, write a letter explaining how the relationship will be different.

9. Write in your journal or talk to a friend about the reactions you receive from others.

Closing

Your relationships will continue to change as you continue to transform. Use this exercise to address changes in the relationships to those close to you.

9

DEVELOPING ONGOING RELATIONSHIPS WITH YOUR CHILDREN WITHIN

Your work with your inner children will never completely be done because they represent your feelings from childhood. You will always be in a position to experience those feelings. However, by cultivating these relationships with your inner children you will be able to deal effectively and efficiently with these feelings from your past. Cultivating these relationships takes time and constant effort. Few people are in the habit of visualizing their inner children whenever they feel discomfort. Many collapse into the discomfort or talk themselves out of feeling that way. But you can work and heal your inner children if you are willing to spend time with them on a daily basis.

DAILY CHECK-IN

Purpose and Directions

Having daily contact with your inner children will enable you to build a relationship with them. This contact only takes a few minutes, but it is that consistency that will build trust.

It is helpful to have a journal in which you can record your daily responses. It enables you to review your journal entries and gives you an idea of the progress you are making in your healing. The following exercise helps you do this. Begin by determining if there are certain times when your inner children may be at risk. You may have a meeting with a business associate who always intimidates you, or you may be going to a job interview and the inner child who carries your inadequacy may be at risk to vulnerability.

For instance, I once had a client who was preparing for a job interview. She felt nervous and was afraid she would appear inadequate and inept. I asked her which self carried that fear. She replied that it was her teenager, who had done poorly in school and always felt inadequate.

I had her picture her teen self in her mind's eye. She told this inner child that she was going out on an interview and assured the self that she did not have to go along—only the adult self had to attend. The teenager within could do whatever she wanted for that period.

In her imagination, she made plans for the teenager just the way a parent would make plans for his or her own biological child. This enabled my client to separate her feelings of inadequacy (her teenager) from her feelings of competence (the responsible adult). Instead of going to the interview with feelings of fear, she was able to go from a position of strength.

You too will want to objectify your fears as the inner children and make plans for their needs. The only difficult aspect of doing this is to remember to *do* it. Your consistency is essential if you hope to build the trust necessary to maintain the caretaking role you have established with your children within.

Preparation

You can either record these directions and listen to the tape daily, or you can simply use these questions as a writing exercise which you will do daily. Go to your private place, play soothing music, and have your pen and journal nearby.

1. Close your eyes and take a few deep breaths.
2. Imagine a protective Light all around you.
3. When you feel relaxed, imagine you are walking down a path in a meadow.
4. As you are enjoying the beauty in this meadow, imagine that you see a small figure walking on the path towards you. See if you can determine who this inner child is.
5. Record in your journal the age of this inner child. Is there just one child, or more than one?
6. Ask the inner children what is needed from you that day. Record their responses in your journal.

7. Ask the inner children if there is anything they need to talk to you about. Are there any concerns that need to be addressed? Record their response in your journal. If you have a dialogue, make a note of that as well.

8. Now think about your day and see if there are any times that the children within might be at risk.

9. Are there times you need to plan ahead for the needs of your inner children? If so, make those plans. Jot them down in your journal.

10. Then bring your focus back to the Light that surrounds you.

11. When you feel complete, take several cleansing breaths, put away your materials and proceed with your day.

Shame

I had an experience with my shame one time when I was in a therapy group for women. In one particular meeting we were giving each other feedback. When one woman spoke to me, I heard her say, "There is absolutely nothing about you I feel I could like." To this day I do no know if these were her words. All I know is that is what I heard. My reaction was predictable. I froze. All the blood in my body rushed to my head, and I went blank. I could not respond. It felt like all systems inside shut down. This reaction, of course, was not apparent to anyone else. And I certainly didn't say anything. Fortunately, the group ended soon after. Once I was at home I went straight to my room and sat down in front of the mirror.

I was gasping for air. It felt like I had not taken a breath since she had spoken. My stomach was in knots and I started to rock back and forth slowly. Finally, I was able to look myself in the eye. I heard my voice gently say, "It's okay. We don't need her to like us. We have five other women in that group who value us. It's okay that she feels the way she does. It doesn't mean we are bad." Repeating those words over and over, I felt a sense of calm and the knots in my stomach relaxed.

At the next meeting, I realized I was ready for her to criticize anything I had to say. She might not say anything, but I "knew" she would think it. Each week, before the meeting I imagined I had a wooden barrel around me. Behind this barrel I would picture my little girl. This barrel blocked any of her judgments from piercing into me. I would continuously have an inner dialogue with her, reminding her it was going to be okay. By doing this, I was separated from my inner child and didn't collapse into her shame. I did not ignore my fear of being disliked, but I didn't shrink in response to the "perceived" disapproval. I concentrated on acting from my adult self and not dissolving into my shame for being disliked.

It worked. I proved to myself and to my little girl that I could withstand that kind of feedback without losing my sense of self-worth. My attitude changed toward the woman, too. And even though disapproval still triggers my shame, it doesn't reduce me to a state of shame. You are in a state of shame when every move you make is motivated by not feeling "good enough." There is no relief from the feeling because everything you do is based on shame. One way to deal with shame this poisonous is to work with it *in the moment.* One suggestion is to come up with a one-liner to say to your young inner child whenever your shame gets triggered.

Rokelle Lerner, in her taped lecture entitled "Journey Through Shame," talks about a statement she uses when she feels that she is not okay just the way she is. She repeats to herself, "I am different; I am not deficient!" I usually repeat, "I am okay just the way I am." I suggest you come up with your own one-liner.

QUICK REPARENTING TECHNIQUES

Purpose and Directions

Developing a relationship with your inner children when you are calm and already coming from your adult self will give you the experience of separation that you need when the needs of the inner children get triggered. This can happen anytime you find yourself in a threatening or unpredictable situation. It may be planned, such as a job interview, or it may be spontaneous, such as a friend getting mad at you. But whenever you feel emotional discomfort, restlessness or fear, an inner child's needs have been triggered and you are most likely operating in an unconscious way.

Having used the formula to work with each of your children within, you will already be familar with some of the way to work with their pain in private. These methods will give you ways to cope with your inner children's needs when they surface and you are out in public.

1. Detecting The Inner Child's Needs. One of the most effective interventions to use when your inner child's needs get triggered is to stop and take the time to detect its needs. Simply bring your focus to the center of your being and ask, "Who's there?", "What are you feeling?", and "What do you need me to do?" See, sense, or feel a response. Using "you" establishes a separation between the healthy adult self and the discomfort of the inner child and helps you objectify the feelings that have been triggered. Once you understand what the need is, determine how it can best be filled. You can use this technique while driving in the car, at your desk at work, or anywhere and anytime an inner child's issue gets triggered. It is all done silently, no one will be aware of your having this internal dialogue.

2. Acknowledging The Inner Child's Feelings. If you find yourself feeling uncomfortable, then it is helpful to get a moment alone and determine if an inner child's needs have been triggered. If it is not convenient to deal with the feelings at that time, simply acknowledge the feelings of your inner child but explain that you cannot work with the feelings at that moment. Ask your inner child what he would like to do until you can tend to the feelings. He may want to go be with friends, stay with the nanny, or go visit the zoo. The important thing is to imagine removing your inner child from the situation.

If earlier in your daily check-in you have already made plans for this possibility, then simply remind your inner child of the plans that had already been made and picture him or her back at the zoo, at the beach or wherever you had originally planned. Having made these plans earlier in the day, you can deal very quickly with the discomfort if it does surface.

3. Looking in The Mirror. If you get caught in a traffic jam or somewhere away from home, and you feel yourself getting riled, find a mirror. Silently or verbally, check-in with whoever is upset inside. Talk to him or her. Work with this inner child until the tension is released.

4. Calling Council. If you find you feel uneasy and confused, you are probably experiencing conflicting simultaneous feelings. We sometimes believe that if we are happy, we cannot feel sad; if we are angry, we cannot feel compassion. But it is simply not true. We have many different voices within. When they arise, it is helpful to "call council." This technique takes some time, so go to a place where you can do some internal work and get a bit of time alone.

Start by focusing on the loudest voice you hear or the most predominant feeling you are experiencing. Write down what that part of

2. Begin your session as usual. Take a few deep breaths, and in your imagination, surround yourself with protective Light. Have your pen and journal ready.

3. Before you check in with your inner children, reflect on what this special day means to you as an adult. Record your feelings in your journal.

4. When you feel ready to proceed, close your eyes and ask the inner children who have needs or feelings about this special day to come forward.

5. Make a note in your journal of each child who appears.

6. Now, take one child at a time and talk with him about what is needed. Write each response down in your journal, so you'll have a list.

7. Look at the list and see if there are any requests that need to be discussed. Remember, because you are working in the realm of the imagination, one child can choose to go to Paris and another can go with her imaginery friend to the movies!

8. After you have made plans for each inner child, make a list of the activities that will take place in your imagination and which ones you will actually do. For instance, if one child wants a special dinner, or flowers to be sent to her at home, you can go to a florist and order flowers or make reservations at a restaurant.

9. Once you have determined the needs of the children within, decide how you, as the adult, want to celebrate this day. Determine which of these adult needs fits in with those of your inner children and plan accordingly. Make any necessary arrangements.

10. When the day comes, have another session with your inner children; see in your mind's eye the imaginary plans taking place, and reassure your inner children that the non-imaginary needs will get met.

Closing

Once you have done this process for awhile, it will becomes second nature. It is truly an act of taking responsibility for yourself. It is self-caring, not selfish. You deserve to have special days and you deserve to plan them. Don't be afraid to ask others to participate, but keep in mind that the ultimate responsibility is yours.

CHRISTMAS, HANUKKAH, OR NEW YEAR'S

The Christmas and Hanukkah season seems to bring about a special set of feelings. It is the time of year when everyone is supposed to be merry. On your birthday you can hide and get away from it. But at this holiday season expectations are everywhere. It is difficult to watch TV or go to a store without being reminded. This is why the rate of suicide is so high during the holiday season—expectations are defeated and the contrast between what you are supposed to feel and what you actually feel is so grave.

It seems that during this time of year grief surfaces the most. We grieve about what we didn't have. We grieve about what we had and no longer have. If you feel lonely anyway, this season will provoke those feelings even more. If you tend to feel competitive, the holiday season may accentuate this as well. You may compare your ability to purchase gifts with the abilities of those around you.

You may also come face to face with your shame; you fear you will not be good enough. If you are unable to find just the right present or select just the right dress for a gala event, then this must mean that you are worthless. You attempt to be perfect and when you fail, you feel shame.

And, of course, greed can rear its ugly head. You can start judging how much others value you by putting a price tag on the present they give you. You can try to impress others with gifts that are beyond your budget.

All of these issues can surface and make the holiday season a nightmare. The following exercise offers suggestions on how to deal with this time of the year.

EXERCISE ONE: DEALING WITH CHRISTMAS OR HANUKKAH

Purpose and Directions

These exercises give you a way to *work with* your feelings, rather than just trying to live with them. This time of year can trigger a great deal of grief. I suggest you make use of these feelings and work through the grief. Many people I've worked with on this particular issue have commented on how good it felt not to have run from the loss they felt at this time of the year, but rather to embrace it and resolve the left-over pain. I hope these suggestions will enable you to do the same.

Exercise

1. Dedicate one day to grieve the holidays of the past. Let yourself really *feel* what you miss, or long for what you did not have. Play records, look at pictures. Do anything that will trigger your feelings of grief. Then express these feelings and release them. Ritualize the process and then let it go. Hold to your commitment of exploring these feelings for an entire twenty-four hour period.

2. Make an obligation list. On a piece of paper, write down what you feel obligated to do. For instance, you might feel obligated to buy a present for a relative whom you don't particularly like. Next to the obligation, explain why you feel obligated. In other words, what consequences would occur if you didn't do it? Then ask yourself if you can live with those consequences. If not, what action could you take that would feel less obligatory? With each obligation, continue to explore until you feel a sense of choice about the action you want to take.

3. Make a tradition list. If you feel loss because your family was so dysfunctional that you had no family traditions, take the time to create them for yourself now. Go to the library and research different cultures. Adopt traditions that have meaning for you. Or invent your own. Make a certain kind of cookie every year, or attend a particular service. Anything you do from one year to the next can be your own tradition. Allow your creativity to emerge and guide you, but figure out ways you can make the holiday season special.

4. Do the following on a daily basis through the holiday season.

• Spend ten minutes acknowledging and letting go of painful feelings. Any other time they come up during the day simply remind yourself to wait to work through them until the time you've set aside.

• Spend ten to fifteen minutes talking with your inner children to see how they are feeling. Check in with them about what they need or want. Record this in your journal.

• Have a holiday buddy. Call this person and check in at least once a day for five minutes.

5. Last, but not least, here are some general hints to help you through the holidays.

• Let your inner child plan the gift list.

• Have a non-monetary holiday; prepare a meal for friends, give a backrub, offer to wash their car, or clean their house.

• Keep a gift-wrapped box by your door. When a feeling comes up that you want to release, simply write that feeling on a piece of paper and insert it in the box. On New Year's day do a ceremony to release them.

• Volunteer for some kind of service during the holidays; working with the handicapped, or homeless, or with a senior citizens group.

• Take advantage of friends or Twelve Step marathon meetings.

• Allow yourself to spend time alone.

• Be responsible for your own loneliness!

6. Take a dollar a day for a week and pass it on to someone anonymously. (Pay the bridge toll for the person behind you. Pay for the cup of coffee of the next person in line. Treat the person in the car behind you at the fast-food place to

6. Take a dollar a day for a week and pass it on to someone anonymously. (Pay the bridge toll for the person behind you. Pay for the cup of coffee of the next person in line. Treat the person in the car behind you at the fast-food place to a soda. Enclose a dollar in each of your monthly payments with a note saying it is for the person who opens the envelope. The list is endless. Let your inner child have fun giving.)

Closing

If you have the tools to deal with the painful feelings that arise, you can be open to the excitement that the holiday season *does* bring, and make it meaningful for you. You don't have to be a victim of your past or of the commercialism of the present. If you are open and creative and willing to clear up the blocks that keep you locked into old and unresolved pain, you can beat the holiday blues and transform this time of the year into a true season of personal joy.

10

INTIMATE ADULT RELATIONSHIPS AND YOUR CHILDREN WITHIN

The unresolved issues of our children within are most evident when we begin to examine the conflicts we experience in our romantic relationships. Even if we have resolved some of these issues when we are on our own, they tend to emerge again the minute we get romantic. No matter how much we can contain the needs and fears of our inner children in our friendships, it seems to be a different story when we are talking about romance. Romance means risk: risk of being hurt, and risk of recreating the patterns of love or abuse we learned in childhood.

Still, most of us do have a deep desire to connect. It may be the infant who operates from an urge to merge, or it may the teenager who operates from the myth of marrying and living happily ever after. Most of us find ouselves engaged in romance. But often, we are not prepared to deal with what follows.

We are drawn to relationships because we hope that they will bring us greater fulfillment. And they do, initially. As long as we are in that intoxicated, totally absorbed first stage of the relationship, it *is* blissful. And there's nothing wrong with this feeling of being swept away. It is perfectly natural to be preoccupied with each other in the initial stage of a relationship. It is natural to want to look good and to please each other. It only becomes addictive when we are spending all of our time with the other person because we are afraid to say no. It is addictive when we begin to experience feelings that we fear may jeopardize the relationship, but out of fear, we deny these feelings and act in ways that betray ourselves. It is addictive when we refuse to risk being who we really are, because we assume that it would result in abandonment, humiliation or abuse. To feel these fears, however, is not addictive. It is human. And it is reflective of the inner child's pain.

The healthier we get, the more aware we seem to be of this pain. It is as if that blissful, intoxicated, first stage of the relationship begins to diminish because we become aware of how painful it is to attempt intimacy! In fact, in some ways it begins to feel like emotional suicide. And perhaps it is a suicide of sorts. Intimacy does call for a continual exposure of our hidden parts; what dies is our childhood need to hide.

INTIMACY

The word intimacy can be read as 'in-to-me-see.' For most of us, that means 'see my pain, my shame and my fear.' Few are able to trust another person that much. We become frightened; we feel a need to close down and remain safe. And usually we don't close down gracefully. We are too frightened; we shut down angrily, or we silently withdraw, giving no explanation for our sudden retreat.

It is appropriate to protect yourself. It can be harmful to trust too quickly; it can leave your inner children at risk of being hurt. It can be harmful to reveal too much too soon; it leaves your inner children too vulnerable. What you can do, however, is use the tools you have developed in working with your inner children so that they can feel protected by the adult within you. In working with your inner children's fears, you can open up at a pace that enables you to manage the feelings of your children within. You will not have to collapse into their fears, overreact, or become immobilized.

If you can separate yourself from your fears and work with the inner child's pain, you can move through these feelings with ease—or, at least, you can move through them without sabotaging the relationship!

It is important to realize, however, that you will probably recreate whatever you learned about intimacy in childhood. No matter how much you convince yourself you will behave differently, there is a part of you that will behave the same. This is the inner child who watched his or her parents and learned what it meant to love. If you saw your parents fight, your inner child may equate love with violence. The inner child may act in ways that recreate this pattern or may block closeness because he or she is afraid.

2. Ask your young inner adult what he feels about love and marriage. Record the response in your journal.

3. See how this part of self responds when your partner enters the room.

4. How do the two of them relate?

5. What does this part of self need from you to feel safe with your partner?

6. What is needed from your partner?

7. When you feel complete, imagine that you and your partner say goodbye and leave the room.

8. Pause for a moment to record your experiences in your journal.

Once you have done your inventory, you can begin to examine the unhealthy patterns that you may be recreating in your relationships. For instance, my partner in my first primary relationship was very promiscuous. He would get up early and leave the house before I was awake so I could not question where he was going. I would wake up feeling panic-stricken and abandoned.

One day, my partner in my current relationship woke up before me and left the house early. He had to change the oil in his car and he decided to get it done early. When I woke up and saw that he was gone, I panicked. When he returned later, proud that he had completed the task early, I laid into him. My reaction was extreme; I couldn't figure it out. Finally, I went to do some work in the mirror to see if I could determine who inside had been so alarmed. I got in touch with the child within who had been so wounded by my first partner's infidelity. Because my current partner's behavior looked the same, she assumed the motivation was the same. Once I realized who inside was so frightened, I was able to work with her. I accepted her panic but explained that the situation was different. I also reassured her that no matter what my current partner did, I would make sure her needs were met. I took responsibility for her feelings regardless of his actions.

This is a point I really want to stress. I sincerely believe that if you take responsibility for the feelings of your inner child, then you do not have to fear getting hurt anymore. Your inner children have needs, and it is nice when those needs get met through the relationship. The problem begins when we expect our partner to be *responsible* for those needs. The problem is also staying in touch with yourself enough so that you are aware of what your inner children need. In my experience, this is a continuous challenge. To do this, you have to remain cognizant of your inner children's cues; those pangs inside that alert you that something is not quite right, that someone inside has gotten hurt. This takes a lot of work. In fact, I believe that other than parenting a child, relating intimately to another human is the hardest emotional task that we face.

Relationships are difficult. They demand that you examine places within yourself that are wounded. Being intimate means you share your pain and you risk being hurt. Being intimate means feeling vulnerable yet being able to cope. Just as children must fall down and bump and scrape their knees as they learn how to walk, so must you too take your bumps and falls if you choose to trust and be close. I am, however, *not* talking about abuse. I am not talking about being hit or being belittled. I am talking about being in a discussion in which both parties are scared. I am talking about both people responding to the needs of their inner children and wanting those needs to be filled by the person with whom they are involved.

It is my experience that the closer you get to another person the more risky it becomes, because the more you are experiencing fear. The person you care about is probably also feeling fear. So you often begin to open each other's old wounds. Your fear of abandonment triggers his or her rage. The anger frightens you, and you want to leave. On and on it goes, and you continue to collapse into your inner children's fears.

The problem is that your inner children often do not want to be intimate. They want to be loved and protected. What started out as a discussion between two adults turns into a battle for whose needs are going to get met. Each inner child looks to the person across the room to fill his or her needs, and there is no adult on either side to reply. You have both collapsed into your inner children's fears.

How many discussions end this way? How many times have you and your partner attempted to talk about painful situations only to walk away feeling wounded, unsafe, and unheard? At what point in the discussion did you disappear into your inner child's fears and leave your adult behind? How many times do you blame your partner because he or she never responds? We all get scared and sometimes trigger each other's core fears. If you hear youself saying, "This always happens to me!" or "You always do this to me," you have hit a core issue. That core issue is a recreation of something you experienced as a child. When you react from this anger or hurt, you become that inner child. You fall into those old fears and leave that inner child alone to handle the conflict. Unfortunately, your inner child is, at that point, just as defenseless as in childhood. Once again, there is no one around for protection.

When these core issues get triggered, it is necessary to work with them in two ways. One is to respond to and to confront the immediate cause. It is also important to give the other person an idea of the source—sometimes deeply buried—of your reaction. To do this, though, you must first understand your own patterns.

EXERCISE TWO: EXPLORING YOUR CORE ISSUES IN RELATIONSHIPS

Purpose and Directions

This writing exericse helps you examine your core issues and develop the tools necessary for you and your partner to create healthy ways of working with these issues when they get triggered. It may be more beneificial if you and your partner can do this exercise together.

What may affect you will not necessarily affect your partner. For instance, you may feel very hurt if you partner says he or she will be home at a certain time and then arrives an hour late. Histories are different and, therefore, core issues are different. By sharing your core issues with your partner you will hopefully both be better able to treat these with care.

Never use these core issues against each other. Make sure that you share this information with the understanding that it takes great trust to expose yourselves. If you treat the information as sacred, you will begin to build the foundation of a trusting and loving relationship. Use it to hurt each other and you will be sabotaging the very closeness you are attempting to achieve.

If you do not feel safe enough at the present time to share the information with each other, then don't. If your partner is not interested in doing this exercise with you, then do it alone. It will still benefit you to know which of your inner children are involved and which of them needs your support when these issues surface within you.

Allow approximately forty-five minutes to an hour to work. If you need more time, take a stretch break and then proceed. You will need your pen and journal. I suggest you meditate or pray for a few moments before you begin. Surround yourself with protective Light if you choose, take a deep breath, focus on one question, and respond.

Exercise

1. Make a list of your most intimate relationships. (They do not necessarily have to be sexual.)
2. Are you still involved in some way with each person? If not, how did each relationship end? How did you feel about its ending? Are there patterns or similarities to the endings of your relationships? If so, how do these patterns fit into your experience of childhood?
3. If you are presently in a primary or committed relationship, what are the issues that the two of you disagree about most? What are your themes?

4. What is your position and on these issues and what is your partner's position?

5. Now, close your eyes and see which of your inner children responds to this situation. Who gets hurt or angry or afraid?

6. Talk to that child within you to try to understand the pain that surrounds this issue.

7. Ask this part of you what he or she needs from you the next time this issue gets triggered. Make commitments to this younger self on how you will protect him or her.

8. Now write down your understanding of your partner's issue.

9. Check it out with your partner. Ask what this issue brings up in your partner. Is your partner interested in hearing your perceptions? (Remember, these are your *perceptions*, not your judgments!)

10. Share what you learned about yourself as well.

Closing

Make a commitment to yourself or each other that the next time this issue arises you will take a fifteen-minute break and check in with your inner child. This will give you the time to disengage and separate from the feelings of your inner children so you can respond to instead of act out those inner fears.

It is important for you to remember that each time you engage with your partner from a rageful or hurtful place, you are abandoning your inner child, leaving it just as defenseless as when you were young. Once you have acknowledged and worked with the issue from the past, you can respond to the issue in present time. You can reclaim the projections you have placed on your partner. Reclaiming these projections and working with them enables you to learn from your past, rather than to recreate it.

Romantic relationships are exciting. There is no other area that provides so much opportunity for growth. But few of us know much about how to make them work. We are all pioneers in intimacy. There are no true teachers. The dynamics of each relationship are as unique as the relationship itself. We have to teach ourselves and that means being willing to learn from our mistakes.

If you are choosing to be intimate it is necessary to commit also to the process of change; a new relationship always brings change. And you have to commit to this process because you see value in it. If you attempt to change to please someone else, it will backfire. You have to be willing to do it for yourself. You have to be willing to be intimate with your inner children. The result is enhanced closeness with others, but the goal must also be enhanced closeness with the self. This concept is new to our generation. There is no model, no past experience to draw on; there are simply tools to assist you in doing your inner work.

sponsor. A sponsor has been in the program for a while and assists newcomers by answering questions, being available, and guiding them through working the Twelve Steps.

There are other ways an individual can confront addictive behavior. Supportive therapy is one. Behavior Modification and Desensitization Therapy are others. But none, I believe, are as effective as a Twelve Step program, because a Twelve Step program not only confronts the behavior but addresses, on a twenty-four-hour-a-day basis, the need for a new support system as well.

THE THREE STAGES OF RECOVERY AND THE INNER CHILD

If you have recently identified your behavior as addictive, then no matter how you deal with this addictive behavior you will most likely experience three distinct stages of recovery. The first stage involves intervening in your destructive behavior. It means breaking denial and being honest about the consequences that resulted from your addiction. It also means sharing your story with others, as well as discovering new ways to cope with life nonaddictively.

The second stage of recovery occurs when you are ready to deal with the pain that has been camouflaged by your addictive behavior. This book will be most useful during this stage of recovery because it is at this point that you confront and heal your past. As the pain of your past is resolved you explore ways to establish and maintain a sense of serenity. You begin to pursue a sense of spirituality as you determine meaningful ways to live your life. These pursuits constitute the third stage of recovery.

Each stage of recovery involves working with and responding to each inner child's needs. This work begins the moment you get into recovery because you are usually overwhelmed with confusing and powerful feelings. This emotional confusion is the result of the build-up of disowned feelings from childhood. Released from the numbing effect of your addictions, you are very quickly thrown back to the coping mechanisms of childhood.

When you experience a sudden rush of anxiety, it is usually your inner child's grief announcing itself. When you sit in self-help or therapy meetings rehearsing what you want to say, it often means your inner child is seeking approval. When you fear rejection or exposure, it can be a reflection of your inner child's shame. When you re-

experience your compulsion to act out or return to your addictive behavior, it may be your attempt to numb the inner child's pain. When
you sit in meetings and fantasize about that piece of chocolate cake, or
that cigarette or drink, it can be your inner child's ambivalence about
even *wanting* to recover.

Those moments when you most want to act out addictively
are the times you are closest to the repressed feelings of your children within. Until you learn how to deal with and heal the feelings of
your past, you are forever vulnerable to returning to your old addictive ways.

When you first get into recovery, however, there is no separation
between you and your feelings. You don't have to *find* your inner child
because you *are* the inner child. You can't separate from your emotions
because all you are is your addiction or your raw, turbulent emotions.
Until you bond with a group and begin to identify with others who
are recovering, you usually have no healthy or responsible part of self
from which you can separate. You *can* begin to label your feelings and
identify them with your inner children, but the healing will usually
come only through your association with a group who can provide the
safety you need as you move from the distraction of your addictions to
a power greater than yourself.

RECOVERY AND THE DEVELOPMENTAL STAGES
OF CHILDHOOD

When you first get into recovery or begin to intervene in your addictive behavior, you will see the emergence of the unresolved tasks from
the developmental stages of childhood. The first sign of an inner
child's issue emerging will be the panic you experience. Remember,
panic is anxiety; it is the first stage of loss. The loss is giving up your
addictive behavior. This panic is the feeling of the infant part of self
because it is the infant within whose survival depends on a connection
to something outside of self—in this case, your addiction.

Early Recovery and the Infant Within

If, in your early childhood, your basic needs were met, then perhaps
your dependence will not be as dramatic. There will be some panic as
you are in transition from the addictive behavior to your new connection with the group; however, it will not be as frightening as it would

be if, as an infant, you had never experienced safety. If trusting the program and the process of recovery *is* an issue in the beginning of recovery, then it is probably indicative of the lack of safety you felt as a child.

The consistency of the group, the structure of the meetings, and the people making up the meetings will all help address the needs of your infant self. Unknowingly, the structure itself provides the safety you need as you begin to bond and become symbiotic with the program. If you get completely immersed in the program, and the program becomes your whole life, you are, most likely, unconsciously tending to the needs of that youngest part of self and are unwilling, just yet, to move beyond that infant stage.

Early Recovery and the Inner Toddler

Some go first through the issues of the infant self and then later move into the issues of the toddler within. Others just go straight to the toddler behavior. You know you're experiencing this part of self when you come face to face with your ambivalence. Remember that at the toddler stage you wanted both your mother's protection and your independence. In recovery, you want to give up your addiction but at the same time you want to hold onto the numbing protection of that addictive behavior.

You may find yourself torn between wanting to say no to your addiction while still feeling ambivalent about recovery. Giving up the support system that enabled your addiction to exist is difficult. Saying no to your addiction means saying no to your group of former friends. In early recovery, that's not necessarily easy. Your addiction has been your life. As you begin to separate from it, you may feel unsure and part of you may try to find differences between yourself and the other people in the Twelve Step program. You will look for those differences so that you can go back to acting out. But part of you will also want to identify with those who are in recovery and are successful at saying NO!

You may also be wary of talking about your feelings of uncertainty, and assume that, to be part of the program, you have to want to give up the old behavior one-hundred percent.

But in fact, this is not so. Acceptance is what is important, not judgment. You will discover that you are accepted even if you do relapse. You come to understand that being part of the group means you have a desire to stop your addictive behavior, but does not mean you necessarily can stop cold. The group's lack of concern about the pace of your recovery, mixed with its acceptance of you as a person, will help you move through your ambivalence.

Once, when I was at an AA meeting, a man stood up and spoke for fifteen minutes on why he did not believe he was an alcoholic. No one stopped him or ridiculed him. He was allowed to vent his doubts. Twelve Step meetings or support groups can give you the unconditional love that your younger selves so desperately need. That doesn't mean that every person in every meeting will be able to do so but, at this stage, it is not the individuals with whom you are bonding; it is the group or structure itself.

A common motto in Twelve Step programs is "One Day at a Time," meaning that you only have to worry about how you are going to abstain from your addictive behavior twenty-four hours at a time. This twenty-four-hour commitment also becomes a healing factor because it makes the abstinence more manageable. Committing to a life of recovery is too overwhelming and would most likely result in failure.

There is also a guideline which prohibits crosstalk. In other words, if someone shares something, others do not respond—they just listen. This can be very comforting. For many people, it is the first time they have been able to talk without being interrupted, corrected, or challenged. With time, the doubts tend to subside, and being able to talk freely greatly augments the process.

Early Recovery and the Young Inner Child

Each of you will experience these feelings differently. Some parts of the discussion may hit you in the gut, other things won't trigger a thing. Just "take what fits you and discard the rest," as Betty Bethards, a spiritual teacher in Northern California, so eloquently put it. You may go to three meetings that day and stick rigidly to your recovery plan. The next day, however, you may reject the whole program. You may not want the structure and think it's too limiting. If you find yourself criticizing everything about the program, you are probably experiencing the residual feelings of your three-to-five-year-old within. One day you may be very enthusiastic about the program. These mood swings can be overpowering, and you will most likely have little tolerance when they appear. In working through the steps you may want the process to be exact and feel frustrated with yourself when you don't get it. This could result in feeling shame.

The Fourth Step

When you get into recovery, you begin to break your denial about your behavior. In the fourth step, you are asked to take a searching and fearless inventory of your life. Few are able to do this without triggering that shame. But to get beyond your shame, you must first feel it. Completing the fourth and fifth steps enables you to separate your behavior from who you are. It enables you to transform your shame into guilt and your guilt is something you can learn to manage.

The dysfunction in your family will determine the intensity of these issues, but the needs that result can be met in the first stage of recovery. In time, you will hear others share their criticisms, and you will learn it is acceptable to criticize. You will not be ostracized or asked to leave. The only way to learn how to have a balance of feelings (as opposed to only feeling extremes) is to see this balance in another's behavior. Then you can mimic what you see. Having balanced feelings also involves talking about them. The more you do this, the farther you are from acting them out. You learn that it is healthy to experience and express both positive and negative feelings.

You can heal your sense of exposure and shame during this phase of recovery by sharing your feelings. Anonymity helps because you feel less visible. Using only first names provides a sense of safety, as does not talking about what goes on in a meeting outside of that meeting.

The fourth step asks you to look at yourself honestly and without judgment. You list your assets and liabilities. You begin to take stock of who you are. The fourth step changes shame into guilt by separating the addictive behavior from your core self. As you begin to accept that your addictive and maladaptive ways of relating to your environment rendered you powerless, you begin to see your behavior as a product of that powerlessness, not as a product of who you are.

By sharing your inventory in step five, you break the silence. Sharing helps you tolerate the anxiety you feel about yourself. It allows you to feel the support of another human being, and the support of your Higher Self.

The fourth and fifth steps are a healing, and prepare you for steps six and seven, where you release all the old garbage you have carried around. As you begin to accept the good and bad parts of yourself, you begin to feel more at ease with sharing. Being in a group where you feel safe enough to reveal your behavior also helps you cope with your shame. You get more comfortable with your own shame as you see others sharing theirs.

Early Recovery and the Six-to-Twelve-Year-Old Within

The feeling of not being good enough may get you in touch with your six-to-twelve-year-old within. These feelings may surface in early recovery when you are afraid of not fitting into the group. You may find yourself monitoring your actions, trying to figure out exactly the right thing to say. This is a good time for you to begin "impression management," as Anne Wilson Schaef calls it in her book, *Codependence: Misunderstood, Mistreated*, because it is a time when you may try to control what others think of you. You may also feel very cocky—a defense against being afraid of not being accepted. You may be embarrassed by the idea of having to go get a chip to mark an anniversary. You may feel embarrassed that everyone yells hello when you state your name. You may find yourself saying, "I don't need this," while fearing the group might be saying, "We don't want you."

This developmental stage centers around mastering the tasks of peer relationships. If in childhood you were never taught this, then a part of you might resist working the steps, fearing you would only fail. Of course, with time and with the support of your sponsor, you will succeed. In fact, the structure of the twelve steps is one of the chief healers at this stage of development. It lets you complete a task with direction from someone you trust.

Once you get accustomed to meetings and you feel familiar with the people, this part of self feels very much like a part of the gang! The jargon appeals to that part of you who wants to be in groups or activities. The slogans help enhance the sense of being in recovery and being a part of something bigger than your addictions. The structure and ceremony that accompany Twelve Step programs help this part of self begin to heal. Soon, you may find yourself looking forward to the chip ceremony. You may begin to feel comfortable with the hellos after you introduce yourself. You may begin to take on small jobs in the meetings, such as being responsible for coffee, or literature; anything that increases your sense of belonging will help this child within to heal. You will know this part of you is feeling comfortable with the program when you begin to steadfastly work through your program, actively working the steps with your sponsor. You may suffer through the fourth step, but you will experience the fifth, sixth, and seventh steps as a tremendous relief.

Early Recovery and the Thirteen-to-Fifteen-Year-Old Within

When you begin to feel the urge to merge with others but feel an awkwardness about doing so, you have probably moved into the issues carried by your thirteen-to-fifteen-year-old within. Even if you are already in a relationship, these issues will still surface, because you will find yourself attracted to people in new ways.

The best way to deal with this stage of recovery is to follow the program guideline—abstain from focusing on intimate relationships. It soothes the awkwardness for those who never learned to negotiate intimate feelings. For those who learned to love addictively, to initiate a romance at this stage of recovery would simply activate your secondary addiction to love and sex. Although you may find yourself resentful of the guideline and inclined to break the rule, it will best meet your needs to go along with the program until you feel more settled in your recovery. A relationship would only distract you from your main task, which is learning how to cope without re-engaging in addictive behavior.

You will know you have successfully met the needs of your thirteen-to-fifteen-year-old within when you accept the awkwardness and feel protected by the guideline. The year will give you time to sort things out, to learn to put yourself and conquering your addiction first. You will feel comforted at same-sex meetings, where these issues can be discussed. It is important to remember that your recovery uncovers whatever was not resolved during these periods of development. If your development was smooth in childhood and you were able to master most tasks successfully, then there may be some readjustment but the impact would not be nearly as profound as it would be if these tasks were not successfully mastered. If a trauma did occur during any time of your childhood, then recovery will offer you a second chance to resolve that pain.

Early Recovery and the Fifteen-to-Seventeen-Year-Old Within

The rebellious part of you will emerge when you find yourself confronting the unresolved issues from when you were fifteen to seventeen. To this part of self the whole program is seen as a threat. The structure will feel limiting and ridiculous. Since surrender is experienced as letting go of one's ego—and since ego is essential at this age—the idea of surrender will almost feel like a near death experience to that part of you. Every aspect of your fifteen-to-seventeen-year-old within at the initial stage of recovery will fight the program.

This part of self is not really healed in the first stage of recovery. It is "pulled along" by the younger parts of self who need and want to identify with recovery. In stage two, where the past is reworked, the rebellious feelings begin to subside.

Recovery and the Young Adult Within

As you move to the older part of yourself, the young adult within, you may sense a certain restlessness. This restlessness is actually a concern of being swallowed up by the structure of the program. This part may also carry your fear of being one-dimensional. Early recovery demands a surrender of individuality; this late childhood stage is about developing individuality. So there is a conflict.

The earlier needs are met first. They are the primary focus of the first stage of recovery. Slowly, surrender does occur. The bonding takes place, and a sense of safety is established. You begin to work with your shame and guilt and as you work with your sponsor and go through the Twelve Steps you begin to find your place in the program.

At a certain point in recovery you may begin to feel ready to sponsor someone else. You will feel you have *your* story to tell. You will have weathered the first stage of recovery and feel courageous enough to begin to heal and help others heal.

At that point, the earlier chapters will be helpful in reclaiming and reworking your past. I encourage you to stay with the tasks of early recovery until you feel you are truly able to abstain from your destructive behavior and until dealing with old feelings does not threaten your abstinence. Sometimes you will find that you will start your second stage of inner work only to discover that it will reactivate your desire to use, or act out. If that desire becomes unmanageable, then back off momentarily and return to the basics of your early recovery tools.

Go to more meetings, make the necessary phone calls, work with the steps until you feel ready to once again move forward.

Most of your focus will be on tasks involved in working your Twelve Step program and below is a worksheet that can enhance this. It can be used in conjunction with your sponsor to help you stay aware of each inner child's needs so those needs do not sabotage your early recovery.

FIRST STAGE RECOVERY EXERCISE

Purpose and Directions

This worksheet can help you take a daily inventory of each inner child's needs. The questions can also help you identify themes your inner children may carry.

Determine with your sponsor when it is appropriate for you to begin to use this worksheet. In the first months of recovery you may be too concerned with just making it through the day to be bothered by this tool. When you feel like you want to begin to identify the source of your feelings, however, this worksheet can be useful. Keep a record of your daily responses because they can serve as a kind of diary which will reflect the progression of your work.

I suggest you re-type or re-write the worksheet, make copies, and put them in a folder. Be sure to date each sheet. Then allow ten to fifteen minutes daily to respond to the questions. Ask each inner child to write down its feelings about the questions you ask. Share your answers with your sponsor when it feels appropriate to do so. Keep in mind, however, that the needs of your inner children are best met through your association and involvement in a group. This assessment simply helps you stay in touch with what those needs are.

Exercise

1. Ask your infant, What do you need from the program today? Did you get it?
2. Ask your toddler, How did you feel about your addiction today? How did you feel about your recovery?
3. Ask your three-to-six-year-old within, What did you like about the program today? What did you dislike?
4. Ask your six-to-twelve-year-old within, How did you fit into your recovery group today?
5. Ask your twelve-to-fifteen-year-old within, Did you feel any embarrassment about your recovery today?
6. Ask your twelve-to-fifteen-year-old within, What was it like to be around others to whom you were attracted? How did you deal with it?
7. Ask your fifteen-to-seventeen-year-old within, Was there anything you felt like rebelling against today?

8. Ask your seventeen-to-twenty-one-year-old within, Did you feel committed to your recovery today, or impatient with a sense of wanting to get on with your life?

9. Did you contact your sponsor today? Did you use the phone list? Did you do your reading?

Closing

This worksheet will augment your experience of early recovery. Remember that your initial task is to arrest your destructive behavior. The healing and transformation will begin once you have managed your behavior and you have acquired the skills necessary to cope with your day-to-day life nonaddictively.

Epilogue

LIFE AFTER THE PAIN

I have thought a great deal about how I want to end this book. I have theories and predictions, assumptions, answers, and advice all lined up to give you a glimpse of how you will be once you have dealt with your past. I have quotes from clients and quotes from leaders in the field, all of which would contribute nicely to the completion of this work.

But I suddenly realized I cannot say what it will be like for you. I wish I could. I wish I could give you guarantees, promises, and a vision of what your life will be like. But I cannot. It is not my place to do so. Your future is in *your* hands, not mine. Your healing process is between you and your Higher Power, not between you and me. I would only limit the possibilities you can attain. All I can offer are tools, which if used will enable you to make choices about how you want to be.

I can, however, give you a glimpse of what my life is like having healed much of my pain. It is not painless, but it is not without joy either. I feel more like a student of my suffering rather than a victim of my pain.

I continue to feel depression, anger, jealousy, and hate. But I also feel joy and love, compassion, and appreciation. Every feeling, both pleasant and unpleasant, is felt more fully. I have the tools to identify the pain from my past and respond to it accordingly by attending to the needs of my children within.

I am able to deal more effectively with the pain generated from my current life as well. I am more able to see events in their entirety. It is no longer necessary to compartmentalize—experience my life as mere fragments—although I still sometimes choose to do so.

There are times when I behave addictively, but I am no longer "addicted" to any person, substance, or behavior. Grieving has become a part of my everyday life, and I now know what it takes to maintain my sense of peace, although I often choose to ignore what I know and then have to struggle to regain my serenity.

When I am accepting of my own human limitations I am, in turn, much more understanding of the shortcomings of others.

I am less tolerant of abusive behavior and more equipped to disengage and walk away. If someone cuts me off on the freeway, I view it more as his or her problem than as my personal vendetta.

I enjoy being alone and often prefer solitude to the insanity that can be found in crowds.

I still have a great deal to learn about money, but rely solely on myself for support.

I like to write. I love my work, and sometimes I still feel bored.

Spending time on simple activities is important to me. Predictability is important to me. So are waking up with my dog and spending time with loved ones.

I meditate, I run, I work out and can really tell the difference when I don't.

I am more aware of how my body reacts to what I put in it, but there are still times when my body says no but my mouth says "I would love some."

I am happier with my body, however, and can look at myself in the mirror with appreciation instead of shame. In fact, the reflection I see has become one of my best friends.

I still feel threatened and can overreact, but I notice this sooner and can come back and express what I really felt.

My infant self still searches for closeness in most interactions I encounter; my toddler self still feels fear when I neglect to set clear limits and say yes when I should be saying no; my three-to-six-year-old within can still feel competitive, critical, and afraid; my grade-school self can still freeze up when I am about to speak publicly; my teen self at times feels awkward; my adolescent self can still rebel; and my young inner adult has many tasks she yet needs to master. But these feelings do not paralyze me. They can exist, and I can still cope. In fact, these voices contribute to my creativity because they keep me honest, humble, and aware.

I feel capable of more intimacy, each moment seems a little more enriched, and I feel I could die tomorrow with no regrets.

I am intrigued with metaphysics and am expanding my beliefs. My inner child work seems to have served as a bridge to exploring the pain from past lives. Working with this pain, whether real or imagined, has been very fruitful to my growth. I could not have delved into the pain from my past lives, however, without having first worked with the wounds from this one.

What will it be like for you? What will you put your energy into when it is not so wrapped up in your past? It will be what you want it to be. You are not responsible for what happened to you in the past, but you are responsible for what you do with your life now. Do you have the courage and strength to be the expert of your own life? Do you have the courage to be who you were meant to be? These are questions only you can answer. My hope is that this book has given you the opportunity to have more options about how you answer those questions and more choices about how you want to live your life.

THE GIFT OF THE SELF

There are no more maps, no more creeds, no more philosophies. From here on in, the directions come straight from the Divine. The curriculum is being revealed millisecond by millisecond—invisibly, intuitively, spontaneously, lovingly.
AKSHARA NOOR

Appendices

APPENDIX 1: GLOSSARY

ACTING OUT   Exhibiting destructive behavior that discharges the energy of your emotions, but results in negative consequences for yourself and others.

ADULT SELF   The responsible part of yourself that governs your daily life.

CENTER OF YOUR BEING   For most people this is the place in your body at the very bottom of your diaphragm. It is where your breath leads you when you inhale deeply.

CODEPENDENCY   An inability to fulfill your primary needs because your focus is always on meeting the needs of the person upon whom you are emotionally or financially dependent; ordinarily this is due to patterns of behavior learned in childhood to ensure survival and that result in low self-esteem.

DEVELOPMENTAL STAGES   Predictable stages of emotional growth that occur in the natural progression from birth to adulthood. Each stage has specific tasks that need to be mastered if this progression is to occur successfully.

GUIDED IMAGERY   A structured imaginative fantasy whose purpose is to aid your internal exploration. You create images or scenes in your mind's eye and then relate to those images, directing them much as you would a play. Guided imagery does not always elicit visual responses; sometimes the scenes are evoked by recalling certain smells or tastes, or by hearing sounds of the scene being described.

GENERALIZED GRIEF   Grief that extends beyond your personal experience; feeling the pain of others that is similar or the same as your own.

HIGHER POWER   For some it is the image of a wise old being; for others it may be a sphere of light, a guardian angel, or a spirit guide. For some it is experienced as part of the self; for others it will be something outside of the self. The image may be based on religious beliefs, appearing in the form of Jesus, Buddha, Mohammed, or a guru; others may experience it as an abstract symbol of a Higher Self such as a cross or a mandala, or the intuitive or spiritual part of self within you. Some may picture it as an aspect of nature, or a group to which one belongs.

HIGHER SELF   The spiritual dimension of self.

INHERITED GRIEF   Unresolved grief that is passed on from generation to generation until someone finally breaks the cycle and resolves the feelings of loss.

INNER CHILD   Small voices inside that carry childhood feelings.

INNER CHILDREN   The personification of the different feelings and issues that emerge as one progresses through the developmental stages of childhood.

INTERNAL SUPPORT GROUP   Supportive characters, real or imagined, that you bring into your guided imagery to support your exploration.

JOURNAL   A notebook that is used for personal reflections about your emotional and spiritual journey.

MIND'S EYE   Your imagination; what you see in your head when you close your eyes and play imaginative scenes.

PROCESSING   Word used to describe the act of identifying, expressing, and releasing feelings.

PROTECTIVE LIGHT   A healing light connected with your Higher Power that you call on imaginatively to aid your internal explorations; a metaphor for the healing power of the universal spirit.

RECOVERY   The process of learning how to break addictive behavior patterns and live with feelings non-addictively.

RITUAL   A ceremony performed for the purpose of celebrating the completion of a phase of your internal work or to provide a tangible way to release pain.

SELFESTEEM   Describes your level of self-worth; how you feel about yourself. These feelings are based on how you were treated as a child. If you were treated with respect and you received love, you will have high self-esteem. If you were neglected, abused or abandoned you will have low self-esteem and not feel very worthy.

SELF–HELP GROUPS   Leaderless groups that meet regularly and provide a place for individuals to share and grow. They are most often associated with Twelve Step programs.

SPONSOR   A person in a Twelve Step program who can assist an individual in working through the program outlined for his or her recovery; this person is also recovering from addictive behavior.

SUPPORT SYSTEM   Friends, family and others who believe in and encourage your personal growth.

TWELVE STEPS   Steps or principles laid out by Bill W. and Dr. Bob that were first used in Alcoholics Anonymous as the prescription for staying sober. They have been used in AA for almost fifty years and are now applied to many addictive behaviors.

TWELVE STEP PROGRAMS   Self-help programs that use the Twelve Steps outlined by Alcoholics Anonymous and consist of self-help meetings.

APPENDIX 2: THE TWELVE STEPS OF ALCOHOLICS ANONYMOUS

1. We admitted we were powerless over alcohol—that our lives had become unmanageable.

2. Came to believe that a Power greater than ourselves could restore us to sanity.

3. Made a decision to turn our will and our lives over to the care of God *as we understood him.*

4. Made a searching and fearless moral inventory of ourselves.

5. Admitted to God, to ourselves, and to another human being the exact nature of our wrongs.

6. Were entirely ready to have God remove all these defects of character.

7. Humbly asked Him to remove our shortcomings.

8. Made a list of all persons we had harmed, and became willing to make amends to them all.

9. Made direct amends to such people whenever possible, except when to do so would injure them or others.

10. Continued to take personal inventory and when we were wrong promptly admitted it.

11. Sought through prayer and meditation to improve our conscious contact with God *as we understood Him,* praying only for knowledge of His will for us and the power to carry that out.

12. Having had a spiritual awakening as a result of these steps, we tried to carry this message to alcoholics, and to practice these principles in all our affairs.

The Twelve Steps are reprinted with permission of Alcoholics Anonymous World Services, Inc. Permission to reprint the Twelve Steps does not mean that A.A. has reviewed or approved the contents of this publication, nor that A.A. agrees with the views expressed herein. A.A. is a program of recovery from alcoholism. Use of the Twelve Steps in connection with programs and activities which are patterned after A.A., but which address other problems, does not imply otherwise.

APPENDIX 3: HERBS FOR WORK WITH YOUR INNER CHILDREN

Fill a muslin bag with the herbs of your choice. For tea, simply use the bag in your tea pot. To use the herbs in your bath, hang the bag over the spout in your tub, and let the water run through it. While bathing, remove the bag and place it in your bath water; periodically squeeze the muslin bag so you can release more of the herb's healing properties. Or brew the herbs as tea and pour into your bathwater.

Burning frankincense and rosemary incense can also aid healing. Frankincense is associated with overall protection and purification. Rosemary's aroma helps release memories.

Infant
Rose—love and balance
Clove—wards off evil spirits (especially good for infancy)

Toddler
Lavender—overall healing
Rose—love and balance
Horehound—increases clarity and trust while warding off outside influences

Young Inner Child
Chamomile—protection, healing, love
Yarrow—deals with negativity
Star anise—negotiations between opposites

Six-to-twelve-year-old
Peppermint—protection
Thyme—courage, ambition; increases ability to engage in childlike fun

Twelve-to-fifteen-year-old

Hyssop—wards off negativity
Calendula—purification, protection
Cinnamon—aids in concentration and in easing communication

Fifteen-to-seventeen-year-old

Borage—courage, bravery, and fortification of inner self
Basil—elicits inspiration needed in finding sense of self
Horehound—increases clarity and trust while warding off outside influences

Young Adult

Sandalwood—inspires confidence, success, and protection
Cedar—associated with prosperity, and being grounded and centered
Motherwort—encourages purpose, joy, inner strength, and confidence
Ginger—a touch of ginger in your bath is an overall soothing agent for fatigue and for relaxation.

Bibliography

ADDICTIONS

Bowden, Grairtz. *Guide to Recovery.* Holmes Beach, Fla.: Learning Publications, 1985.

Bradshaw, John. *Bradshaw on: The Family.* Deerfield Beach, Fla.: Health Communications, 1988.

Johnson, Vernon. *I'll Quit Tomorrow.* San Francisco: Harper & Row, 1980.

Klass, Joe. *The Twelve Steps to Happiness.* New York: Hazeldon Foundation, 1982.

Larson, Ernie. *Stage II Recovery: Life Beyond Addiction.* San Francisco: Harper & Row, 1985.

Maxwell, Milton. *The AA Experience.* New York: McGraw Hill, 1984.

Milan and Ketcham. *Under the Influence.* New York: Bantam, 1981.

Norwood, Robin. *Women Who Love Too Much.* Los Angeles: Jeremy P. Tarcher, 1985.

Orbach, Susie. *Hunger Strike.* New York: W. W. Norton, 1986.

Phelps and Nourse. *The Hidden Addiction.* Boston: Little, Brown, 1986.

Schaeff, Anne Wilson. *Codependence: Misunderstood, Mistreated.* Minneapolis: Winston Press, 1986.

——. *When Society Becomes an Addict.* San Francisco: Harper & Row, 1987.

Wegsheider, Sharon. *Another Chance.* Palo Alto, Calif.: Science & Behavior, 1981.

——. *Choicemaking.* Pompano Beach, Fla.: Health & Communications, 1985.

Whitfield, Charles. *Alcoholism and Spirituality.* New York: Resource Group, 1985.

——. *Codependence: Healing the Human Condition.* Deerfield Beach, Fla.: Health Communications, 1991.

Zimberg, Wallace and Blume. *Practical Approaches to Alcoholism Psychotherapy.* New York: Plume Press, 1978.

GRIEF

Bozarth-Campbell, Alla. *Life is Goodbye, Life is Hello.* Minneapolis: Compcare Publications, 1982.

Kubler-Ross, Elizabeth. *Working It Through.* New York: MacMillan, 1982.

Miller, Alice. *The Drama of The Gifted Child* (originally, *Prisoners of Childhood*). New York: Basic Books, 1981.

INCEST

Bass, Ellen, and Laura Davis. *The Courage to Heal: A Guide for Women Survivors of Child Sexual Abuse.* New York: Harper & Row, 1988.

Bass, Ellen, and Louise Thornton, eds. *I Never Told Anyone: Writings by Women Survivors of Child Sexual Abuse.* New York: Harper & Row, 1983.

Butler, Sandra. *Conspiracy of Silence: The Trauma of Incest.* San Francisco: Volcano Press, 1985.

Gil, Eliana. *Outgrowing the Pain: A Book For and About Adults Abused as Children.* San Francisco: Launch Press, 1983.

Lew, Mike. *Victims No Longer: Men Recovering From Incest and Other Sexual Child Abuse.* New York: Harper & Row, 1990.

Maltz, Wendy, and Beverly Holman. *Incest and Sexuality: A Guide to Understanding and Healing.* Lexington, Mass.: Lexington Books, 1987.

McClure, Mary Beth. *Reclaiming the Heart: A Handbook of Help and Hope for the Survivors of Incest.* New York: Warner Brothers, 1990.

INNER CHILD

Abrams, Jeremiah. *Reclaiming the Inner Child.* Los Angeles: Jeremy P. Tarcher, 1990.

Bloom, Michael. *Adolescent Parental Separation.* New York: Garden Press, Inc., 1980.

Bradshaw, John. *Healing The Shame That Binds You.* Deerfield Beach, Fla.: Health Communications, 1988.

——. *Homecoming: Reclaiming and Championing Your Inner Child.* Deerfield Beach, Fla.: Health Communications, 1990.

Branden, Nathaniel. *How To Raise Your Self-Esteem.* New York: Bantam, 1987.

Briggs, Dorothy Corkille. *Celebrate Yourself.* Garden City, N.Y.: Doubleday, 1977.

——. *Your Child's Self-Esteem.* Garden City, N.Y.: Doubleday, 1970.

Clark, Jean Illsley, and Connie Dawson. *Growing Up Again.* San Francisco: Harper & Row, 1989.

Gessell, Ames and Bullis. *Infant and Child in the Culture Today.* New York: Harper & Row, 1974.

Hay, Louise L. *You Can Heal Your Life.* Santa Monica, Calif.: Hay House, Inc., 1984.

Kaufman, Gershen. *SHAME—The Power of Caring.* Cambridge: Schenkman, 1985.

Lerner, Rockelle. *Daily Meditations for the Inner Child.* Deerfield Beach, Fla.: Health Communications, 1990.

Pollard, John K. *Self-Parenting.* Malibu, Calif.: Generic Human Studies Publishing, 1987.

Masterson, James. *Treatment of Borderline Adolescent: A Developmental Approach.* New York: John Wiley & Sons, 1972.

Missildine, W. Hugh, M.D. *Your Inner Child of the Past.* New York: Simon & Schuster, 1985.

Whitfield, Charles L. *A Gift to Myself.* Deerfield Beach, Fla.: Health Communications, 1989.

———. *Healing the Child Within.* Deerfield Beach, Fla.: Health Communications, 1987.

INTIMATE ADULT RELATIONSHIPS

Anand, Margo. *The Art of Sexual Ecstacy.* Los Angeles: Jeremy P. Tarcher, 1989.

Hendrix, Harville. *Getting The Love You Want.* San Francisco: Harper & Row, 1990.

Lerner, Harriet Goldhor Ph.D. *The Dance of Intimacy.* New York: Harper & Row, 1989.

Luthman, Shirley Gehrke. *Intimacy: Essence of Male and Female.* San Rafael, Calif.: Mehetabil & Company, 1972.

Napier, Augustus. *The Fragile Bond.* New York: Harper & Row, 1988.

Sanford, John. *The Invisible Partners.* New York: Paulist Press, 1980.

Vissell, Barry, and Joyce Vissell. *The Shared Heart.* Aptos, Calif.: Ramira Publishing, 1984.

Woititz, Janet. *Struggle for Intimacy.* Pompano, Fla.: Health Communications, 1985.

SPIRITUALITY AND CEREMONY

Bach, Richard. *One.* New York: Silver Arrow Books, 1988.

Bethards, Betty. *Be Your Own Guru.* Novato, Calif.: Inner Light Foundation, 1977.

Blum, Ralph. *The Book of Runes.* New York: St. Martens Press, 1987.

Bly, Robert. *Iron John: A Book About Men.* New York: Addison-Wesley, 1990.

Bolen, Jean Shinoda M.D. *Goddesses in Everywoman.* New York: Harper & Row, 1985.

———. *Gods in Everyman.* New York: Harper & Row, 1989.

Campbell, Joseph, with Bill Moyers. *The Power of Myth.* New York: Doubleday, 1988.

Cunningham, Scott. *Magical Herbalism.* St. Paul, Minn.: Llewllyn, 1982.

Dass, Ram. *Grist for the Mill.* Santa Cruz, Calif.: Bantam, 1977.

Gawain, Shakti. *Creative Visualization.* Mill Valley, Calif.: Whatever Publishing, 1983.

Gawain, Shakti, and Laurel King. *Living in the Light.* Mill Valley, Calif.: Whatever Publishing, 1986.

King, Laurel. *Women of Power.* Berkeley, Calif.: Celestial Arts, 1989.

Lazaris. *Audio Series of Spiritual-Psychological Teachings.* Palm Beach, Fla.: Concert Synergy.

Millman, Dan. *The Way of the Peaceful Warrior.* Walpole, N.H.: Stillpoint Publishing, 1980.

Nobel, Vicki. *Motherpeace: A Way to the Goddess Through Myth, Art and Tarot.* San Francisco: Harper & Row, 1983.

Roberts, Jane. *Oversoul Seven.* New York: Simon & Schuster, 1979.

Ross, Nancy Wilson. *Buddhism: A Way of Life and Thought.* New York: Random House, 1980.

Roth, Gabriel, and John Louden. *Maps to Ecstasy: Teachings of An Urban Shaman.* San Rafael, Calif.: New World Library, 1989.

Sams, Jamie. *Sacred Path Cards.* San Francisco: Harper Collins, 1990.

Starhawk. *The Spiral Dance.* San Francisco: Harper & Row, 1979.

Zukav, Gary. *The Seat of the Soul.* New York: Simon & Schuster, 1990.

RESOURCES

The following organizations may be of help as you begin to heal your past. Inclusion on this list does not necessarily indicate a recommendation or endorsement. *Incest Survivor Information Exchange,* Box 3399, New Haven, CT 06515. Produces a newsletter for adult survivors. Open to submissions. Sample issue, $2.00; yearly rates, $10.00 bulk mail or $12.00 first class. *NACOA (National Association for Children of Alcoholics),* 31706 Coast Highway #301, South Laguna, CA 92677, (714) 499-3889. Provides referrals, networking, and literature for adult children of alcoholics.